C000134180

Scrapbooking
with Adobe®
Photoshop® Elements 3

Carla Rose

que®

800 East 96th Street
Indianapolis, Indiana 46240

Scrapbooking With Adobe® Photoshop® Elements 3

Copyright © 2005 by Que Publishing

All rights reserved. No part of this book shall be reproduced, stored in a retrieval system, or transmitted by any means, electronic, mechanical, photocopying, recording, or otherwise, without written permission from the publisher. No patent liability is assumed with respect to the use of the information contained herein. Although every precaution has been taken in the preparation of this book, the publisher and author assume no responsibility for errors or omissions. Nor is any liability assumed for damages resulting from the use of the information contained herein.

International Standard Book Number: 0-7897-3411-7

Library of Congress Catalog Card Number: 2004117284

Printed in the United States of America

First Printing: May 2005

08   07   06   05   4   3   2

Trademarks

All terms mentioned in this book that are known to be trademarks or service marks have been appropriately capitalized. Que Publishing cannot attest to the accuracy of this information. Use of a term in this book should not be regarded as affecting the validity of any trademark or service mark.

Warning and Disclaimer

Every effort has been made to make this book as complete and as accurate as possible, but no warranty or fitness is implied. The information provided is on an "as is" basis. The author and the publisher shall have neither liability nor responsibility to any person or entity with respect to any loss or damages arising from the information contained in this book.

Bulk Sales

Que Publishing offers excellent discounts on this book when ordered in quantity for bulk purchases or special sales. For more information, please contact

U.S. Corporate and Government Sales
1-800-382-3419
corpsales@pearsontechgroup.com

For sales outside of the U.S., please contact

International Sales
international@pearsoned.com

Executive Editor
Candace Hall

Acquisitions Editor
Betsy Brown

Development Editors
Betsy Brown
Kate Small

Managing Editor
Charlotte Clapp

Senior Project Editor
Matthew Purcell

Production Editor
Heather Wilkins

Indexer
Erika Millen

Technical Editors
Lisa Lee
Jennifer Burke

Publishing Coordinator
Vanessa Evans

Designer
Anne Jones

Page Layout
Eric S. Miller

Contents at a Glance

Table of Contents

About the Author

Carla Rose started her photography career at the age of eight with a Brownie Hawkeye. A graduate of the School of the Museum of Fine Arts in Boston, she has been a TV news photographer and film editor, as well as an advertising copywriter and graphic artist, before discovering the Macintosh. She has written all or part of about thirty computer books, including *Maclopedia, Adobe InDesign for the Mac, Sams Teach Yourself Digital Photography in 14 Days, Sams Teach Yourself Photoshop 4 in 14 Days, The Whole Mac, Managing the Windows NT Server, PageMaker 6.5 Complete, Sams Teach Yourself Photoshop 4, 5, 5.5, 6, 7,* and *CS in 24 Hours, Mac Online, The First Book of Macintosh, The First Book of PageMaker 4 for Macintosh, It's a Mad, Mad, Mad, Mad Mac, Turbocharge Your Mac,* and *Everything You Ever Wanted to Know About the Mac.* Her books have been translated into more than fifteen languages. She has written for publications ranging from the *Atlantic Fisherman* to *Photoshop User* to *The New Yorker.* She lives near Boston, with her husband, audio guru Jay Rose, and three large, friendly cats. She welcomes email addressed to author@graphicalcat.com.

Dedication

For all the funny people in my life. Thanks for all the laughs.

Acknowledgments

This is my last computer book. It's been interesting and fun, and I'm very grateful to all the people at Que and Pearson who have kept me working on these books since 1987. Special thanks to Betsy Brown, Matt Purcell, and Heather Wilkins who worked so hard on this one. Big thanks to the people who supplied photos, ephemera, and/or their own faces for use in the illustrations, including Carole Harrison, Judy Storgaard, Suzanne Hecker, Judy Blair, Ann Cartee, Linda Standart, Josh and Melissa Rose, Dan Rose, Kara Marzahn, and Jay Rose. Profound apologies to anyone I forgot to mention. Apologies and a hug to everyone I had to ignore or chase away while I worked, especially all the cats. And the biggest hug and deepest gratitude of all to my wonderful husband Jay, who always does what needs to be done. Please watch for my first scrapbooking mystery, *Scraps of Time*, coming soon to a bookstore near you.

We Want to Hear from You!

As the reader of this book, *you* are our most important critic and commentator. We value your opinion and want to know what we're doing right, what we could do better, what areas you'd like to see us publish in, and any other words of wisdom you're willing to pass our way.

As an executive editor for Que Publishing, I welcome your comments. You can email or write me directly to let me know what you did or didn't like about this book—as well as what we can do to make our books better.

Please note that I cannot help you with technical problems related to the topic of this book. We do have a User Services group, however, where I will forward specific technical questions related to the book.

When you write, please be sure to include this book's title and author as well as your name, email address, and phone number. I will carefully review your comments and share them with the author and editors who worked on the book.

Email: feedback@quepublishing.com

Mail: Candace Hall
           Executive Editor
           Que Publishing
           800 East 96th Street
           Indianapolis, IN 46240 USA

For more information about this book or another Que Publishing title, visit our website at www.quepublishing.com. Type the ISBN (excluding hyphens) or the title of a book in the Search field to find the page you're looking for.

Introduction

The Lure of Scrapbooking

As Simon and Garfunkel said, "Preserve your memories. They're all that's left you."

A *scrapbook* is, literally, a book full of scraps. The main content is usually photos: weddings, baby pictures, and travel photos. Of course, scraps are all kinds of things, not just photos, but ephemera of all kinds—ticket stubs, pressed flowers, menus, pamphlets, post cards, souvenirs—whatever helps you to remember the places, events, and people they're tied to.

A scrapbook can also be a journal, a way of displaying your thoughts, as well as your favorite things and pictures. Scrapbooks are about people, places, pets, or whatever tickles your fancy or tugs your heartstrings.

Scrapbooks have been around in one format or another for many years, but the concept of creating them digitally is new and exciting. With even a simple digital camera or scanner and some inexpensive software, you can jump right in and have reasonably professional-looking pages in a couple of hours.

If you love scrapbooking, you're not alone. About 25% of households now have scrapbooks, compared to 13% three years ago. The current craze is thought to have begun in 1981, in Utah. Mormons, always big on genealogy, started gathering family photos to go with the family tree. Scrapbooking really started back around the turn of the 20th century, as photographs printed on paper became readily available. Prior to that, photos were made on glass plates, elaborately framed with embossed metal edges and tooled leather covers.

Grandma's scrapbooks were nothing more than large books with black or manila construction paper pages holding neat rows of photos, sometimes labeled, unfortunately sometimes not. Pictures were inserted at each corner into small triangular pockets, or were too often glued in place with anything from wheat paste to mucilage or even rubber cement. These glues destroyed most of the pictures to which they were applied. They stained. They cracked. It was usually impossible to remove the picture from the page without tearing it. The acids in the papers mixed with the chemicals in the photos and inks to bleach out the pictures or even eat holes in them.

Today, we have better adhesives that can be peeled off if you want to move a picture and are free of acids and chemicals that might eat the images right off the page. We have acid-free papers, better photo materials, and we can even save our scrapbooks on CD or DVD discs or send them out into cyberspace for the ultimate in long-term storage.

Scrapbooking brings people together, not only to enjoy the finished scrapbook but also to help create them. Scrapbooking parties, called *croppings* for the picture cropping or trimming that's a necessary part of the craft, are much like old-fashioned quilting bees. Groups of family members or friends get together to share snacks and memories as they work on their pages. It's fun, and there are always a few experienced scrapbookers in the crowd to give advice on making pages more interesting. There are even "cropping weekends" held at fancy resorts and "cropping cruises" to allow scrapbookers some working time while their spouses and kids have something else to do.

Just as the scrapbook originally evolved as a place to show off the then-new art of photography, our current obsession with digital photography led to digital scrapbooking. It's the next logical step forward. A digital scrapbook can even contain digital video and music clips, spoken journal entries rather than written, animation, and whatever else you can think of.

There are other virtues to digital scrapbooking as well. Unlike regular film photography, it's very easy to retouch a digital picture. You can remove anything that shouldn't be there, including dead tree branches in a landscape or Uncle Harry's tacky girlfriend. If the photo is crooked, you can straighten it. You can use the same picture as often as you want. If it's in black and white, you can color it; or you can remove some or all of the color from those overly bright 1960 Kodachrome prints.

If you make up the pages on the computer instead of with scissors and glue, you can set the type for captions, quotes, or journal notes right on the page. There are thousands of typefaces available, and you can make the type any size you like, knowing it will look professional. You can choose from all the millions of colors your computer screen displays, and you can, if you have access to an inkjet color printer, print copies of your pages to put in a "real" (non-digital) book.

Digital scrapbooks are easy to share. You can put them up on a website for family and friends. Use password protection if you don't want to open your scrapbook to the public. You can send your scrapbook as a CD-ROM with sounds and movies for less than the cost of an annual Christmas card. Distributing copies of your scrapbooks digitally is good insurance against losing all those precious memories in a flood, fire, or other catastrophe.

Why has scrapbooking become such a hot topic? In an interview in the *New York Times,* Deidre Bullock, a consultant for the Minnesota-based Creative Memories, the largest nontraditional retailer of scrapbooking products, says simply, "It keeps the art of storytelling alive." Even beyond that, sociologists have noticed a trend towards "cocooning" that started somewhere in the 1990s. Home and family are more important to us now than in the wild and crazy years that came before. Scrapbooking is a great family activity, as well as a good excuse to get together with friends for cropping parties and to teach each other new techniques.

Also, of course, there's money to be made. With one in four Americans making scrapbooks, it's now a 3-billion-dollar-a-year industry. That includes materials sold at general craft store chains such as Michael's and A.C. Moore; internet businesses that sell scrapbook supplies; and home scrapbooking parties, much like Tupperware parties, where a consultant demonstrates techniques and sells kits to make a specific page that features the user's photos. Finally, for those who can't, or haven't the time, to do it themselves, there are *S4Os.* That's short for "scrapbook for others," and it's becoming a lucrative home-based business. Typically, a professional scrapbooker charges about $20 a page to assemble your old photos into themed pages, or upwards of $200 to do a whole scrapbook or album. The latter are in turn moneymakers for the bakers, photographers, landscapers, and muralists who commission them. You can find a professional scrapbook maker by asking at your local crafts shop or on the Web at http://a.webring.com/hub?ring=customscrapbooka.

Whatever the cost, whether you do the work yourself or hire someone to do it, whether you work with a computer or scissors and glue, scrapbooking is time and money well-spent. After all, you're saving memories, and memories are priceless.

What You Need to Get Started

You've already got the most important thing—your pictures and the memories that go with them. The next four chapters will help you turn them into scrapbook pages you'll be proud of. First, you need to develop a theme and a "look" for your scrapbook, and then you need to locate and assemble all the stuff you've thought about putting into it. If you're going to build your pages on paper, you need such basic tools as scissors and glue, paper stocks, and rubber stamps, and embossing powder, charms, stickers, glitter, and more to "fancy up" the pages. You need a comfortable, well-lit workspace, ideally one that can be kid- and animal-proofed, and doesn't need to be packed away between cropping sessions. Next, we'll look at the hardware you need: a computer, a color printer, either a scanner or a digital camera or both, and a CD or DVD reader/writer. Finally, there's software: You need a copy of Adobe Photoshop Elements 3 in order to get the most benefit from this book.

Got all that? If not, you get to do some shopping after you know what to look for. Get ready to have some fun.

Starting a Scrapbook

If you have been scrapbooking for a while, you already know how important it is to plan ahead. If this is your first scrapbook ever or even your first digital scrapbook, although you're eager to start work, you need to stop and think first. Maybe even make a few notes.

What's It About?

Does your scrapbook have a purpose? Or are you just collecting your old pictures to save in one place? Scrapbooks look best when they're telling a story rather than just displaying pictures on a page. What kind of story does yours tell? A scrapbook about your baby's birth tells a story. So does one on your wedding, or your kids in general. You can scrapbook your family vacations. Building or renovating a house is a fun topic, with lots of opportunities for comments and progress pictures. You can make a scrapbook of recipes, with photos and/or comments about the people who gave them to you. You can even include a digital photo of the finished dish, or of the family enjoying it. When you're telling a story, don't skip the punch line. Similarly, plan to end your scrapbook with a photo that sums up the earlier pages. Consider a picture of the newlyweds heading off on their honeymoon, or the baby's first year ending with her first birthday.

Organization

Organization is another aspect to consider before you start. Most scrapbooks seem to be more or less *chronological*. That is to say, your baby book might start with an ultrasound picture and several photos of the expectant mother trying on her first maternity clothes. Several scrapbook pages can be devoted to the preparation of the baby's crib and nursery area, and go on to show family and friends celebrating at the baby shower. When the baby arrives, depending on circumstances, you might be able to capture a few pictures from the labor and delivery room, of the doctor or midwife, and of course, several first photos of the baby. You then continue on through baby's first year, and then start a new one for year two, and so on.

Of course, you're not limited to making your scrapbook a timeline. Suppose you want to make a scrapbook about your cat or dog, and you don't have, or can't find, those first kitten or puppy pictures. Start with him now, in a nice pose. Show some of his daily activities; perhaps playing ball with the kids, eating, napping, or doing tricks for treats. Keep that camera handy so you can catch him in the funniest or most characteristic poses he takes on.

The point is that your scrapbook needs to be organized in some logical way; otherwise, it's simply a collection of stuff. You might even consider including an index. I saw one really neat scrapbook a mom had done for her daughter. It was organized into four sections, each on a different color background. The index page was divided into four sections, each using the appropriate color to identify the categories: family, friends, school, and sports.

I found a unique way to organize the scrapbook that a friend wanted to make of all her favorite 60s and 70s musical groups. She's a pack rat, too, and saved the ticket stubs from every concert she attended. Bingo. There's the unifying factor. I scanned bunches of tickets to make several page backgrounds, and then scanned some of the most important ones by themselves. Now she has a *themed page background* (actually several similar but different ones so that the scrapbook doesn't get boring) and a bunch of embellishments ready to work with. She simply needs to add her photos and possibly some titles and bits of song lyrics. Figure 1.1a shows one of the ticket stub backgrounds and Figure 1.1b shows the background made into a page.

Figure 1.1

All you really need is imagination. (Ephemera courtesy of Ann Cartee.)

Style Is More Than Fashion

What about style? There are two factors to consider here: your *personal taste* and the *subject* of the scrapbook. Do you love the country look? Are you a Martha Stewart fan? Martha's scrapbook pages reflect a style of elegant simplicity, whereas the country look might have pastel pinks and blues, with flowers and calico or chintz accents.

Did you go nuts for Care Bears, Strawberry Shortcake dolls, or the Hello Kitty line? If so, your style might be "cuteness." Or perhaps you love all things Victorian. Your pages will have lace and lots of the deep mauves and grayed colors so beloved in those days. Dried flowers make nice embellishments for a Victorian-designed book.

The subject of the book might decide the style, too. You can use the Victorian look on a wedding album quite nicely, unless the wedding featured the bride in a decidedly modern mini-dress or the groom in a polyester leisure suit. In that case, it might be better to try a different, more modern look. Pages featuring really old photos almost demand an antique background. It doesn't have to be elaborate, but consider limiting your colors to some that do not overwhelm the black-and-white or sepia (brown-tinted) photos.

Color Schemes

After you've decided on a style, your color choices are the next major decision. For each page you need, at a minimum, one background color, a bright accent, and a third color that works with both. Choosing colors is easy for some people but difficult for others. I sometimes think color sense is something you're either born with or not, like having perfect pitch. I can look at a piece of khaki-colored paper and know immediately that it will look quite good with a bright turquoise and a related shade of cream. Or I could take a deep cranberry red, combine it with a pale pink and a warm gray, and have a very different looking page, even though the layout might be exactly the same.

Warm gray? Yes, colors have temperatures. Reds, yellows, oranges, and even browns are all *warm colors*. If you were doing a page about a day at the beach, you might want to try mixing red, yellow, and orange to stress the heat of the sun and sand. *Cool colors*, such as blues, greens, and violet tones, suggest cooler temperatures, perhaps cool water or leafy forest glades. Warm grays have a touch of one of the warm colors in them. Cool grays include some blue or purple to cool them off. In between is neutral gray, which doesn't lean toward either warm or cool.

Colors also have moods and even cultural associations attached to them. Hot colors are bright, bold, and jazzy. Cool colors are restful and calming. Some colors are associated with particular holidays, and some with moods or places. For instance, purple and yellow together always make me think of Easter. Red and green suggest Christmas. One good way to experiment with color schemes is to drop by your local Lowe's or Home Depot or other store with a large paint department. Grab a handful of those color chip strips. Go for a broad color range from pastels to brights. When you get home, cut them into single colors and then just move them around on a piece of white paper until you find color combinations that please you or remind you of moods or places that suggest pages in your book.

Many avid scrapbookers keep a *color wheel* to refer to. I've placed a small one on the first page of the color insert section for you. Here's a diagram (Figure 1.2) to help you see what I'm talking about. Colors on the color wheel are divided into three categories: primary, secondary, and tertiary. The *primary* colors are red, blue, and yellow. These are the "pure" colors. *Secondary* colors are an equal mix of two adjacent primaries. Red and blue make purple. Red and yellow make orange. Blue and yellow make green. It's fair to say that *any* combination of a primary color and a related secondary color, like blue with purple or blue with green, harmonizes nicely.

Tertiary colors are the colors that would be wedged in between the adjacent primary and secondary. For example, blue-green and blue-violet; they harmonize with the colors that make them. So you can happily combine turquoise blue and lime green because they have green in common, or dark blue and any shade of violet because they have blue in common.

Figure I.2

The color wheel in black and white. (See the color insert for the wheel in full color.)

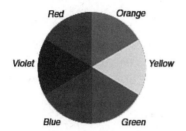

Complementary colors are the ones that are opposite each other on the color wheel, like red and green, blue and orange, and so on. They can also work as combinations, either in their bright form or often more happily as pastels. Red and green can be an effective combination, but come on too strong for some uses. Instead, think pink and pale mint green, or dark blue against tan. Remember that there's more to color than just the color. There are *tints* and *shades* and differences in *brightness*. Think of mixing white with a color to reduce the amount of pure color, giving you a pastel tint. Mix black or gray with a bright color to darken it or mute it, making a shade—for example, mauve instead of hot pink. Grayed or softened colors are particularly effective with a country or Victorian look.

If your photos are in color, make sure the colors you choose for your pages are similar to the colors in the photo. For instance, suppose you have a picture of your son ready to go trick-or-treating in his purple dinosaur suit, carrying an orange pumpkin-shaped candy bucket and posed against the shrubbery in front of your house. Got those colors in mind? Now, put him on a traditional orange-and-black Halloween page and you've completely overpowered the photo. Instead, how about using muted shades of the green, orange, and purple together? Sounds rather strange, but it works nicely. See this and some other good color combination swatches on the first page of the color section.

What to Include on a Page

Now that you've done some thinking about your scrapbook in general, you can start putting together a page. Back to square one again. What's the page about? Let's say your daughter's doing a fancy dive off the high board at the pool. What are the colors in the photo? Blue sky, blue water, red swimsuit. Okay, the red's a nice accent for lettering or for an eye-grabbing patch of color behind the photo. The background probably needs to be something in the blue to blue-green range, with a deeper value of the same color to set off a title. Decorations? Maybe a bit of clip art, such as a curling wave, a silhouetted lifeguard's chair, or whatever you happen to find. Maybe punched out sunglasses.

While you're thinking about your page, start assembling the stuff that goes on it. Do you have more than one photo? Is one enough? Sometimes it is. If it's a busy photo with a lot going on, you can make several copies of it and crop smaller pieces to use as accents around the big picture. See an example in Figure 1.3.

Figure I.3

These are all the same picture, cropped to show different scenes.

One of the great things about going digital is that you can cut copies of your photo and reuse them indefinitely, without risking damage to the original.

What's Your Format?

After you know what your book is about and why you're making it, the final question is "how?" Will the pages be printed and bound into a book, maybe fitted into page protectors for safety? Will you work on your photos digitally and then paste them on a paper page, or design and print the entire page on the computer?

What about paper? Do you need glossy photo paper to make your prints look more like snapshots? Or do you want to try specialty papers in the printer? What about paper size? Many scrapbookers prefer the 12-inch square pages, and are therefore limited to printing only parts of the page with a standard printer. You need a wide body printer like the Epson Photo Stylus 1520 shown here, in Figure 1.4, or the Canon i9100 or Hewlett-Packard CP1700 to make pages wider than 8.5×11 inches. These are a little more expensive; all three are in the $500 range. Your other option is to have your wide pages printed at a commercial copy shop like Kinko's.

Figure 1.4

The Epson Photo Stylus 1520 prints on paper up to 17×22".

If you intend to distribute your scrapbook on a CD-ROM, what format will you use? Remember, HTML (.htm) and PDF (.pdf) are the most likely types of electronic documents to be opened by any kind of computer. Unfortunately, every scrapbooking program seems to have its own way of saving pages, and each one is different enough that you can't use one program to view another program's files. If you know your friends and family use the same scrapbooking software you do, you can confidently send pages in that format. Otherwise, they might not be able to see your work using any other brand of viewer. Alternatively, standard graphic file formats like .tif, .jpg, or .png can be read by just about all graphics viewers on both Mac and Windows platforms, assuming your scrapbook program offers any of these file types as a Save option.

Putting your pages on the Web requires that you either have a website of your own or that you sign up with a service that offers web hosting as part of their package, such as Earthlink.net, Comcast.net, or Delphiforums.com. A web builder service, such as Moonfruit SiteMaker (http://www.moonfruit.com) or Site2you (http://www.site2you.com), helps you assemble your pages online, so you don't need to buy or even understand web design software. Or you can ask a Web-savvy friend for some help. I'll discuss this stuff in detail in Chapter 11, "For Web/CD-Based Scrapbooks."

If you want to put individual photos on the Web, look into websites such as Snapfish.com or ofoto.com (a Kodak company). They help you get your film photos developed, let you upload your digital photos, perform minor repairs (such as fixing red eye), and so on. After you establish an account, they provide you with a password or specific address you can send to family and friends. Then, anyone you have shared your photos with can order their own prints or high-resolution digital downloadable photos—for a fee, of course. For instance, ofoto.com offers prints from wallet size to 16×20". This is obviously not scrapbooking, but it does let your friends see some of your photos.

What's the Difference Between a Scrapbook and a Journal?

The only real difference between a scrapbook and a journal is the ratio of words to pictures. A *journal* goes further than the who, what, and when kind of photo captions you often use in a scrapbook. A journal entry tells a story, describes a place or a feeling, and includes a joke or a poem or whatever helps explain to someone else why you made the page. Journaling is sometimes more difficult for the average person than simply scrapbooking because there's usually more writing involved. Your journal entries needn't be perfect. They should reflect your thoughts and feelings, but it's okay if you want to check spelling before you commit the words to the page. I happen to like to write haiku, a very short and fun kind of poem. To write a haiku, you need to express your idea as a poem in three lines, respectively of five, seven, and five syllables. Here's one:

> *Scraps of old paper,*
>
> *The story of my childhood*
>
> *Stuck down, just one page.*

You can also "borrow" quotes from other people. When my kids were small, I liked to write down in a notebook some of the cute, funny, or profound things they said. That notebook is a wealth of quotes for pages. I especially remember my son Joshua watching Grandma's cat's new kittens.

> *"Look, mommy. They're playing with their chothers."*
>
> *"Do you mean brothers, Joshie?"*
>
> *"No. Chothers, like brothers and sisters both. Each other has their chothers."*

Made sense to me. And it made an amazing quote for the kitten pages. I cherish those little bits of childhood, especially now that both boys are grown up and out of here.

You can put together a scrapbook about anything if you have the basic materials to use for accents. I am especially fond of travel scrapbooks because I never get tired of seeing new places. One of my friends spent a lot of time in the Middle East, back when travel there wasn't so dangerous. I am very glad she made scrapbooks of Baghdad, Istanbul, Jerusalem, and other beautiful cities while they were relatively unscathed.

Scrapbooks about family members are always a big hit, and become projects you can keep on adding to as the years go by. For this kind of project, make sure you always have a camera nearby. I've never heard anyone say, "I wish I hadn't taken so many pictures."

Recipe books are a useful and fun kind of scrapbook. Do you have favorite recipes that have been passed along by family and friends? One of my friends used to make a very special apple pie every year on April 1st. It tasted great, but had no apples in it. So I got the recipe and an old photo, and made a page for Grandma Figg's Mock Apple Pie. Here it is, in Figure 1.5, and it's also in the color section.

Figure 1.5

I've made the pie and it's good. (This figure is also in the color section.)

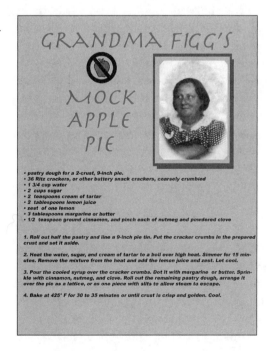

If you have or know someone who has small children, you can make *board books* or scrapbooks specifically for the kids to enjoy. Place your pictures on heavy book-binder's board, and then use sheets of laminating plastic to cover and protect the pages. Make them two sided, and to bind them, punch holes through the sides of the pages and use steel rings from the stationery store. The plastic ones can break and be swallowed, so stick with metal here. These books can be wiped clean as needed, and new pages can be added after the child has learned all the pictures and words on the first set. Magazine cutouts work well here, as do copies of photos of family members and pets. Don't use any original or one-of-a-kind photos you care about because the laminating sheets are impossible to remove.

Books and Book Covers

If you check out a large crafts store, you'll be amazed at how many choices you have for scrapbook covers. There are premade scrapbook sets with either ring binders or binders that clamp the pages together. There are bound journal-type scrapbooks with a lined page to write on and a blank page to paste on. There are, of course, book-binding supplies available to do it yourself, and then there are my personal favorites, the ubiquitous three-ring binders. They come in lots of styles, sizes, and colors, but I always look for the ones that have a clear acetate panel on the cover and end spine. What I like about these is that I can customize the fronts and spines by slipping a printed cover page under the acetate. It's also very easy to add pages or change the order if you think of or discover something else that can go in there. I also like to use acetate page protectors rather than trusting glue and good luck to hold everything together. On pages that are strictly computer generated, it's not as critical, but I still like to be able to pass the books around and not worry too much about fingerprints or somebody bending a page and popping off my carefully applied decorations.

tip

Check out online office supply mega-stores like Staples (http://www. staples.com) or Office Depot (http:// www.officedepot.com) or wholesale clubs such as Sam's Club or Costco for good prices on three-ring binders.

Binding Your Own Book

If you really want the book to be completely your own, here's a simple way to bind it. At your local art supply or craft store, you can buy what's called *bookbinder's board*. It's a heavy cardboard, almost an eighth of an inch thick. You can cover it with paper or fabric. Putting a thin layer of cotton batting under the fabric gives you a nice puffy cover. Cut the cover material (cloth or paper) about an inch larger than the book cover all around. Turn it face down and place the cover on top. After folding in the corners, glue the material to the inside of the cover as in Figure 1.6. Either miter the corners as you fold them in (as if you were making a bed) or make a V cut at each corner to reduce the bulk. Be careful not to cut your V too closely, or you might end up with a frayed corner. After that's dried, cut a piece of paper just slightly smaller than the cover and glue it, neatly centered, for an inside cover. Marbled papers look really awesome here, especially if yours is a Victorian style or traditional scrapbook. Look for whimsical prints or even nice wrapping paper for a country or "cute" look.

Don't forget to make a back cover too, repeating the steps you used for the front cover. You can make covers out of anything stiff enough to protect the pages. You might need to use a drill on very heavy or thick material to punch the holes for binding, but after the holes are in place, you can assemble the book and bind it with ribbons, heavy yarn, hemp twine, or even those clip-on rings. The crafts stores have plastic ones in a wide range of colors and sizes.

Figure 1.6

Step 1, the basic cover board. Step 2, place cover material under it. Step 3, fold material neatly over to the inside and glue. Step 4, cover with end paper and glue.

If you're sending out your scrapbook on a CD-ROM, investigate label templates. You can design a custom label and *j-card* (jewel box cover) for the CD, and print them out yourself. Go check out the paper section of the computer store, where you'll find precut CD labels that go through your regular printer, as well as cards to insert into the plastic boxes. The info on the package guides you to a web page where you can download the appropriate templates. If you go to http://www.avery.com, you can find both blank templates to use with your own art or nicely thought out sets of pre-designed templates. Insert your own information in MS Word, and print them out. Nothing can be much easier than that.

Got your pictures gathered up, your color scheme picked out, and the ideas flying? Good! Let's go look at some tools.

Summary—What You Need to Remember

The main thing to remember is to have a plan. Decide ahead of time what your scrapbook is about, how you want to organize it, how you'll display it (on paper, on the computer screen, or both), and what photos and other items you want to put into it. Decide on a style that suits the subject and a color scheme that fits the style. Gather your tools and scraps and do it!

Traditional Scrapbooking Tools

Whenever I walk into a scrapbooking store or a crafts store like Michael's or A.C. Moore, I start to feel like a kid in a candy shop. There's so much of everything you can imagine for scrapbooking and paper crafts in general, and of course, I want it all! These places can be very hard on your wallet or credit card, so it's a good idea to plan your project and make up a shopping list before you go, and then at least try to force yourself to stick to the list. I also carry a small notebook and sometimes a digital camera when I shop. If I see something I like for a future project, I'll make notes or snap a photo for later reference. I don't need to buy it until I'm ready to use it. If it's a patterned paper, perhaps I can re-create something similar on my computer at home and just print it on a light card stock, saving a dollar or so per page, and making my work even more my own. (If you're going to carry a camera with you, watch out for—and obey—signs that say "No Photography.")

Storage

Storing the paper and all the goodies and tools you have gathered for your scrapbooking projects can become a problem. I've learned the hard way that an expensive piece of vellum or handmade paper is a cat magnet and will become covered in fur and dust in the course of just one afternoon catnap. Sticky-fingered kids are another problem. Your scrapbooking papers and tools seem like fair game to them, and until they're of an age to start their own projects, you might need to declare some things strictly off limits. For households with children, I recommend storing all your scrapbooking supplies in a locking file cabinet. Because my own two boys are grown up and gone from the house, I get by with a sturdy, plastic three-drawer rolling stand (see Figure 2.1), which keeps my tools and supplies organized and keeps the cats out—unless I forget to close a drawer tightly.

Figure 2.1

A good storage container protects your scrapbooking supplies, and can serve as a printer or scanner stand, too.

What sort of scrapbooking supplies do you need most? Well, three things are basic. You need something to put on the scrapbook page, such as photos or other mementoes; something to put these things on, namely paper or card stock; and something to attach them with. Let's start with papers.

Taking Stock

Stock is how designers and printers (the people, not the machines) traditionally refer to papers. It's a question of thickness or weight. *Card stock* is generally used as a basis for scrapbook pages because it is thick enough to support attached items. It comes in a variety of colors, and might be available with preprinted designs. If not and you want a pattern on your card stock, you can run it through most inkjet printers with no trouble as long as you feed one sheet at a time through your printer. If your inkjet printer is more than a couple of years old, you might want to check the manual to see whether it can handle card stock. If not, you can take your stock and a CD or Zip disk of your pattern file to a place like Kinko's and they'll print it for you.

Text weight papers, such as copy paper or inkjet paper, are often used as layers of a page design, to set off titles or photos, or to add some color and texture to the page. If you look in any office supply store or craft store, you'll find tons of preprinted or pretextured papers just waiting to inspire you. These papers might be a bit flimsy to use as a background if you're adding lots of stuff to your design. That's why it's best to either back them up with card stock or make sure that your pages go into protective plastic holders. (We'll talk more about those in a minute.)

Tissue papers come in wonderful colors and are great for cutting designs from. They are, however, a real nuisance to attach to the page. I like to use them with thinned out Elmer's school glue to make interesting covers for my scrapbooks and for decorating memory boxes. Building layers of translucent tissue creates a stained-glass-like covering. Check out the color insert section to see an example of this kind of tissue work.

Don't neglect any part of the craft or office supply store when you're looking for ideas. I picked up the most amazing paper doilies, even some in gold and silver, in the candy-making section of one of the big craft stores. These work beautifully on a Victorian design or on any kind of romantic wedding or Valentine page. You can use the smaller ones, or pieces of a large one, to frame a baby picture too. Figure 2.2 shows some of these.

Figure 2.2

Shops that sell candy-making or cake-decorating supplies are a good source for paper laces.

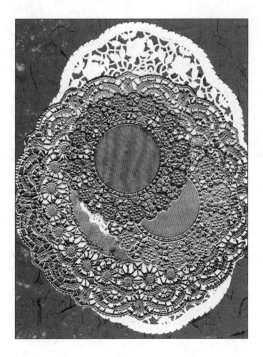

Vellum is a scrapbooking basic. It's a translucent paper designed to resemble the antique parchments that were actually made of animal skins scraped thin. Don't worry. No animals are involved in today's vellum process. It's purely synthetic. Some kinds of vellum have a rougher texture on one side than the other. If you are using vellum with an inkjet printer, be sure to print on the rougher side, and give the ink plenty of time to dry before you touch the printed vellum page. You can speed up the drying time, if you need to, with a hair dryer on low or a heat gun purchased from the craft store. If you do use a heat gun, please be careful. They get very hot. Keep it a safe distance from your project. You can actually set fire to delicate papers, according to one of the editors of this book who's had an unfortunate experience.

The Acid Test

Whatever materials you select to work with, it's very important that you make sure they are safe for scrapbooking. After all, you want your scrapbooks to protect your pictures, not destroy them. Many papers are made with a process that uses an acid to help break down the fibers and give the paper a smooth finished surface. Also, wood pulp often contains a natural substance called *lignin* that breaks down into an acid over time. You know what acid does—and it's not pretty. Acid in the paper can react with chemicals present in all photographs and even in such things as ribbon or dried flowers that you might use for decorations. So you need to avoid direct contact between acid and your photographs whenever possible.

Be sure your papers are either acid-free or lignin-free, or at least acid-fast, meaning the acid won't migrate into your photos and other scraps. Hammermill, a paper manufacturer, uses a non-acid process in the making of all its papers, so that brand is generally safe for scrapbooks and other photo preservation projects. If you are unsure whether the paper you have is acid-free or acid-fast, you can get an acid testing pen at the craft store. To use it, just make a tiny dot on one corner of the paper. If it changes color, your paper isn't the best choice for a scrapbook. Use it for shopping lists or something else noncritical.

To make the job even easier, just look for the letters "CK OK" on scrapbook materials you buy. Creative Keepsakes, one of the better scrapbook and paper craft companies, developed a program to test materials and places their stamp of approval on those that are safe. Other companies are welcome to submit their products for testing, and if they pass, can display the same seal. Creative Memories, another of the leaders in the scrapbooking industry, makes a strong point of repeatedly mentioning that all of their products are acid-free, lignin-free, and chemically buffered to have a neutral acid/alkaline ratio.

Newsprint, used by newspapers and some magazine publishers because it is less expensive, is almost always full of acid. That's why it turns yellow and crumbly as it ages. If you're including newspaper clippings in your scrapbook, copy them onto safe paper, or put them in archival plastic sleeves from the craft store. The sleeves won't stop the yellowing, but they'll protect the rest of your book.

The computer store is another good place to look for papers. In addition to the usual wide variety of inkjet papers and glossy photo paper, you can find a really cool selection of items such as print-on stickers, tags, CD labels (in case you decide to distribute your scrapbook as a CD-ROM), some specialty inkjet papers with a canvas, linen, or silk finish, and even some *art papers*. These are heavyweight textured papers like the ones artists use for pen and ink or watercolor work.

> **tip**
>
> You can also get iron-on transfer paper to place photos and designs on your t-shirts, caps, or tote bags. (If you try these, remember to reverse or flip the design so it reads correctly when you iron it on.) If you happen to have an item that's difficult to iron on, such as a baseball cap, iron the design onto a small cloth patch, and then sew it on the hat.

Booking It

At some point you'll need a book to keep your pages in. If your pages are completely printed, you can take the easy way out by punching them with a three-hole punch and using a three-ring binder. If you crave something a bit more interesting, or if your pages are full of stuck-on stuff and you worry about damage, look for a book with plastic page protectors included. You can usually buy packs of these page protectors in case the book doesn't come with enough sleeves for all your pages. There are also books that clamp together to hold pages firmly in place. Some are *binding systems* that have you drill holes through the pages and a front and back cover, and then bind your book with plastic rings. These can be kind of fun, given the right book. There are also bound books with paper or card stock pages you can paste directly onto. I don't recommend these except for writing journals because they are small and, I think, too flimsy for heavily decorated scrapbook pages.

If this is your first scrapbooking attempt, I strongly urge you to start with a premade scrapbook. There's time enough to master the art of book binding when you have several books stacked up and you have more experience. Sleeves come in several sizes, up to 12×12 inches. If you have a printer that accommodates a wide page, these are fun because you have more space in which to place your designs than on an 8 1/2×11-inch sheet.

Stay far away from *magnetic photo albums*. Those were one of the worst ideas to come out of the 1960s and 1970s. Photos that were stored in such albums can sometimes be rescued by scanning the images, without attempting to remove the photos from the album page. But, contrary to the claims made when they were sold, you often can't just peel the pictures out of such albums again. They're stuck in there, and the adhesive might have caused some unexpected and nasty color shifts in some older photos.

Sticky Stuff

Okay, you have a photo and a page to put it on. You need something to attach the picture to the page. First of all, no matter what the men in your life might say, don't use duct tape! Also, don't use super glue, rubber cement, or regular scotch tape. They'll all eventually destroy your pictures.

There are a variety of glues that are safe and do the job very well. *Safe*, in this case, means they are acid-free and of archival quality. Anything that calls itself *archival* is supposed to be able to be used "without deleterious effect in the conservation or care of important artifacts." Figure 2.3 shows some of the sticky stuff from my work chest. They come in different styles according to how they're applied. The simplest is the *glue stick*. It's a tube not unlike a lipstick tube. These are available almost everywhere. I think I bought my current one at the supermarket. They're cheap, not too messy, and stick without lumps or clumps. There are also *liquid glue pens*. You press the pen on the paper, and a dab of glue is released. Press harder and longer for a bigger dab. These are great for gluing small objects, such as buttons or ribbon, because you have good control over where you put the glue. You can even draw or write with a glue pen, and before the glue dries, dust it with glitter or colored chalk powder for some cool textured lettering.

You can also buy *bottled liquid glues* for scrapbooking. They come in dispenser bottles with a very small nozzle, like the glue pen, and are also easy to control when gluing small bits of stuff on a page. Some of these liquid glues can be used like rubber cement, in that you can make them form either a permanent or temporary bond between your materials. If you stick the photo down with wet glue, it forms a very strong bond. But if you apply glue to the general area where you want the photo and allow it to dry completely, you can put the picture down, and peel it up again and move it if it doesn't look right. Follow the package directions to make sure you end up with a permanent bond.

Figure 2.3

Stick with these and you won't get stuck.

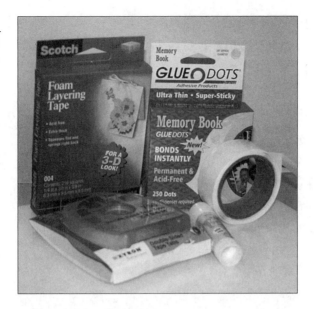

Finally, there are *glue dots* in various sizes. They come on a paper backing. Peel them off and stick them to the item you are gluing and then just press it down on the page. These too are moveable. They come in several thicknesses, letting you give a page some dimensional quality by mounting things on thick dots to stand out. *Double-stick tapes* involve the same concept, only in a line instead of a dot. Easily applied with a tape roller, double-stick is often a good way to go. It's ideal if you are scrapbooking with your kids because it's spill-proof and not messy, and if you drop it, you just pick it up again. Also, look for what's called *photo splits*. They come by the box, and you pull off as many as you need from the dispenser, stick them on the page, and then peel off the protective top layer and stick your pictures on them. Nothing can be easier than that.

The easiest and least destructive way to attach your photos to your pages is the same method grandma used—those little *stick-on corners* that hold the photo in place. You can make your own corners or buy them precut. If you had a bunch of envelopes you don't need, you can cut off the corners and recycle them. Because that's rather unlikely, you can make them yourself from whatever scraps are handy. Take a small piece of paper, as in Figure 2.4. This one's a used sticky note. Fold the corners toward the center at a 45-degree angle, making a pyramid shape. Then cut the pyramid to a nice square corner. Or use scissors with a scalloped or other fancy edge to dress up or add style to your scrapbook page.

Figure 2.4
Stick-on corners
work best with glue
dots or photo splits.

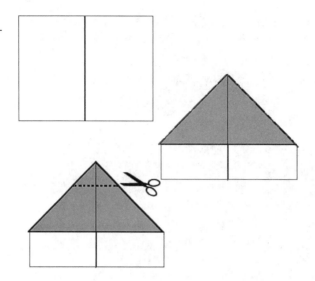

You can buy corners in a range of colors and styles—preglued, too. It saves time, and when you use them, you can be sure they won't put your precious family pictures at risk. Using corners also lets you pop the picture out of its holder to read the writing on the back, which is important in the case of very old photos that have been handed down through several generations.

Don't Run with Scissors

Scissors are a necessity unless you're working entirely on the computer. Then, of course, you need a graphics program that enables you to crop your pictures on the screen. I always have at least two pairs of scissors available, large ones for cutting corners or trimming bigger pieces of paper or other material, and a pair of manicure scissors or sharp-tipped embroidery scissors for cutting out small designs or whatever is too difficult with the big ones. Get the best scissors you can, and keep them in a safe place. (Henckels and Fiskars are both good brands.) If you go to classes or croppings and carry your tools in a bag, for heaven's sake, cover your scissors with a sheath. Otherwise, you can damage the tips (or yourself). You can even improvise one by folding a piece of card stock or heavy paper and stapling or gluing it to form a pocket. See Figure 2.5 for an example.

You can also get, as mentioned previously, scissors with fancy edges. They come in all kinds of patterns, from zigzags to scallops to the old-fashioned deckle edges reminiscent of drugstore-processed photos from the 1950s. If that's a look you're trying to achieve, print your photos on glossy paper and trim them with the photo edge scissors. The only drawback I've found to this tool is that you do need to carefully watch what you're doing. I make a light line with a pencil and ruler to cut along, and with successive cuts I have to try very hard to match the pattern. Sometimes it's perfect, sometimes it's not. You can always put a sticker or some other little embellishment over a goof, so don't worry too much if you get off-track while cutting a decorative edge. By the way, don't try to use these scissors as pinking shears, if you also sew. They're not strong enough for cloth, and they can't easily be resharpened; so after they are dull, they're gonzo.

Figure 2.5

This protective sheath was made by cutting a corner from a Manila envelope.

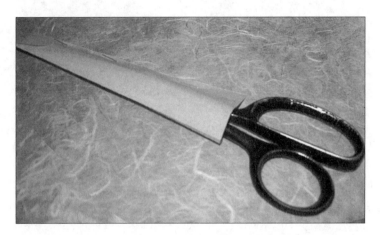

In the same general category of sharp stuff, look for a good sturdy art knife, such as an X-ACTO brand knife, and a cork-backed metal ruler for cutting straight edges. You also need a piece of scrap cardboard to cut on, or even better, one of those self-healing cutting mats from the craft store. You'll most likely find them near the scissors and knives. They have a smooth, slightly resilient surface that accepts even very deep cuts and then reseals itself. Pretty amazing technology, if you ask me. Anyway, it's not an absolute must, but a very nice addition to your toolkit that helps to protect the table where you work on your projects.

And then there are *punches*. I can get punchy describing all the different kinds. Seriously. Name a holiday, name a shape, name a critter, and you can find little punches to cut them out of paper. Hearts, dinosaurs, cats and dogs, umbrellas (for when it's raining cats and dogs, I suppose), and so many more, you have to see them all to believe it. Don't forget you can use both the shapes you cut out, and the stuff you cut them from. A strip of hearts punched out of a red ribbon is a cute addition to any romantically themed page. Save the hearts for some other use and mount the punched ribbon on the page as a decorative accent.

Figure 2.6 shows one of my punch tools, and some precut stick-ons, too.

Figure 2.6

Try punching colored papers, ribbons, foils, and even hologram papers.

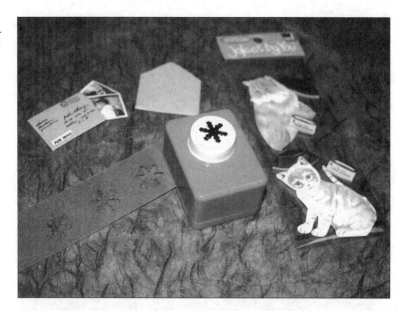

I'd certainly be remiss if I didn't mention *edge trimmers* and *paper cutters* somewhere in here. You probably remember paper cutters from your school days. I remember being warned to stay away from them because you can lose a finger in a split second. "Let the teacher do it," we were told. In one dramatic experiment, our teacher sliced a potato, just to show us she wasn't kidding around. The good news is that today there are safer ones that won't leave you missing a digit. If you're not good with a knife and straight edge, look for a safety trimmer. The cutter slides back and forth on a bar and gives you a smooth edge, every time. Some even come with deckle edge and scallop edge cutters that do the same tricks as the fancy scissors, only without your needing to cut extra carefully and line up the patterns.

Finding the "Write" Tools

When you're using a computer to create your scrapbook pages, you won't need as many of the calligraphy pens, markers, and other writing tools used by nondigital scrapbookers. What you do need, though, is a good source of *computer typefaces*, also called *fonts*. There are, of course, tons of free versions on the Web. Some typefaces are more amateur in appearance, whereas others are professionally created by artists and designers. Figure 2.7 shows a single page from one of the many free font sites.

Figure 2.7

To find pages like these, do an Internet search for "free fonts PC" (or "Mac," as appropriate).

You can also find inexpensive, but well-indexed, CD-ROM collections of fonts at your local computer store, in the ads in the backs of computer magazines, and so on. Stay away from the professional ones like Agfa, ITC, and Adobe unless you want to pay a lot of money for a single font. Such expensive fonts are intended for professional use and are not a good value for most scrapbook projects. By the way, most of the scrapbooking programs, such as PhotoExpress My Scrapbook by ULead and Art Explosion Scrapbook Factory by Nova Development, come with a collection of fonts. These are generally pretty good ones, chosen specifically to be useful for scrapbooking.

One of the many advantages of computer lettering is that, if you set your type using a word processor or a program such as Photoshop Elements, you can check your spelling as you work. Nothing says amateur like a misspelled word. It's like a blot on the paper.

The one warning I always give about fonts is not to get carried away. Remember that, first of all, the purpose of putting words on a page is so they can be read. If the font you choose is illegible, either because it was made that way or because you've set it in yellow on pink, well…nobody's going to bother to decipher the text. So what's the point of putting it there? If you use more than two unrelated fonts on a page, you'll end up with a different kind of mess, but one that is just as confusing for the viewer. Remember that the words have meaning and the way you choose to display them determines how important the message is. You wouldn't use the same font for a wedding page as for "Billy's Baseball Adventure" or "A Visit from the Great Pumpkin." At least, I hope you wouldn't. Don't feel limited to plain vanilla fonts, either. There's a lot of variety and character, or comic, fonts suitable for all occasions. Just use them wisely, and let the message and the reason for the pages help you decide the lettering styles you use.

On the other hand, if you are a master calligrapher, or just someone with really nice handwriting, you can have a lot of fun and make something truly unique by hand lettering your titles, journal entries, and photo captions. My own handwriting is awful. I don't even try. Which means I don't have a good excuse to buy many gel markers, glitter markers, metallic pens, and other kinds of pens, pencils and such found on the shelves of the arts and crafts stores. That hasn't truly stopped me. You can see some of my toys in Figure 2.8.

Figure 2.8
Colored markers and such are both useful and fun.

Stamping Grounds

Rubber stamping is a legitimate craft of its own, but it's also a good technique for scrapbookers to have in their bag of tricks. Stamps are one of the best ways for non-artists to get pictures on their pages. Rubber stamps come in just about every imaginable design, from alphabets to art. You can purchase bugs, beasts, butterflies, cats and dogs, Celtic designs, all holidays, drawings and etchings from the Renaissance masters, Victorian art, and much more. Do a Web search on rubber stamps or just check out http://www.rubberstampsclub.com, http://www.aboutrubberstamps.com, or http://www.addictedtorubberstamps.com. These are three of the best sites I've found for a good selection of stamps and accessories.

Accessories? Oh, yeah. You don't get away with just the same old standard red or black stamp pad you might use at the office. Serious stampers collect stamp pads almost as much as they do the stamps to go with them. There are all kinds of colors and color combinations. Figure 2.9 shows just a tiny sample.

Embossing is a stamper's technique for creating a raised surface from the stamp. First you stamp, using a special pad. Then you dust the stamped design with powder. Shake off the excess, and warm the design with a hot air gun, melting the powder into a slightly raised shiny or matte line that clings only where the lines of the stamp were pressed to the paper.

Figure 2.9

Stamps come in all kinds of sizes and designs.

After you have stamped a design, you can use a variety of markers or watercolor paints to add color to it. Just be careful to stay within the lines and not to let the paper get too wet. Doing your stamping on a heavy paper stock or on watercolor paper helps prevent wrinkling and warping.

The computer version of rubber stamping is called *clip art*, and you can find pretty much the same variety of stuff and probably lots more. Print Explosion and Art Explosion, both published by Nova Development, offer thousands of pieces of art you can use in your scrapbooks. No matter what you're looking for, it's there somewhere. If you don't want to spend money, look on the Internet for free clip art. Here again, make sure it's free or pay the (usually) small shareware fees. It's not nice to steal.

Embellishments

Embellishments is a big word for little odds and ends of stuff. Do you need them? Not really. Do they add to a page? Sometimes. We're talking now about the items such as charms, ribbons, tags, eyelets, and other goodies you might want to stick on your pages. Some of them, like ticket stubs and souvenirs of your travels, are entirely appropriate. Others, just stuck on for no particular reason, might not really add anything but clutter to the page. Use them, but use them sparingly.

What should you look for, and where should you look? Well, your jewelry box might be a good place to start. Charms from old charm bracelets are fun. You can pry fake stones from broken junk jewelry. Just make sure it's really junk and not valuable before you use it in your project. Check the notions section of a fabric store for small buttons, spangles, tiny pearls, and of course, rickrack, ribbons, seam bindings, and odd bits of lace. If the stuff is too thick or sharp-edged to mount on the page or if you're sticking to computer designed pages, scan the trinkets, and paste them in on the computer. If you use scans, you can also resize them, which you can't do with the real thing.

tip If you scan an object to put on a page, try adding a drop shadow behind it. It looks more 3D that way. Drop shadows are explained in Chapter 6, "Backgrounds."

Military medals, service ribbons, and collar bars and buttons all make nice decorations for a page about your favorite military person or veteran. Scan them rather than applying them directly, as they can otherwise damage adjacent pages.

Glitter can be messy, but it can also be lots of fun to use. Draw or write with a glue pen, and then sprinkle glitter over the lines. Let it dry thoroughly and then give the paper a good hard shake over a wastebasket to remove the loose bits. Finally, be sure your glittered pages go into a book with plastic sleeves to keep the shedding down to a minimum.

Stickers are a favorite of many scrapbookers. They are easy to use and add color and character to a page. They are also an easy way out if you want art on the page, and can't draw or paint even enough to fill in a rubber stamp design. Kids started sticker collecting as a craze about the same time their parents started scrapbooking, probably about 20 years ago. I certainly remember mine asking for certain stickers, and then finding them stuck on everything in the house. Some of the better known sticker companies include Mrs. Grossman's, Suzy's Zoo, Stickapotamus, and Sandy Lion. For one of many good sources, check out http://www.stickersgalore.com. They have more than 75 sticker brands, plus probably a lot more scrapbooking stuff than you even dreamt was possible. I've found tons of ideas on their pages, too.

Ephemera

Ephemera is a term that describes all the stuff you have collected in desk drawers, little boxes, envelopes, and wherever your own inner pack rat takes you. A lot of it is surprisingly good for scrapbooking. I love to mix in things like foreign coins and stamps from my trips abroad, and even baggage tags from the hotels I stayed at, and the collections I made on my first European trip as a teenager. One such collection included hotel Do Not Disturb signs and another included lumps of wrapped sugar from the various cafes, restaurants, and even the trains we rode on. Those didn't travel too well, so I ended up peeling them and sticking all the wrappers in the back of my travel diary, and they were eventually thrown out. I'd love to have them now. They'd make an awesome page, along with some cups of coffee, tea and chocolate, and perhaps a cutout of a cookie or two and a scrap of poetry about sugar or sweetness, or even lyrics to the "Java Jive." You could add a photo of two people under a Cinzano umbrella in wire chairs at a tiny table, and a (carefully painted) ring from a spilled espresso.

These are the kinds of things that make interesting pages. You must have a ton of them tucked away. Why not dig them out and put them to work for you?

Summary—What You Need to Remember

Here the bottom line is really basic: You need papers, something to put on the paper, and something to hold it there, preferably not duct tape or staples. Always look for acid-free or lignin-free supplies. Acid in paper eats pictures. Glues and double-stick tapes are good for keeping your pictures in place; so are corner pockets, which you can make or buy. After you have the basic page, you can add all kinds of embellishments to make it more interesting. If you have valuable or bulky items, scan them, rather than putting them directly on the pages.

Digital Tools: Hardware

Hardware includes all that computer stuff—the computer itself, its keyboard, monitor, mouse or trackball, and the printer. Chances are you have all that if you're reading this book. You don't need the world's fanciest or most powerful computer to build scrapbooks. And you should know how to make it perform common tasks such as copying, pasting, and saving your work. If you're a real newcomer to the computer world, consider getting a good book on your particular computer and operating system and working through it before you start scrapbooking, or at least having such a book handy for reference as you go along. The *Sams Teach Yourself in 24 Hours* series is a good place to begin. It's not really important whether you use a Mac or a PC. I prefer Macintosh for graphics myself, and you'll find that many of the screen captures in this book have obviously been taken from a Mac. The software I'm recommending and working with for the rest of this book, Photoshop Elements 3, comes in both Mac and Windows versions. The bottom line is to use the computer you have.

The Computer

If you're really a beginner, let's start here. At its most basic, a computer includes a box called a *CPU* (central processing unit , essentially the brain of the machine), a *monitor* (a video display that lets you see what you're doing), and a *keyboard* (to input text and commands). It can, however, be a lot more than a "smart typewriter." By adding a mouse, trackball, or graphics tablet with a stylus, you can begin to use the computer as a writing and drawing tool. The mouse or trackball moves the pointer (or cursor) around on the screen so you can easily edit text, navigate the Internet, draw and paint, and so on. Drawing with a trackball is very difficult, and using a mouse isn't all that much better, so artists often have a graphics tablet and stylus in addition to a keyboard and mouse. The plastic stylus acts and feels like a pen, and is much easier to use than a mouse or trackball for creating and editing artwork or touching up photographs. I strongly urge you to try one at your local computer store and buy it if you like it. I wouldn't use anything else now that I am used to the tablet. Wacom (http://www.wacom.com) makes high-quality tablets in various sizes.

Computers also need a way to get data in and out, and a place to keep it. These functions are served by an internal and/or external hard drive and some sort of disc reader/writer. Today, software comes on CD-ROMs and your computer likely has a built-in CD-ROM drive. If not, or if you want extra input, you can usually install another CD and/or DVD reader and writer. You can also add bigger and faster hard drives for more data storage, which you'll probably need if you choose a high resolution camera or scanner.

Resolution? I Resolve to Explain...

The term *resolution* comes up every time I talk about cameras or scanners, and even monitors and printers. Resolution refers to the quality of the image produced by a camera or scanner, displayed by a computer screen, or created by a printer. Resolution measures the number of dots or *pixels* (which stands for picture element, the preferred term for dots on the computer screen) per square inch of image. A higher resolution means that the image is made up of more, smaller pixels per inch.

When you look at a picture on your computer or television screen, you're looking at a bunch of relatively large colored dots. (The typical screen resolution for an inexpensive monitor is 72 *dots per inch*, abbreviated as dpi.) Each dot measures 1/72 of an inch across. Your eye and brain work together to blur the dots into an image. Each dot or pixel has slightly different amounts of the red, green, and blue phosphors that give off light in those colors. They mix visually to make each dot a different color.

If you're familiar with the paintings of Georges Seurat, the famous pointillist painter, you'll remember that he placed tiny, individual dots of color on his canvas. Because you can actually see the little dots and count them, his paintings are at a very low resolution. He was probably working at about 25 dpi, or 625 (25 squared) little dots of paint per square inch of canvas. With patience like that, he should have been a scrapbooker. Figure 3.1 shows a greatly magnified view of a small piece of a Seurat painting. As you can see, every dot is a different shade of color, translated by your eye and brain into a unified image.

Figure 3.1

This is blown up to show the dots better. (Georges Seurat, "Sunday Afternoon on the Island of La Grande Jatte")

A similar kind of dot is found on the *sensor*, the "film" part of the digital camera. These sensor dots analyze the light that falls on them, determining its percentage of red, green, and blue. Then the digital camera records this info along with the position of the dot in the captured image. That gets to be a lot to remember. So when you upload the picture to the computer from the camera, all that information is included. The more pixels per square inch you have to deal with, the higher the resolution of the image, and the more memory it takes to hold it all. So, higher resolution means bigger files as well as better-quality pictures. Of course, it takes more time to open and process a large file. It takes more storage space, both on the camera's flashcard and on the computer itself, to save them. You can actually save a little money here by not buying more camera than you need. Think about what you want to do with it other than scrapbooking, and whether you really need 5-megapixel resolution. If you're going to be shooting outdoors, in a variety of lighting situations, it's more important to find a camera with a flash and a zoom lens.

So, What's a Megapixel, Anyway?

A megapixel is *not* a single pixel that's been super-sized. Megapixel is shorthand for one million pixels. So a 5-megapixel camera captures 5 million pixels worth of information. A 3-megapixel camera captures 3 million pixels worth. You can expect to pay more for higher resolution, but you get photos that are very clear even when enlarged. If you're not planning to enlarge the photos to a size larger than 8×10 inches, you don't need a 5-megapixel camera. A 2- or 3-megapixel model does the job.

Digital Cameras

When consumer-level digital cameras first came out, somewhere in the early 1990s, they were more of a gimmick than a useful tool. The resolution wasn't good enough to make a print more than a few inches wide. Photographers weren't ready to give up their film cameras, and computer fanatics weren't into photography except as a way to fancy up their websites. But as a relatively short time passed, several things happened. Digital cameras improved and became more affordable, and picture-editing software also improved and became easier to use. Meanwhile, the scrapbook craze was growing bigger and bigger. It seemed logical to combine them.

Today's digital cameras are amazing. Most of them don't look much different from the ordinary 35mm and pocket-size snapshot cameras you're used to. They slide right into your handbag, brief-case, fanny pack, or jacket pocket without weighing you down. They mostly run on AA batteries, which are available anywhere. Most use inter-changeable compact flashcards or the newer, even smaller SD (secure digital) cards or xD picture cards for memory. A single card smaller than a matchbook can hold several hundred or more pictures. These cards can be reused indefinitely, and come in sizes from 32 megabytes to 1 gigabyte (1000Mb).

tip The price of memory cards has dropped significantly over the past year. Buy the biggest cards you can afford, memorywise, especially if you're planning to travel and take a lot of pictures. A 5-megapixel camera with a 512Mb memory card can hold 204 photos.

Digital cameras work somewhat the same way film cameras do. Light passes through a lens, but instead of exposing a piece of film, it touches a sensor panel. On both kinds of camera, you can focus the lens and adjust the lens aperture and exposure, or let the camera do it for you. The lens aperture determines how much light is allowed to pass through the lens, and the exposure is the length of time (in fractions of a second) that the light reaches the sensor. One nice feature that most digital cameras include is a *view screen* that lets you see your photos immediately, so you can erase the ones that you consider a waste of film.

Figure 3.2 shows a couple of my favorite digital cameras, along with their flash-cards. You can get a camera with a 5-megapixel resolution for what you paid for a 640×480 (less than one megapixel) resolution model only five years ago.

Figure 3.2

I really like my Nikons, but there are less expensive cameras that do the job just as well.

Why Go Digital?

The advantages of digital photography are many. Digital cameras are typically lighter weight and easier to carry around. You don't need to buy film or pay for processing. And you're not contributing to the chemical waste the processing plants dump into the sewers, which eventually end up in the water supply.

Digital photography is faster than traditional film photography. There's no need to wait for film to be processed into prints and scanned into electronic format. You can look at your digital photos as soon as you've taken them. If there's a TV set handy, you can display your pictures on the TV screen just by plugging in a cable that's included with the camera. Transferring the photo from the camera to the computer takes only a few seconds. All you do is plug a cable from the camera into the computer (following the instructions included with your camera), open the downloading program that came with the camera, and choose the picture that you want to import.

Most digital cameras also let you throw away bad shots so they don't waste memory space. The photos you decide to keep last as long as the hard disk, floppy, CD-ROM, or other storage medium you save them on lasts—virtually forever—without scratching, fading, or color shifting.

Another advantage is the space you'll save. Nearly all digital cameras save pictures to a *flashcard*, a piece of plastic about half the size of a business card and only a little thicker. You can pack 20 of these flashcards in the space occupied by just two rolls of 35mm film, and carry as many as 5,000 high-quality pictures, instead of the 72 that the film holds. The new xD cards are scarcely larger than a postage stamp, and have up to a 512 Mb capacity. If you carry only a couple, and have access to a computer, you can upload your pictures and recycle the flashcard to hold more, an ideal situation for the world traveler or roving photo-journalist as well as the family on vacation.

In the long run, digital photography can be cheaper. After you're past the initial investment—the camera, the computer, image-manipulation software, and a color printer—your pictures don't cost you anything. You'll never run out of film, and you'll never need to buy any.

Having said that, you won't be paying for film, but you might want to find a place to buy AA batteries by the case. (Costco and Sam's Club have bulk packs at reasonable prices.) Whenever possible, run these cameras from their AC power packs. Lithium batteries give longer service, but because they cost more, it's a toss-up whether you save anything by using them. A few sets of rechargeable batteries and a charger are definitely a wise investment.

When You Go Camera Shopping, Consider...

If you think that you'll need to take several pictures of something in rapid sequence, choose your digital camera very carefully. Not all models can handle *high-speed recovery* between shots. Most require a delay of anywhere from 3–10 seconds or more between pictures while the camera compresses and stores the image it's just captured. A better way to take a sequence of pictures is to use a video camera. It freezes the action every 1/30th of a second, so you can analyze a golf swing or watch the figure skater take off and land the triple Salchow as well as catch her at the peak of the jump. Such sequential photos are a fun addition to a scrapbook page, too.

If you are planning to buy a digital camera strictly to capture images for scrapbooking, any kind of point-and-shoot camera suffices. You're not going to be worrying very much about image resolution because you're not going to be using big prints. However, after you see how easy digital cameras are to use, and how good the pictures are, even from an older model, you're probably going to want the best one you can find. Digital cameras are sold in camera stores, computer stores, and catalogs. You'll find about the same prices everywhere. You can also usually save a few bucks by shopping on eBay for a slightly older but higher-resolution model. Beware of exceptionally low-priced cameras. They might be "gray market" merchandise brought in from third-world countries and therefore not covered by warranty. Or they might be cheaply made imitations of the good ones. I still remember buying what I thought was a really good calculator for just five dollars on a bargain table, and then getting it home and noticing that the brand name was "Shrap." Not very sharp of me!

Other considerations when digital camera shopping include the flash and the zoom. Although most experts don't use built-in flashes on cameras, I have found them to be very useful. You simply need to be aware of the shadow the flash casts, and position the photo subject where a cast shadow won't matter. The built-in zoom lens is a must-have in my opinion. You can't always stand as close to something as you want, but you can zoom in closer on it, or you can pull back for a wider angle shot without moving the camera—and yourself—into a possibly dangerous location. Generally speaking, digital cameras use a *multiplier* (shown as 2×, 5×, or 10×) to represent their capability to "zoom" in on a subject. For example, a normal non-zoom lens shows what you can see with your unaided eye. A 10× zoom is 10 times better, revealing more detail and making a subject appear that much closer to the camera. Always look for the words *optical zoom* rather than digital zoom. An optical zoom changes the length of the lens, whereas a digital zoom is just a gimmick that makes the pixels bigger so whatever you're shooting looks bigger than it is. It lowers the picture quality in the process.

A *macro*, or *close-focus*, lens setting is also very desirable, especially for scrapbooking. You can use your digital camera as a quick-and-easy scanner to copy pictures and small objects that you want to put on a page. Because the lens, set to macro and fully zoomed in, lets you make nice clean copies of things at their full size—or larger in some cases—you can enlarge a picture to the point where you can use it as a background for a page. Figure 3.3 shows a quick example of this really neat effect. You'll read more about this later, when you get into designing pages.

Suppose you just want to shoot a few digital pictures and you aren't ready to spend a lot of money on a camera. There's a solution for your problem, a *one-use digital camera*. You can take a picture, view it in the camera, and either keep it or discard it. When the camera's full (it holds 25 photos), you take it back to the store, and they give you—for another 10 bucks—a set of high-quality 4×6 inch prints and a CD-ROM with all your pictures.

Figure 3.3

You can fade the colors of the photo to make it a better background.

Scanners

The typical desktop scanner looks and acts very much like a photocopier. In fact you can get multipurpose boxes that scan, make photocopies, and also print from your computer. Some can also serve as fax machines. A typical scanner has a flat glass bed, and a lens inside that moves back and forth to read whatever you have placed on the glass plate. The machine gathers the image, one line at a time, and records the data the same way the digital camera does, but directly to the computer. Figure 3.4 is a picture of my current scanner, a Microtek ScanMaker 5700. I chose this one mainly because it is fast and reasonably accurate colorwise.

Figure 3.4

The Microtek
ScanMaker 5700.

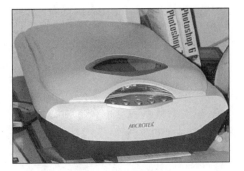

These days you'll find scanners that connect to your computer by FireWire, as well as USB, parallel port, and SCSI. Some can even connect via radio frequency to an AirPort wireless network (an Apple product). The HP PSC 1350 is typical of the combination scanner, printer, and copier. For its size, it's remarkably good at both scanning and printing, and is ideal for scrapbookers because you can plug a camera or compact flashcard directly into it. This helpful device is shown in Figure 3.5. You can print directly from a flashcard, with no computer involved.

Figure 3.5

The HP PSC 1350
and the Epson CX
6400—both small,
but effective.

The process of printing directly from a Compact flashcard is really quite simple. First, you plug the card into a slot in the printer. Then you print a proof page that shows all the images on the card. Finally, you simply select the ones you want to print, and run them off in any size from 4×6" to 8 1/2×13". Refer to the owner's manual for your printer to learn how to choose and load different paper sizes, and how to print the proof.

Epson also makes several good combination printer, scanner, and copiers. The CX 6400 does all the same tricks the HP does, and costs about the same. Comparing the same photo printed from both printers, I preferred the Epson version. The color seemed smoother, and the image appeared to have less grain, as if the Epson used smaller ink drops. However, either one suffices.

You Gotta Have Connections

Computers need to be able to "talk" to their printers, scanners, cameras, external drives, and to the Internet. They can make these connections several ways. It used to be that SCSI (small computer system interface, pronounced "scuzzy") and parallel ports (LPT 1 and LPT 2) were pretty much the only way to do so. SCSI had a lot of problems, sometimes needing a bit of magic to make it work. If the cable was too long, the signal faded out before it got where it was going. If the signal was too strong or not properly terminated, it caused misleading echoes that the computer would try to interpret. That didn't work either. Then came a newer, faster kind of connection called USB (universal serial bus). USB seems to be free of most of these problems and is faster and uses less expensive cable and connectors. Then Apple gave us FireWire, for PCs as well as for Macs. It's faster than USB, and even more reliable. Finally, there are wireless hubs, such as Apple's AirPort and AirPort Extreme, that connect your keyboard, mouse, and other devices using radio frequency technology. PC users can find similar wireless technology at the computer store or using an online merchant.

Because most of the photos you'll be adding to a scrapbook are from old paper prints, owning a scanner saves you both money and time. They're not expensive, and using one is about as complicated as making a photocopy. You place the item you want to scan on the scanner's glass plate, close the cover, and click the Scan button. By installing the proprietary software that came with your scanner, you can begin a new scan, preview the image, and choose how to save data to your computer's hard drive. Image editing programs like Adobe Photoshop Elements let you scan directly into a new document in the program. In fact, the majority of scanners on the market today come with Photoshop Elements or another picture-editing program as well as their own proprietary scanning software.

You can use your scanner to photograph small objects, too. Old jewelry, coins, medals, and other small mementos scan just as well as photos and can then be printed as photos and mounted on foam core board to give your pages some depth. Figure 3.6 shows a few examples. Notice how clear they are. When you are scanning objects, make sure they don't scratch against the scanner's glass plate.

Figure 3.6

These were all scanned with the Microtek scanner.

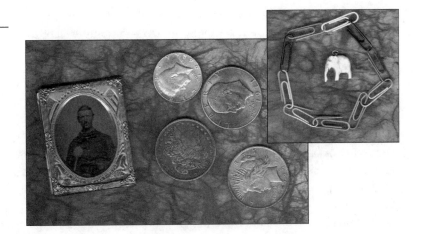

In addition to image-gathering software, most scanners come with software that lets you scan text into an *optical character recognition (OCR)* program and edit it in your word processor. If you have old documents that you want to share via email, such as old family newspaper clippings, this is a good way to transfer the content to your computer. OCR scanning doesn't preserve the look of the document, though. It's just for getting the words into the computer without having to retype them.

tip

Several scanners, including some Microtek and Epson models, come with special software, which actually repairs damaged photos as they are scanned.

Accuracy depends on how clearly printed the original text is. Typically, OCR software attempts to guess at letters that it cannot read clearly, sometimes with unusual or funny results. Newspaper and book print usually come out pretty well. Hand lettering, unless it's in nice clean handwriting, doesn't work for OCR. Sorry, but the program's not quite that sophisticated.

No Camera? No Scanner?

The digital camera and scanner are both great tools for the scrapbooker, but if you can't afford them, don't give up. There are many services, including PhotoQuik, Ritz Camera, and the photo kiosks at Wal-Mart, Walgreens, CVS, and other similar stores that scan your prints or rolls of film and give you the scanned photos on CD-ROM. Kodak offers this service, too, and it's a perfectly good way to get your pictures into the computer.

If you have friends or relatives who have a scanner, ask them to scan your pictures and to email you the scanned photos or burn them onto a CD-ROM. The point is simply to get them into the computer. After you've done so, you can work on them whenever you want. Check with family and friends to see whether they have already uploaded any pictures you want to use, such as the annual family picnic potluck, the neighborhood yard sale, or the soccer team's games. Many people create online web pages, which are a kind of scrapbook, or they upload their pictures to a service such as Snapfish (http://www.snapfish.com), Shutterfly (http://www.shutterfly.com), or Ofoto (http://www.ofoto.com). These services—and there are several more of them listed in Appendix C, "While You're Wandering the Web..."—not only develop and send back your prints but upload your photos to a password-protected website where you can view the pictures, download them to your computer, and order reprints. The storage of your online photos is typically free and there's no limit to the number of pictures you can send for posting.

You can take other pictures from the Web, too, and some of them are quite awesome. Anything from the government files can be borrowed for free and without even asking permission. Remember those beautiful pictures of Earth from out in space? You can use them. Check out http://www.earthdvd.com/links.htm to see one of the most famous, and then scout around that site to see what else you can find. Pictures from the White House? Sure. Go to http://www.whitehouse.gov and have a look. The Library of Congress has a treasure trove of maps and photos for your enjoyment and use. You can find these at http://www.loc.gov.

What you can't legally do is use anything that has a copyright notice attached. This includes pictures, textures, designs, icons, and other bits of graphic art you find on other people's websites, commercial or otherwise—unless they've posted it along with permission to help yourself. Of course, if your scrapbook isn't going outside your circle of family and friends, you're probably okay anyway. You just can't do anything that makes money for you without the consent of the copyright owner, usually the artist or author involved. If you want to quote some appropriate poetry or a song lyric on a page, you can do so as long as you aren't going to sell the page or make it available for other people to use. The bottom line of fair use is that you can't do anything that might deprive the original creator of making money from his or her creations.

Suppose you're a new bride, putting together a scrapbook of your wedding. Your song was "Wind Beneath My Wings." Fine, go ahead and typeset or hand letter that song on a scrapbook page. It's not going to harm the songwriter in any way. But suppose your scrapbook turns out really well, and you decide to assemble and sell a kit for other new brides to do the same, adding their wedding photos where your photos were. Now you're profiting from your work, and you can't do that without the songwriter's permission—which you're probably not going to get without spending some of your own money. You need to find out who the publisher of the song is and send a written request to their permissions department. Depending on how popular any given song is, and how new it is, they might ask for a fee or just give you permission and wish you luck. It never hurts to ask.

Printers

If your scrapbook is only going onto the Web, or being distributed on a CD-ROM, you probably don't really need a printer for your projects. However, there are many reasons, aside from scrapbook making, that you might need a printer. Several types of color printers are available, but color inkjet printers are by far the most common and the least expensive. You can also find color laser printers, but they tend to be very expensive, and don't give as natural looking results. Inkjets, as the name implies, work by firing tiny jets of ink at the paper. Generally, printers use four colors to create any image: cyan, magenta, yellow, and black. Other printers use a six- or even seven-color system, adding light cyan, light magenta, and light black to improve the reproduction of delicate flesh tones and light sky blue. In addition, some printers now can use either a matte finish or regular black ink. The matte black makes a very definite difference in the quality of any black-and-white work you might need to do, mainly because it looks more dense and black. Color laser printing uses the same process as color copiers. A powdered toner is fused to the paper as it passes over a heated wire on its way through the copy machine or laser printer.

tip
While you're visiting the Epson website, take a look at their section of craft ideas. They have some beautiful photographic backgrounds for your scrapbook pages, as well as templates for pages and tips on how to fix bad pictures. Go to http://www.epson.com and look on the left side of the screen to explore solutions for craft projects. It's worth the time.

Some printers only take standard 8 1/2×11" paper; others can handle much larger sheets. If you like the traditional 12×12 scrapbook pages and want to create your page layouts digitally, you need a printer capable of handling that page size. In my opinion, Epson makes the best of the wide-body printers. Check out the Epson Stylus Photo 1280 at http://www.epson.com and in Figure 3.7.

The Epson Stylus Photo 1280 has a six-color photo ink system, and gives you BorderFree photo printing in six popular sizes. *BorderFree* means that it can print all the way to the edges of the page without leaving a white margin like some printers do. It's compatible with Windows and Macintosh and includes software. You get both Epson Software Film Factory and Adobe Photoshop Elements 2.0. It's a good buy at about $400. You can find other wide-body printers with four-color inks for a little less money. Check your computer store, and ask to see print samples from any printer you're considering buying.

Figure 3.7

The Epson Stylus Photo 1280 is a very good extra-wide printer that can handle 12×12" sheets.

Printers, like scanners and cameras, demand that you install a *driver*. A driver is a simple piece of software that lets the printer communicate with the computer. The driver is what sets up the printer controls and tells the printer how many copies you want to make, the paper size you selected, and any other details it needs to know, such as what kind of paper it's going to print on. Some papers are naturally more absorbent than others, and require different amounts of ink.

Be sure to look in both your computer store and in office supply or art stores for different types of printing papers. There are a great many choices, from basic white copy weight paper to glossy photo paper, matte photo paper, textured papers, canvas, silk, and metallic foil. You can purchase precut stickers to print on, in a fair selection of shapes, plus full transparent or white glossy sticker paper pages to cut out and stick to your scrapbook pages.

If your printer only prints black-and-white images and you aren't ready to consider purchasing a color printer, you can still create interesting scrapbook pages in black and white and add color accents with paints, markers, or stamps after they are printed. And you can, of course, load your pictures or finished pages on a CD and have them printed at a local copy or print shop such as Kinko's.

CD or DVD Writer

Do you really need one of these? It's a matter of opinion and mine is "yes, absolutely." There are a couple of good reasons. First of all, most software these days comes on CD-ROM. And most reasonably new computers already have a CD-ROM drive built-in. But you need a CD drive that writes disks as well as reads them. It's called a *CD-RW*. CDs are the preferred storage method for archival copies of electronic files. CDs are easy to store and, unlike the floppy disk, are unlikely to become obsolete any time soon. If you have commercially processed pictures returned to you on CD, you need to be able to view and retrieve them to the computer to edit. If you're planning to share your scrapbooks with friends or relatives, sending a CD-ROM through the mail is a lot easier and cheaper than sending a bulky book.

The difference between a CD and a DVD is a matter of size—how many bits of information a single disc holds. *DVDs* are frequently used for feature films because they can hold about three to four times more data than an ordinary CD-ROM. The data itself can be any kind: movies, scrapbooks, music, programs, and games. After all, no matter what you're seeing on the screen or hearing from the speakers, it's all just ones and zeros.

For protection of your precious photos, consider putting them on a CD-ROM or DVD and putting it in a safe, disaster-proof place, such as a safe deposit box at the bank or a fire-proof home safe. Office stores and warehouse stores like Costco or Sam's Club sell them. You can even send a copy to a friend or relative in another town. Then, if there's a fire or natural disaster that floods or otherwise trashes your house, your photos are still safe.

You can also safely store photos online at such places as Snapfish or Hotmail. Go to their sites to register and then follow the directions for uploading your files.

But I Don't Have a Computer!

No computer? I might wonder why you chose this book, but here you are and let's review some options. First of all, look around your neighborhood. Schools might offer adult computing classes, which help you learn the basics of using one. Then you can go to the local library or to one of the cyber cafés that seem to be springing up like mushrooms all over the place. These computers generally have a word processor and some kind of graphics program. Use them to crop and edit your photos or to print out your titles and journaling entries, or buy a half dozen CDs and save each session to a CD-ROM until you're ready to go to someplace like Kinko's to get the final prints.

Kinko's and many similar shops let you rent a computer fully equipped with a scanner and printer and the basic text and graphics programs you need for only a few dollars an hour. Be careful if you work on a public machine, though. Some might be infected with computer viruses, and if you save an infected file and then upload it to another computer, you spread the virus. There's a good discussion of computer viruses and how to avoid them at http://www.howstuffworks.com/virus.

Finally, as you saw previously, there are printers that work directly with a camera, using a docking interface, whereby you put the camera on the printer and pictures are transferred, using a cable, and printed. Some work by removing the little memory cards and simply inserting the cards into the printer and printing the pictures you want. This is never going to be the most satisfactory way to do it, but you have digital pictures, printed, for your pages.

Summary—What You Need to Remember

Computer hardware includes the computer itself and all the things that can plug into it, such as the scanner, printer, and CD-ROM drive. Most computers are sold with one CD-ROM drive built in, but if you want, you can add a second one or opt for a CD-ROM burner to make your own CDs. Digital cameras come in many sizes, quality, and price ranges, and feature a wide range of capabilities. For digital scrapbooking, a point-and-shoot type of camera is usually fine. You don't generally need incredibly high-resolution photos for scrapbook size pictures. Look for a digital camera with macro and zoom capability, though. That way, you can use it as a scanner if you need to copy some pictures or 3D objects to include in your scrapbook. Scanners are like copy machines except they send the image to your computer instead of printing it directly on paper. If you have a lot of paper photos you want to put into your scrapbook using your computer, buying a scanner is very worthwhile. Commercial services print your photos for you and put them on a CD-ROM or DVD so you can use them with your computer scrapbook software. You can also download pictures from the Web, as long as you're careful not to use copyrighted material for profit. Anything you find at a Federal government site is up for grabs.

Printers come in different widths. Some can't handle more than an ordinary letter-sized page, whereas others can print up to 13×19". These wide-body printers are ideal for 12×12"-size scrapbook pages. You can print digital pictures directly from your camera to paper with specially equipped photo printers. Or you can get them printed at almost any camera store, and then just use them like regular photos on your paper pages.

Digital Tools: Software

Like an army, the computer needs marching orders to tell it what to do. These orders are variously called programs, applications, or software. For scrapbooking, you need a program that can open up your photos on the computer screen, let you change the size of a picture to make it fit on a page, add embellishments and titles, and then print the page and save it for use on the Web or on a CD or DVD.

Choosing Your Program

A number of specific scrapbook programs are on the market, but I don't like to recommend them. They're not very versatile. They don't allow you to do more than the most minor kinds of corrections when you have photos that need work. The main reason I don't like them, though, is the same reason I warn beginning scrapbookers to stay away from the prepackaged kits—there's little or no room for creativity. You get already-made page backgrounds, somebody else's idea of what colors and type faces you should use, and you're even told where to place the pictures. At the end of the day, you have a completed page that looks just like everyone else's.

If you show your pages to other scrapbookers, they'll recognize the kit trademark or the stuff from the scrapbook program, and they might even have the same pages in their book. You're left feeling like you've both worn the same dress to a party.

Don't feel bad if you already own one or more of these programs. You have to start somewhere, after all. Poke around the program menus and try doing a page. You'll soon see where the limits are, and why you need something more versatile. There are several different possibilities. You could do pages with a web design program such as Macromedia Dreamweaver or Microsoft FrontPage, a page layout program such as Adobe InDesign, or your favorite word processor. But the best way is to use a program that's designed for computer graphics and photo editing.

With the help of photo-editing programs such as Adobe Photoshop Elements, you can incorporate your photographs into any kind of document you want to create, such as a scrapbook page, a printed catalog or report, a multimedia presentation, or a lavishly illustrated web page. One overwhelming advantage a digital camera has over a conventional camera relates to software. Within a matter of a minute or two after you've shot a picture, you can open it in Photoshop Elements 3 and crop, color correct, and place it where you want it. You can handle the entire process yourself. You don't need to send the pictures out to be processed, and then off to a service bureau for color scanning. Just plug the camera into the computer, save the pictures, and carry on.

Programs such as Photoshop Elements are bitmap paint programs and because they work pixel-by-pixel, they are capable of extremely subtle corrections as well as quick, all-over changes. You can achieve effects with these programs you can't possibly manage any other way, certainly not with traditional film-developed photo techniques. Digital retouching is much easier. Standard color correction can be done automatically, or if you're looking for something out of the ordinary, you can try as many variations as you like. Undo is just a keystroke away, and you're not wasting expensive photo paper and chemicals experimenting. And that's the second major difference. Because you're not constrained by the technical limits of the photographic process or the need to economize, you're free to try as many versions of the picture as you can invent. Save them, print them, or dump them in the trash and start over. All you've spent is time.

Making Versus Taking a Picture

When you use a conventional camera, you "take" a picture. You shoot what's there. If the image is not quite right, you have to shoot another photograph and develop it before you know for sure what you have. However, with the combination of a digital camera and software to manipulate images, you're not taking a picture—you're making a picture. Sometimes you know ahead of time exactly what elements you need to make a good picture. Other times, you start with no particular concept and experiment with images until you reach a satisfactory picture. It works either way.

When you look at images in ads, on magazine covers, on packaging, and practically everywhere else, most of the photos you see are made, rather than shot. It's not always convenient, or even possible, to set up some of the shots art directors ask for. A current fashion magazine has a model dressed in some sort of windblown chiffon dress, standing on an iron girder right at the edge of a new building under construction. No guard rail, no obvious safety belt, and she doesn't look the least bit scared, perched there in her four-inch high heels. The photographer probably took the building shot from the building across the street and placed the model on a plain white backdrop with a fan blowing on her dress. From there, it's just a few minutes work with the computer and any version of Photoshop to assemble the desired picture.

Why Adobe Photoshop Elements?

Photo-editing programs open your pictures so you can work on them, and also make wonderful scrapbook pages, web pages, and even book covers and T-shirts. In fact, all of the examples you'll see in upcoming chapters are pages I created with Photoshop Elements.

As we move along, you'll see why I prefer it to any of the scrapbook-specific software. There are several good reasons. First, it's far more versatile. I can use it for page layouts, for setting text, as well as for photo cleanup and repair. Second, it has all the wonderful Photoshop filters and accepts all the equally wonderful third-party Photoshop plug-ins that let me turn ordinary photos into works of art. Third, it's cross-platform, so I can swap files back and forth between my Mac and my Windows XP machine without even thinking about it. And everything's in the same place on both platforms, so I don't have to unlearn any of my shortcuts or tricks.

The current version is Photoshop Elements 3, but if you have a copy of an older Photoshop Elements bundled with a camera or scanner, by all means use it. Adobe used to have other, simplified versions of their professional Adobe Photoshop software. I remember Adobe Photoshop LE, and before that Adobe PhotoDeluxe. Each new version has more power and is easier to use than the previous one. Now you can accomplish nearly everything with Photoshop Elements that you can do in the latest professional release, Adobe Photoshop CS. Those few tools that aren't included in Photoshop Elements aren't anything you are likely to need anyway. Scrapbookers rarely have to deal with channels and paths, for example.

I've been involved in graphics and photography for a good many years now, and tried each new program as it came out. Based on that experience, I can tell you Photoshop Elements is by far the easiest to learn and the best value for your money.

Elementary Elements

Photoshop Elements has two purposes: correction and creation. Use it to solve problems with pictures you've scanned or shot with a digital camera. Very few pictures are perfect right from the camera. You can recompose a picture by cropping away part of it. You can remove people or objects that shouldn't be there. You can fix red eye and remove dust and scratches. You can make technical corrections for color, exposure, and even focus. Then you can get creative and have fun with it. Cure your kid's acne. Change your lemons to limes, or your pink roses to sky blue ones. Liquify a clock face so it looks like one of Salvador Dali's dripping watches. Move your family group shot from the backyard to someplace more interesting. Add type to your pictures, remove backgrounds.... The only limit is your imagination.

Like any other piece of software, you have to work with Elements for a while before you learn all of its tricks. I'm still discovering new ways to make it give me exactly the effect I want. But you can be up and running with it in an hour or two, at least to do basic photo cleanup and cropping.

Figure 4.1 shows the basic Photoshop Elements screen. It has a toolbox on the left and a Shortcuts bar and Tool Options bar stacked together across the top. On the right are some *palettes* (helpful little windows that let you work with some of the program's features such as layers and colors), and on the main work surface is a page I just threw together in about two minutes. I started by choosing a background color that harmonized with the photo I was going to use. The accent on the left side of my page is a combination of a colored stripe I drew by drawing a rectangle and filling it with tan paint. I then drew a narrower box on top and filled it with a gradient colored to look like copper. The lettering is simply placed on the colored background with a drop shadow added. The photo is the real thing, shot in Valley of Fire State Park. Obviously, there are more things I could add to this page, perhaps some pictoglyphs (the symbols carved on rocks by the Native American colonies who lived here thousands of years ago), perhaps a frame around the photo, or even flames shooting up from the words *Valley of Fire*. None of these things are difficult to do, and Elements lets me design the page the way I want it.

Figure 4.1

The Photoshop Elements screen puts all your tools where you can easily find them.

The Shortcuts bar, shown in Figure 4.2, is a big timesaver once you get used to it. Many other programs, including Microsoft Word and Excel, use similar shortcuts on a bar. Select the icon that looks like what you want to do and click on it. This is also where you'll switch to the Quick Fix menu, explained in full in Chapter 7, "Working with Old Photos."

Figure 4.2

Shortcuts do save time.

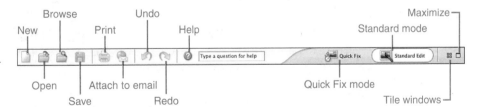

Where Photoshop Elements really excels, however, is in photo repair and editing. Figure 4.3 shows a photo, before and after I did some badly needed repairs.

Figure 4.3

The original photo, on the left, was in bad shape.

I could also have hand-colored this picture, turned it into a charcoal drawing, an etching, or any of a dozen or so other art styles with a couple of clicks. You will learn how to do these repairs and turn pictures to art in the next few chapters.

Opening Elements

Photoshop Elements opens with a welcome screen, which gives you some choices to make regarding how you want to work. In the Windows version, shown in Figure 4.4, your choices are Product Overview, View and Organize Photos, Quickly Fix Photos, Edit and Enhance Photos, Make Photo Creation, and Start from Scratch. You can probably guess what each of these does, but if not, just drag your mouse pointer over the desired action and you'll see more information about it.

If you open the Mac version, shown in Figure 4.5, you might feel a little less welcome. There are only three options. You can Start from Scratch, Open File for Editing, or Connect to a Camera or Scanner. View and Organize isn't an option for Mac users, but don't worry, these three choices get you where you want to go. Adobe introduced Photoshop Album last year as a stand-alone photo cataloging tool. For reasons the marketing department never shared, they developed it only for Windows machines. So when it came time to start work on Elements 3, there was no Mac album equivalent ready to drop in. Mac people simply have to find some other way to keep track of their photos. Fortunately, there's iPhoto, part of the iLife suite for Macintosh. It does everything you want, and more. We'll talk about photo organizing—the pros call it *asset management*—later on.

Figure 4.4

The Photoshop
Elements welcome
screen (Windows
version).

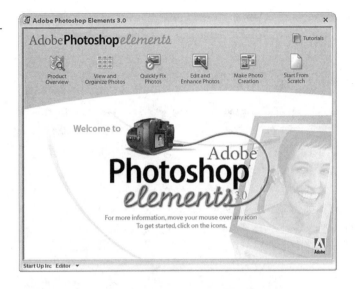

Figure 4.5

The Photoshop
Elements welcome
screen (Mac
version).

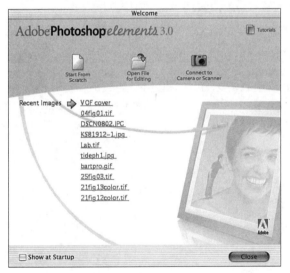

Meanwhile, in either version, you double-click the icon on the Welcome screen that
represents what you want to do. On the Mac, if you choose Open File for Editing,
what you actually open is the File Browser, a slide sorter that shows whatever pictures are in the folder you select. The File Browser is also present in the Windows
version, but when you choose View and Organize Photos, you open the Organizer
instead. After you're in the Organizer, you can download pictures from your camera, scanner, Palm pilot, or cell phone. You can assign your photos to albums and
mark them with keywords to help you find them. To do these things on the Mac,

choose Connect from Camera or Scanner to bring in new photos, or Open File for Editing to work on the ones you've already imported.

Different Programs, Same Commands

One of the good things that came out of the early days of Windows and Mac computing was an informal agreement among programmers that common functions, such as saving your work, opening a new document, and printing, would always use the same commands, even across platforms. This means after you learn how to do something in one application, you already know how to do it in virtually every other one. (There are probably a few exceptions, but I can't think of any.) If you can copy and paste in your word processor, you can do it in Elements. You don't have to relearn each new program. Many of the menu titles will be familiar, too, though what's actually on the menu may be different.

Working on the Elements Desktop

The desktop is nearly identical in both the Mac and Windows versions. You saw the Mac version in Figure 4.1, and Figure 4.6 shows the Windows desktop. As with most other programs, there is a menu bar at the top. Next, there's a Shortcuts bar and beneath it, an Options bar. At the left is the toolbox. There are palettes open on the right side of the screen. A palette is a kind of window that gives you information about your project or lets you choose from a display of colors or styles.

Figure 4.6

The Elements desktop for Windows users looks very much like the Mac version.

What Are on the Menus?

The *File menu*, as in all applications, contains commands for working with your files. Come here to open a file, to use the File browser to locate a specific picture, to close, or to save your work. One especially helpful option on this menu is the Save for Web command. Your printing options are found here as well. Elements can also format your photos as a web gallery, make contact sheets from all of the photos in a folder, and can automatically arrange to print several copies of a single photo in a "picture package" so you use your paper more efficiently. And last, but far from least, it can assemble a series of images into a panoramic photo.

tip If you open Elements and don't see the palettes lined up on the right side of the screen, open the Window menu and check Palette Bin to make them visible again. If you're looking for a specific palette, such as Layers or Color, make sure it's checked on this menu. Otherwise, it's closed and not visible.

The *Edit menu* has the same functions as any other edit menu. You can choose commands here to cut, copy, paste, undo, and redo. The Edit menu also lets you custom design a brush or a pattern. You'll soon learn, if you haven't already, that the cut, copy, paste, and other commonly used commands have (⌘-key) [Ctrl+key] combinations that are easy to learn and much quicker to use than clicking the mouse to open the menu and then selecting the desired command. The *Transform menu* lets you rotate, skew, distort, and change the dimensions of a photo or a canvas. (*Enlarging* a canvas simply means you add extra space around the image.) The *Enhance menu* offers access to all of Elements's color correction tools, and you can choose whether to apply them as auto corrections or to tweak them one at a time until your picture is, well, picture perfect.

Layers are, in effect, sheets of transparent cellophane which can be placed over or under an image letting you add text and brush strokes without damaging the original picture. The *Layer menu* contains commands to work with these layers, eventually merging them or *flattening* the image. You'll learn all about layers in Chapter 5, "Page Layout and Design." The *Selection menu* lets you work with layers or with parts of an image you have selected with a selection tool. If your blue sky looks pink, select it and make it bluer.

The *Filter menu*, shown in Figure 4.7, is one of the most interesting. *Filters* are little plug-in programs that affect your picture somewhat like mounting a filter on the front of a lens, only instead of just adding a starburst effect or blurring the edges of a scene, you can use Photoshop filters to make a photo look like an etching or something created in neon tubing. The Filter menu gives access to close to 100 Photoshop filters and as many third-party filters as you decide to add. They're covered in Chapter 9, "Turning a Photo into Art."

Figure 4.7

If you add any third-party filters, they show up at the bottom of the list.

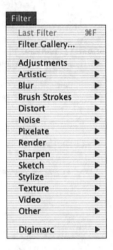

The *View menu* gives you access to rulers and toggles the grid on and off. The *Window menu* lets you open and close the palettes, and makes the photo bin visible. The *photo bin* is a strip along the bottom of the page that shows whatever windows happen to be open at the time. You can then click on one of them to bring it to the top of the pile. It's not especially useful unless you're going to be placing several photos on a page.

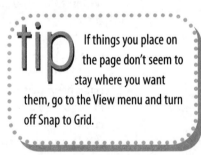

tip

If things you place on the page don't seem to stay where you want them, go to the View menu and turn off Snap to Grid.

Looking at the Toolbox

Menus and palettes are useful, but you can't do anything at all without the right tools. The *toolbox*, shown in Figure 4.8, is like an artist's work table or paint box that holds all the tools you use to draw, paint, erase, and otherwise work on your picture. There are sets of tools to select, to draw and paint, to blur and sharpen, and to place type in the picture. The toolbox can be displayed as either a long single strip of tools or a shorter double strip. Either way, it has the same tools. Click the dots at the top of the bar to change the display.

Figure 4.8

To select a tool, click on it.

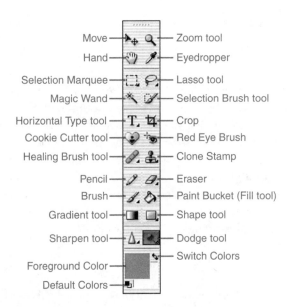

Move — Zoom tool
Hand — Eyedropper
Selection Marquee — Lasso tool
Magic Wand — Selection Brush tool
Horizontal Type tool — Crop
Cookie Cutter tool — Red Eye Brush
Healing Brush tool — Clone Stamp
Pencil — Eraser
Brush — Paint Bucket (Fill tool)
Gradient tool — Shape tool
Sharpen tool — Dodge tool
— Switch Colors
Foreground Color —
Default Colors —

The toolbox has additional tools hidden wherever you see a black arrowhead. Click and hold on any tool with an arrowhead, and the additional tools associated with it pop out on a short menu. Figure 4.9 shows the tools normally hidden under the Type tool.

Figure 4.9

You will learn about working with type in Chapter 10, "Adding Text."

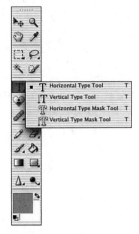

Horizontal Type Tool   T
Vertical Type Tool   T
Horizontal Type Mask Tool   T
Vertical Type Mask Tool   T

Utility Tools

If you look carefully at the toolbox, you can see thin lines that divide it into differ-ent sections. The top section holds what I call Utility tools—the Move tool, Hand tool, Zoom tool, and Eyedropper. The *Move tool* drags a selected object to some other part of the page. The *Hand* moves the entire page, or the portion of the page that's shown on the screen in a magnified view. The *Zoom tool* enlarges or reduces the image. Click it on the picture to increase magnification. Hold down the Option/Alt key as you click to decrease it. When you zoom in, the picture is usually too big to see all at once. The Hand moves it within the window and is helpful after you use the Zoom tool to enlarge the picture. Use the hand to slide the part of the picture you want to see or work on into a convenient spot. The *Eyedropper* picks up a sam-ple of color, which you can make the active color or add to your Swatches palette.

Selection Tools

The next section of the toolbox contains a group of tools called Selection tools. They are used to select all or part of a picture. There are four kinds: the Marquees, the Lassos, the Selection Brush, and the Magic Wand. When you select an area of the screen with the *Marquee tools*, a blinking selection border surrounds it. (The Marquee tools are named after the lights on movie theater marquees that flash on and off.) There are two Marquee tools. Click the tool in the toolbox to open the pop-up menu that allows you to switch between the rectangle and the ellipse. The Marquees make their selections as you click and drag the tool over the part of an image you want to select, drawing a box or circle.

The *Lasso tools*—three in all—draw a line as you click and drag the tip of the lasso across the page. Draw part of a free-form shape, and Elements completes the shape automatically with a straight line from where you stopped back to the start. There are also Lassos used to select an area by drawing straight path segments instead of a free-form line, and to select an area "magnetically" by separating an object from its contrasting background. Figure 4.10 shows the selections that result from using these tools.

The *Magic Wand tool* selects by color. You can set the amount of similarity it demands, and just click to select all pixels of that color.

The *Selection Brush* simply selects anything you paint over. Given that there are hundreds of standard paintbrushes, plus any you design yourself, this tool can be enormously flexible. Select it and drag your paintbrush over anything you want to turn into a selection. This tool doesn't exist in the "big" Photoshop program. I wish it did. You can use it to create masks over areas you want to protect when you're changing another part of the image. For instance, say you're working on a portrait of a lady, and you need to lighten her hair without bleaching out her face. Paint around the hair, or if it's easier, paint only the hair and then invert the selection so you've selected everything *but* the hair. If that sounds a little confusing, don't worry. It will become clear as you read further in the book.

Figure 4.10

Each Lasso and Marquee tool makes a different kind of selection.

Polygonal Lasso

Elliptical Marquee

Magnetic Lasso

Rectangular Marquee

Miscellaneous Tools

I'm not sure how to categorize this section of the toolbox. It has the Type tool, the Crop tool, the Cookie Cutter tool (new in this version), the Red Eye Removal tool, the Healing Brush tool, and the Clone Stamp tool. You'll find yourself using these tools a lot for photo repair.

The *Type tool* puts text on the page. It uses the same fonts your word processor and other programs use, and can set type either horizontally or vertically, and can warp it into arcs, waves, and other funky shapes. There's also a *Type Mask tool* that selects whatever's on the layer below as a selection marquee so you can cut type out of a photo, filling the letters with pictures.

The *Crop tool* works just like the Rectangular Marquee tool, in that you drag a *bounding box* to surround the part of the picture you are keeping. When you do so, the area outside the box turns gray. You can drag a side or a corner to make the bounding box bigger or smaller. When you're done adjusting the box, double-click in the box to remove everything outside it.

The *Cookie Cutter tool* uses the same masking principle as the Type Mask tool. Instead of letters, though, it cuts shapes from your photo. Elements comes with a generous selection of shapes, all the way from animal silhouettes to musical notes, ornate frames, and even cartoon characters. The shapes work with both the Cookie Cutter tool and the Shape tool. Don't confuse these two. The Cookie Cutter removes the background and leaves only the shape you cut from it, and the Shape tool draws a shape you can *stroke* (leaving an outline) or fill with a color or gradient.

The Red Eye Removal tool, the Healing Brush, and the Spot Healing Brush are very helpful for retouching. The *Red Eye Removal tool* simply finds the odd color and replaces it with the correct eye color. Two clicks and your "devil eyes" photos can be pictures of saints. The Healing Brush and the Spot Healing Brush help your photo subjects put their best faces forward by hiding uneven skin tones, pimples, moles, or freckles. We'll cover their use more thoroughly in Chapter 8, "Working with Digital Photos."

The *Clone Stamp tool* copies a piece of the existing picture and pastes it somewhere else. It uses the Paintbrush tool's size and shape. You can stamp (or paint) with a soft-edged brush or a hard one, in any size from a single pixel on up.

Painting Tools

Elements has an impressive set of *Painting tools*: Brushes, a Pencil, an Eraser, and Paint Bucket and Gradient tools. These all apply color to the screen in one way or another, just like the real tools they imitate. You can change the width and angle for the Pencil and Brush tools. The Brush tool and the Impressionist Brush share a space in the toolbox. The latter simulates different kinds of brushstrokes. Though there isn't a lot of use for it in photo correction or enhancement, it's fun to play with. Many of these tools are covered throughout this book, in sections that discuss how to make specific types of repairs on photos.

There are also various erasers that, as you might expect, take away part of the picture. You can use a block eraser, or erase with any of the paintbrush or airbrush shapes. There are two special-purpose erasers, the *Background* and *Magic Erasers*. Use them to automatically erase a selected part of the image. The *Paint Bucket*, also called the *Fill tool*, pours paint (the foreground color) into any contiguous area you select. (If no area is selected, it'll fill the whole image.) The *Gradient tool* lets you create backgrounds that shade from one color to another, or even all the way through the color spectrum.

Lastly, there is a vector tool (the *Custom Shape tool*) that draws shapes as *vectors*. These are shapes defined by their outline rather than as bitmaps (tiny dots that form a shape). When you use these tools, you don't get the jagged effect you otherwise would when building an object from individual pixels because a vector image can be resized and its resolution adjusted without any effect on the clarity of the image.

Figure 4.11 shows the difference between bitmapped and vector text and drawn lines. As you can see, the bitmapped text is ragged around the edges, especially when it's enlarged. Look closely at the curves of the *b*, *t*, *m*, *a*, *p*, *e*, and *d* to see this effect. The bitmapped line shares the same fate—it has bumps along its sides. The vector text and line, on the other hand, is quite smooth, regardless of the size at which you view it.

Figure 4.11
Vector type versus bitmapped type.

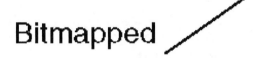

Toning Tools

Toning tools are tools that sharpen, blur, and change the intensity of the image. The *Blur*, *Sharpen*, and *Smudge tools* change the level of focus and the *Dodge*, *Burn*, and *Sponge tools* change the degree of darkness or lightness and the saturation of selected pixels.

Colors

Finally, there are two large blocks of color displayed at the bottom of the toolbox. Photoshop Elements calls them *swatches*. They are your foreground and background colors, and by default they are black and white, respectively. Change them by clicking once on the appropriate square to open the Color Picker. There, you can click to select any color you like. You can, of course, also click on a color from the color swatch palette. The foreground color (logically, the one on top) is the color you apply when you paint a brushstroke, place type, or do anything that leaves a mark on the page.

Starting a New Image

When you work in Elements, you start with an image you have either scanned or imported from a digital camera. You are going to need a blank image file to try some of the tools on. Let's create one now, using the Shortcuts bar. We'll work with other kinds of images and other ways to create them afterward.

1. Point your cursor to the New button.

2. Click once to open the New dialog box shown in Figure 4.12.

3. Click on the Preset Sizes drop-down list and choose Default Photoshop Elements Size.

4. Check to see that the White option in the Background Contents area of the dialog box is selected.

5. Click OK or press Return and the new page opens.

Figure 4.12

Your dialog box should look like this.

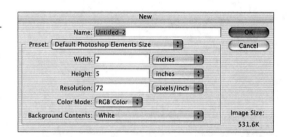

Now you have a blank image on your desktop, and you can start to work with the tools. Go ahead and try them out. You can't break anything. Select something. Draw something. Paint a heart and move it around the screen. Try some colors. When the image gets too full, press (⌘-A) [Ctrl+A] to select everything. Then delete it by pressing Delete and start over again.

Another way to start a blank page is to go the File menu and select New or to type (⌘-N) [Ctrl+N]. These open the same dialog box you just reached from the Shortcuts bar.

Starting at the top of the dialog box, you have the option of immediately naming your image, or leaving it untitled until you save it. Because I am almost always in a hurry, I skip that step and immediately consider page size. This dialog box has a pop-up menu of possible page sizes, shown in Figure 4.13. The default is horizontal, 7×5 inches.

Choose a page size appropriate for what you want to do, remembering that screen formats are horizontal, and magazine covers and illustrations are more likely to be vertical. Landscapes and portraits dictate different orientations because of the shape of the subject. There are even sizes for different kinds of TV and video screens.

If you have something on the clipboard waiting to be pasted into your new image, the dialog box opens with that item's dimensions in place of whatever other numbers might be there. You can still override it and choose a larger size, if you want.

Figure 4.13

Most of the standard American and European page dimensions are included. I've chosen 8×10" as my page size.

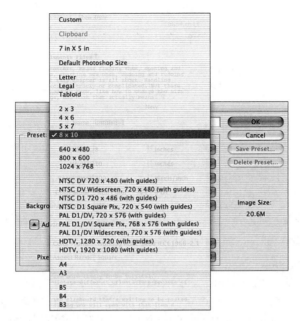

Resolution is a tricky issue we'll discuss in depth in the section, "Adjusting Resolution." Meanwhile, if your art project is to be viewed on the screen, perhaps as part of a PowerPoint slideshow or on the Web, or if you are just playing, as we are now, use 72 pixels/inch as the resolution.

You have only three choices for mode in this dialog box. If you're working in color, you must choose RGB color as the mode. Grayscale lacks color, and Bitmap means simply black or white pixels, with no grays at all. If you want to use Indexed color mode, you need to select that option from the Image, Mode menu after creating the file using RGB color or Grayscale. Indexed Color uses a restricted palette, 256 colors or less. It's not recommended for photo work but is fine for line art with just a few colors.

The Contents options refer to what appears on the first layer of the image when it's created for you. White is the usual choice. Background applies whatever color is the current background color in the toolbox. (By default, it's white.) Transparent backgrounds are normally indicated by a sort of gray and white checkerboard effect. (You can change its color in the Preferences.) Transparent backgrounds are extremely useful when you are creating web graphics.

When you're ready, click OK or just press Return to open the new image.

Browsing for a File

Most of the time, though, you won't start with a blank image. Instead, you'll have a photo you want to work with. If you know where it is, you can press (⌘-O) [Ctrl+O], click on the Open icon, double-click the file, or do whatever you generally do to open a file.

If you don't know where on the hard drive your picture is, or what it is called, opening it becomes a little harder. This is one of the times when you'll turn to the File Browser. Another is when you've shot and downloaded a bunch of similar pictures and want to find the best of the bunch. You really need to be able to see what you've got.

Open the File Browser by choosing it from the File menu or the Windows menu, or by typing (⌘-Shift-O) [Ctrl+Shift+O].

You can select the thumbnail size from the More menu or by clicking the View by button. The File Browser can also show you the file hierarchy, the creation data, and camera file info, as well as a larger thumbnail of a selected image, as in Figure 4.14. Normally, all information about a file is displayed in the Metadata window; to display only camera or scanner information, select EXIF from the menu on the lower right. As I mentioned in the last chapter, you can change the sort order using the options on the Sort By menu.

Figure 4.14
The Metadata window includes creation date, camera used, and so on.

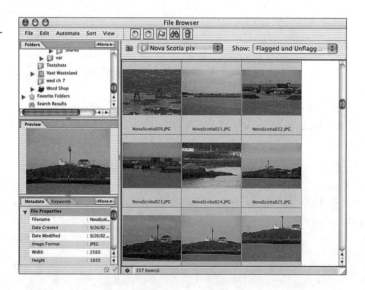

Something new has been added to the Mac version of the File Browser. You can add keywords to your pictures to help find them next time you go looking. Use the Help screens to learn how to do this.

Use the top pop-up menu to locate the disk and folder you think the file is on, and just start scrolling through the folder list on the left until you find it. Drag it into an Elements window, or double-click it and it opens its own window.

To rotate the selected image 90° to the right, click the Rotate button. To delete the file from your computer, click the Delete File button.

Time for a little practice! The following steps walk you through the process of browsing for some picture files on your hard drive:

1. Go to the Window menu and select File Browser.
2. After the window opens, use the scrollbar to review what's on the desktop.
3. Use the pop-up menu at the top of the browser to navigate to a different hard disk, disk partition, or other external storage device. Again, scroll through to see what's there.
4. The top-left browser window shows the file hierarchy. Scroll down until you locate the folder where a photo you'd like to select lives. Then click the file when it appears in the list on the right. It should be highlighted.

> **tip**
>
> If you can't find any other graphic file, try the Samples folder, located in the Photoshop Elements folder.

5. Read through the image information in the bottom pane. If it is a digital photo you've shot and saved to the computer, you can find out a lot about it. What was your shutter speed? Did you use a flash? If you scanned it in, when did you do so? What's the resolution?
6. Double-click the file to open it, or drag it into the Elements window.
7. Notice that the File Browser remains open. If you like, explore your hard drive(s) and locate more pictures you want to come back to and work on later. When you're done, close the File Browser.

Saving Your Work

Saving is the most important step in any project, but you probably don't realize how important it is unless you have had a computer crash while you're working. It happens to everyone, and eventually most of us learn to save our work often, work on a copy of the original, or use other tactics that end up saving our sanity as well as our words and pictures.

Elements has a couple of different Save options. You can save the image in the format of your choice with the File, Save As command, or you can save it optimized for the Web by choosing Save for Web from the File menu. The first time you save

any file, you'll be asked to give it a name (if you didn't already do so when you created the file or imported the scanned or camera image).

Figure 4.15 shows the Save As dialog box. It looks a lot like the Save dialog boxes in
other applications, with a few minor differences.

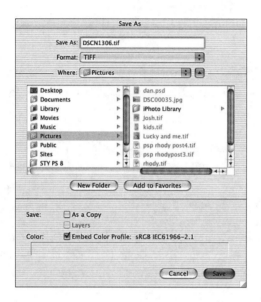

Figure 4.15

Be sure to use a
name that helps you
remember what the
picture is. Raw
camera filenames,
like the one shown
here, don't tell you
much.

Choosing a File Format

The Format pop-up menu, which indicates the current file format, lists about 16 file formats you
can use. How do you choose? That depends on the
kind of image you are working on, and what you
intend to do with it. Web browsers can only display images in three formats: GIF, PNG, and JPEG.
You must choose one of the three if your picture is
for Web use. If you are going to place the picture
into a page of text, such as a scrapbook, newsletter, advertisement, or brochure, you need to save
it in a format compatible with the word processing or desktop publishing program you plan to
use. It must also be compatible with the printing
system you'll be using. Finally, you must consider
whether your image will be printed in black and
white, in full color, or using spot color.

The file format determines how the information
in a file is compressed (if, in fact, it is compressed)

Spot color refers
to individual
accent colors applied by
an artist, as opposed to *full color*, as
in a photograph. Spot color is
printed with a separate offset plate
and a precisely compounded colored
ink for each color. Spot color is often
used by graphic designers in places
where a specific color must appear,
such as on an official logo. Full color,
also called *process color* or *CMYK
color*, is printed with overlapping
dots of cyan, magenta, yellow, and
black inks.

and whether it contains data for multiple layers of the image as well as the color management system used and other important details. Elements can work with files in any of the types shown on its menu, but some you will probably never use.

Let's take a quick look at the formats available and what they actually do (the three-letter combination in parentheses after each format name is the file extension for that format). You'll never need to use most of these, but you might as well know what they are.

- **Photoshop (.psd)**—This is the native format for both Photoshop and Elements documents. It saves all possible data about the picture, and is compatible with Adobe Illustrator and Acrobat as well as Photoshop itself. This is the best format to use while you are working, or if you intend to return to this image some other time.

- **Bitmap (.bmp)**—Bitmap is a standard graphics file format for Windows. Because it must describe each pixel on the screen, a bitmap file can be quite large.

- **CompuServe GIF (.gif)**—GIF stands for Graphical Interchange Format . It was first used (prior to the Internet) by the CompuServe online network to enable members to view each other's graphics. It is still in use as one of the three common graphics formats for web publishing. It compresses file size by limiting the number of colors. Because it is a compressed format, files are smaller and take less time to transfer.

- **Photoshop EPS (.eps)**—EPS stands for Encapsulated PostScript, a format developed by Adobe to go transparently cross-platform to many graphic, page layout, and illustration programs. For best results, use it when your work is printed on PostScript-enabled printers.

- **JPEG (.jpg)**—JPEG stands for Joint Photographic Experts Group, the group that developed this format, which relies on 8-bit color (RGB only) and a *lossy compression* system (a system that selectively removes data from the file). It is a popular format for web publishing because it can produce small files, but each save results in further compression and files deteriorate quickly. Use JPEG as a web format, but never as a working format.

- **PCX (.pcx)**—PCX is a common graphics format for IBM-compatible PCs.

- **Photoshop PDF (.pdf)**—Adobe's Portable Document Format is a system for creating documents that can be read cross-platform.

- **Photoshop 2.0 (.psd)**—This is an early Photoshop format for the Macintosh that doesn't support layers and flattens your image. Use this format only if your files must be opened by a very early version of Photoshop.

- **PICT file (.pct)**—This is mainly a Macintosh format, and is equivalent to PCX.
- **PICT resource (.rsr)**—This format is used by Macintosh for icons, sprites, and other graphic resources.
- **Pixar (.pxr)**—Pixar is the proprietary format used by high-end Pixar graphics workstations.
- **PNG (.png)**—PNG stands for Portable Network Graphics. It's a newer and arguably better format for web graphics than GIF or JPEG. It combines GIF's good compression with JPEG's unlimited color palette. However, older browsers don't support it.
- **Raw (.raw)**—This format saves image information in the most flexible format for transferring files between applications and computer platforms.
- **Scitex CT (.sct)**—This is another proprietary format for a brand of graphics workstation.
- **Targa (.tga)**—Another proprietary format, this one works with a specific kind of Truevision video board used by MS-DOS machines.
- **TIFF (.tif)**—TIFF stands for Tagged Image File Format. Files in this format can be saved for use on either Macintosh or Windows machines. This is often the preferred format for desktop publishing applications, such as PageMaker and QuarkXPress. Enhanced TIFF is a similar format that supports saving layers. This is the format I use most often for scrapbooking as well as for sending pictures to clients.

Photoshop format (.psd) is the default format in Elements, and is the best choice for saving a file you intend to keep working on. As noted, it saves layers, layer style information, and color management information.

Choosing Other Save Options

If you select the Save: As a Copy option in the Save As dialog box, Elements saves a (closed) copy of the current image and allows you to continue working on the open one. Save: As a Copy is especially useful for making a backup copy before you try a drastic change, such as reducing color depth or increasing JPEG lossiness (sacrificing clarity to reduce file size), or for saving the file in a different format.

> # Caution
>
> If you are opening a file in Elements that was created in Photoshop, you do not have access to unsupported features such as clipping paths or layer sets, but the data remains with the file if you later reopen it in Photoshop.

Suppose you create a logo for your business and want to use it in print and on the Web. You should save it as a TIFF or EPS file to print from, and save a copy as a JPEG, GIF, or PNG file for your web page. The word *copy* is automatically added to the filename.

If you select the Save: Layers check box, your file format options are limited to the file types that can save layers separately. These are .PSD and .TIF. The ICC Profile (Windows)/Embed Color Profile (Mac) option saves a color profile with the image file if you choose particular formats that use them. Use Thumbnail (Windows)/ Image Previews Options (Mac) to save a thumbnail of the image in the file. Choose Use Lower Case Extensions (Windows)/File Extension Options (Mac) to save the file with a lowercase extension, which makes it compatible with Internet and network servers that use Unix.

Adjusting Resolution

Resolution is an important concept to understand and can be just a little bit complicated because it means different things in different situations. Resolution is what determines the quality of what you see on the screen and what you see in print. You already know your Elements images are bitmaps. A *bit*, in this case, is a *pixel*, an individual picture element. You can enlarge a piece of your image enough to take a good look at individual pixels. Figure 4.16 shows an image of flowers in various stages of enlargement up to 1600%. At that size, you can see that the image consists of little squares in different colors or shades of gray.

Figure 4.16
A pixel is a pixel, however large or small it is.

 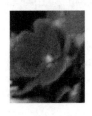 

| 100% | 200% | 400% | 1,600% |

When you shrink the squares down to a smaller size, let's say 1/72 of an inch, they are too small to be seen individually. What you do see at that resolution is the picture as it appears on your monitor. Typical monitor resolution is either 72 or 96dpi (dots per inch). (72dpi is the traditional resolution of older Mac screens. New monitors are more likely to use 96dpi resolution for a clearer picture. However, most people still think in terms of 72dpi screen resolution. So will we.) In the case of 72dpi, a square inch of picture has 72 pixels, squared, or a total of 5,184 pixels per square inch.

When you print a picture, you'll see your printer most likely has a much higher resolution than your screen. So an image displayed in a 1:1 ratio on your monitor appears smaller when printed because the dots of ink per square inch are more numerous and therefore smaller than screen pixels. Also, an image saved with a low-resolution setting does not suddenly become clearer when printed with a high-resolution printer.

Of course, if you have a higher resolution image, you have a lot more data and a much sharper, clearer picture to work with. That also means a bigger file to store and work on. Your hard drive fills up faster. With a larger file, any operation you attempt in Elements takes longer. If you're applying a filter, for example, you're telling the computer to make a specific set of adjustments to each pixel. If the resolution is set to 72dpi, the computer has to change a little more than five thousand numbers per square inch of image. If it's at 300dpi, it has to make the same changes an additional 85,000 times per square inch. That adds up.

So, the problem lies in deciding whether you want to work slowly on a large file with high resolution that prints well, or quickly on a smaller file that looks fine on the Web. If you already have plans for the picture, your choice is simple. If it's only going to be seen on the screen, you might as well work at 72dpi. If you are placing the photo into another document at something close to or smaller than snapshot size, or printing small copies at home on your inkjet printer, you can get away with using 150dpi as a working resolution. For more flexibility or larger prints, keep the resolution at 300dpi while you are cleaning it up, cropping, retouching, and so on. You can always save a low-res (lower resolution) copy later. For instance, if you're saving a copy of the picture for a web page, you can reduce the resolution when you convert it to a JPEG, and end up with a clear *and* very small file.

Most printers do a fine job of adjusting resolution, particularly if the printer's resolution is a close or exact multiple of the file it's printing. Typically, a home/office inkjet printer has a resolution of 300, 600, or even as much as 1,200dpi. If you send a picture that's an exact multiple (for instance, 200, 300, or even 150dpi), the printed result should have nice even tones with smooth transitions from one color to another. You shouldn't see jagged edges or obvious blocks.

There are times when you have to change the image resolution, even though it may mean losing some image quality. If you have access to a high-end digital camera or scanner, it presents you with very large files at a very high resolution. You might find that you have to reduce the resolution of the image before you can work on it, especially if your computer is an older, slower one or doesn't have enough RAM to work on a large file.

Photoshop Elements does a pretty good job of changing resolution by *resampling* the image. When you *downsample* (decrease the number of pixels in an image and thus decrease the image's size), you can reduce the size of the image, or the resolution, or both. Suppose you have a picture that's six inches square. You want it to be three inches square. You open the Image Size dialog box (shown in Figure 4.17) by choosing Image, Resize, Image Size, and change the numbers to make the image size 3"×3" instead of 6"×6". You don't change the resolution. When you click OK, the image shrinks to half the size it was on the screen. Because you haven't changed the resolution, the file size shrinks to a quarter of what it was.

Figure 4.17

You can change the size and/or the resolution in this dialog box.

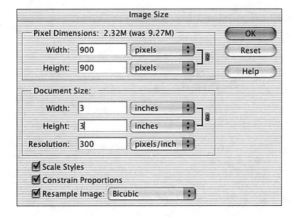

If you increase the resolution while keeping the image the same size, the screen display doubles because you are now looking at an "inch" that's twice as long (144 pixels instead of 72).

Downsampling condenses the file information into a smaller spread of pixels, so you won't lose detail in the image as you might when upsampling. When you increase the resolution, Elements has to invent new values for the pixels you're adding. There are three different ways it can do this, and you can choose which of the three to apply by selecting it from the Resample Image pop-up menu at the bottom of the dialog box. Your choices are

- **Nearest neighbor**—This is the quickest method because it essentially copies what's there, assigning a value to the next pixel based on the average of the ones on either side of it. It works best on edges that are not *antialiased*. (Antialiasing is a technique that's applied to artificially produced edges such as the curve of a letter or a drawn line. It adds bits of gray along the edge to smooth it out and make it less jagged in appearance.) It also produces a smaller file. It may, however, result in lines that appear jagged because of the lack of antialiasing.

- **Bilinear**—This method, considered better than the nearest neighbor method, is based on averaging the four pixels above, below, and to the sides of a target pixel and assigning it the resulting value.

- **Bicubic**—Instead of taking an average of four pixels, the bicubic method takes an average of eight, surrounding the target pixel on all sides and corners. This method produces the best results but takes a longer time to complete.

Figure 4.18 shows the differences between these three methods.

Figure 4.18

This is approximately, but not mathematically, the way it happens.

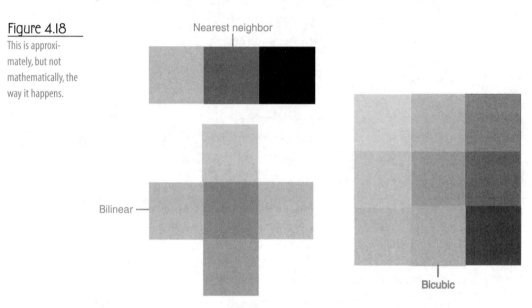

Remember, too, that the program goes through the entire set of calculations for each pixel in the image. When one is changed, all the ones around it must also change slightly.

Saving for the Web

The full-blown version of Photoshop ships with a second program called ImageReady, which is used to prepare images for the Web. It helps you find the best combination of file format, image size, and image quality to place the image on a web page so it loads quickly and looks as good as possible. Elements has a similar feature, which is simply called Save for Web and is found on the File menu. Figure 4.19 shows the Save for Web dialog box.

Figure 4.19

The two views of the image compare the original to the optimized version. It's often hard to see a difference.

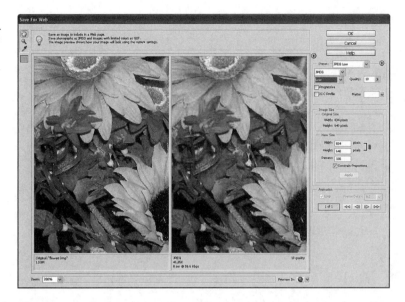

Choose PNG or JPEG for full color art and photographs. Choose GIF only if you are working with something that has a limited number of colors, such as a company logo, drawing, graph, or chart. There's no need to include information on 256 colors if you are only using a handful. Be sure to watch the changes on the screen at different quality settings. You want to find the best compromise between quality and file size. If a file is large, it loads very slowly on an older, slower modem. Most people don't yet have a super fast Internet connection. In some parts of the country they're not even available. As a good cybercitizen, you want to make your pages as accessible as possible for all, and part of that is keeping the download time to a minimum.

On the File menu and the Shortcuts bar, you also see an option called Attach to Email. Use this when you want to send a copy of the picture you've been working on. You are prompted to save the picture, if you haven't already done so, and then Elements locates your email program and opens a blank email message with the photo already attached to it. The file is not modified in any way—its file type, size, and resolution are preserved as they were when you selected this command. Add a message and send it off.

Undoing and Redoing

Before I got my Apple keyboard, I had a third-party model that was cheaply made. The paint started to wear off the letters. As a writer and an artist who works mainly in Photoshop, I use the keyboard a lot, particularly the ⌘-Z combination. That's why the Z was one of the first keys to fade to black.

Mac users know (⌘-Z) means Undo. Windows folk know this combination as [Ctrl+Z]. Same deal. It undoes the last thing you did. To be able to undo with just a keystroke is a wonderful thing. It gives you the freedom to make mistakes, to experiment; and that is how you learn. (I often wish life came with an Undo key.) If the Shortcuts bar is displayed, you can also click the Step Backward button to undo the last action. To redo any change you've undone, click Step Forward or press (⌘-Y) [Ctrl+Y]. To undo multiple changes, click Step Backward as many times as needed, or press (⌘-Z) [Ctrl+Z] multiple times.

note You can also find Undo at the top of the Edit menu, but the keystroke combination or the toolbar buttons are really easier to use.

Using the Undo History Palette

For those people who like to experiment with their graphics, Adobe provides an Undo History palette, which makes it easy to back up step by step or jump back to an earlier state with just one click.

In Figure 4.20, you can see a typical Undo History palette. To display the palette, choose Windows, Undo History, or click its tab in the palette if it's displayed there. The Undo History palette lists all the tools I have used on the image so far. It reflects each use of a tool. If I select a brush and paint several lines, each line shows up as a history step because I have to press and release the mouse button in between lines. If I were to paint one very long continuous line without releasing the mouse button, there would be only one history step to show for it.

Figure 4.20

Changes I've made to an image are stored on the Undo History palette.

If I select a step that's several steps back on the palette, all the subsequent steps are undone. They appear dimmed on the palette and are kept in memory until I do something different to the image. At that point, a new step replaces the ones I backed out of.

If you go to the General panel of the Preferences dialog box, you can enter a number of steps for the Undo History palette to remember. The default is 20 steps. Depending on your working style, you might find that 10 steps are enough, or you may need as many as 50 if you like to draw with short pencil or brush strokes. The limit is 100. You can clear the history if you are about to start a complicated revision to your picture and want to make sure you'll have enough space on the palette to keep track of the steps. Clear Undo History is on the pop-up menu that appears when you click the More button at the top of the palette.

Getting Pictures from a Scanner or Camera

Much of the work you do with Photoshop Elements involves either photos you've downloaded from a digital camera or photos you have scanned. When you buy a camera, it should come with a cable that plugs into the camera on one end and into the computer (usually into a USB or Firewire port) on the other end. It probably also comes with a CD-ROM of software. Each manufacturer has its own downloading system, which displays the pictures in the camera as if they were slides on a sorter and lets you choose which ones to download. Or you can skip this and simply copy the photos as if the camera was an external hard drive. It really doesn't matter.

All of the information for transferring pictures to the computer should be included in either the camera manual or the software manual. (These may even be two sections of the same booklet.) Some cameras also allow you to connect via Elements 3.

Transferring an Image

With the software installed and the camera connected to the computer, you're ready to proceed. Because Olympus Camedia is fairly typical of the image handling software you're likely to use, let's use it as an example. After you start the application, you see a splash screen like the one in Figure 4.21. Click on Transfer Images from Camera. If you are using a different program, don't worry. All of the basic steps are the same. Verify that the camera is turned on and that both ends of the cable are plugged in to the appropriate places.

tip

If you'd rather skip the Splash Screen menu and just get right to work, use the Don't Show this Screen check box at the bottom of the screen. Instead, you'll go directly to the desktop interface. However, if you're planning to download images, don't turn off the splash screen because it's the only way to reach that option.

Figure 4.21

The Olympus
Camedia Splash
Screen menu.

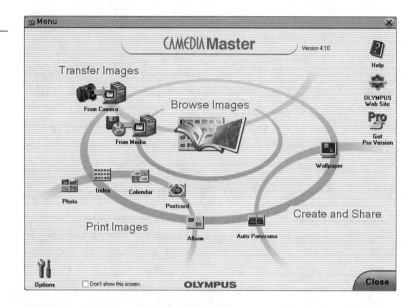

After you ask for a transfer, you see thumbnails of the photos in the camera. Figure 4.22 shows an example. You can transfer all of them or just select the ones you want by clicking on them. First, click the small button that toggles between All Images and Selected Images, and then press the Shift key and click the pictures you want to select before you click the larger Transfer button above it. You also need a destination file for your pictures. Camedia creates albums, as do most image transfer programs. *Albums* are simply folders that keep your pictures organized. You can stick everything into one album and sort it later, or make separate albums for new sets of pictures. In Camedia, you click the New Album button at the bottom right of the screen and enter a title for the new album.

note Virtually all of the digital cameras currently on the market support both the Windows and Macintosh platforms, and supply appropriate software for both platforms.

After you click the transfer button, you see a window like the one in Figure 4.23, telling you that your photos are being copied to your hard drive. In a few seconds or up to a minute or so, depending on how many pictures are in the camera, your photos are transferred to the new album. You can, if you want, delete the images from the camera and free up space on the memory card to shoot new ones. To study your pictures, go back to the menu and select Browse, and then click on the one you'd like to see enlarged.

Figure 4.22

Pictures are displayed as if they were slides on a light table.

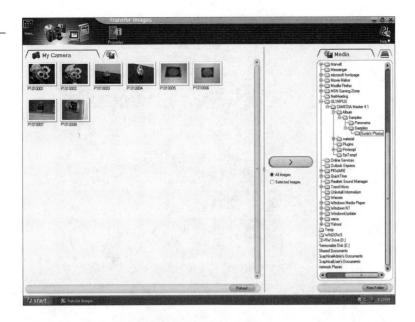

Figure 4.23

This box, or one like it, shows download-ing progress.

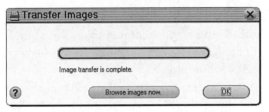

Camedia doesn't give you a lot of options for working on your photos. You can crop, adjust brightness and contrast, and so on, and even add type, but there are better programs for creativity.

The Nikon series of cameras comes with a similar downloading program that actu-ally has even fewer options for photo correction, but has the advantage of giving you the option to open a selected picture in your choice of photo-editing software. Figure 4.24 shows the Nikon interface.

Figure 4.24

Here, again, you click
on a photo to select
it for downloading.

Getting Photos from a Scanner

Your scanner is actually a kind of digital camera that turns your document into a
computer image by photographing and processing one line at a time. Like cameras,
scanners come with their own proprietary software. Some types of scanner also
come with a plug-in that, after it's installed in the proper Elements folder, allows
you to import a scanned image directly from the scanner into Elements. Follow the
install instructions on the scanner's CD-ROM and you're good to go. We'll talk more
about scanner use in Chapter 7.

Other Ways to Make Pages

Acting on the theory that a page is a page is a page, there's no real reason why you
can't use any page layout software you happen to have as a way to assemble scrapbook pages. Some, like Adobe InDesign, make the job a snap, letting you place
grids for your layouts and duplicate pages until you're bleary-eyed. Of course, for
the price, which is about $700, it should also make coffee and massage your back
while you work. Quark Xpress and Adobe PageMaker are also high-priced applications intended for professional use in page, newsletter, newspaper, and book design.
If you have access to one, and have a fairly good idea of how it works, go ahead
and play. Placing and resizing photos is a cinch with any of these, and you can certainly add all the backgrounds and embellishments you can design.

An all-purpose office suite, such as iWork, Microsoft Office, or Corel WordPerfect Office, has enough basic tools to turn out scrapbook pages, too. I sometimes use Microsoft Word for page design, but PowerPoint is good, too, and very easy to use. Corel's WordPerfect Office has a program called Presentations that's very much like PowerPoint. As long as you can place art and type on the same page, you can print the results as a scrapbook page. If you like, just print the pieces you need, and assemble them with traditional scrapbook papers and tools. There's no good reason not to mix your media, so to speak. Computer type and computer-printed photos can be awesome on a page with some real elements as well. Remember, the only limit to what you can do with computer art is your own sense of creativity and fun.

Programs for Sharing Pages Electronically

This final category of software to consider for your scrapbooking pages includes the programs you use for web page design or cross-platform page distribution. The following is an overview, but in Chapter 11, "For Web/CD-Based Scrapbooks," you'll learn much more about putting your pages on the Web or on a CD.

Portable Document Format (.pdf)

The best known program for creating portable, cross-platform documents is Adobe Acrobat. Because a great many other programs rely on Adobe Acrobat to create universally compatible manuals or Read Me documents, you might already have several copies of Acrobat Reader installed on your hard drive. Adobe Acrobat Reader, of course, is not for document creation, but if you have a Mac running OS X, virtually any program you can print from can save your pages as a .pdf file. (Unfortunately, this doesn't work in Windows. It's a function built into the Macintosh printer drivers.) Figure 4.25 shows the Mac's Print window. To make a PDF, simply click on the Save As PDF button.

Those using PCs have to invest in Adobe Acrobat to create PDF files, but if you're going to be sending your work out on a CD-ROM, it's a smart investment. Otherwise, your family and friends might not be able to see your work unless they have the same software you used to create your digital scrapbook.

Figure 4.25

Making a PDF is simple for Mac users.

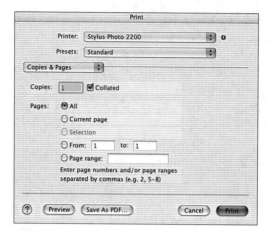

Web Pages

There are a lot of good web page creation programs. Even if you end up printing your pages, you can still lay them out in the .html file format with your favorite web design software. If you're planning to put your scrapbook up on your website, this is the most obvious way to do it, but even if you're not, you can load your HTML pages onto a CD or DVD and be fairly certain your friends and relatives have some kind of web software that can open the pages you send. I use Netscape Composer for my own web page work. It's easy and free, as is the rest of the Netscape package. I've been told, however, that Netscape might not be around forever. So I might have to look at Microsoft FrontPage or some other good and easy web page package. They all work pretty much alike. You can also design and save web pages with the word processor programs I mentioned earlier.

My husband enjoys coding web pages by hand and can put together a full page in HTML with nothing more than a text editor, while I'm still entering a title for mine. Fortunately, design is not his strong point. Otherwise, I'd be out of a job. He uses a program called BBEdit for the Mac, but the fact is that almost any word processor can save your text as HTML, even Microsoft Word.

Summary—What You Need to Remember

All you need to remember about software is that you need some, at the least a dedicated scrapbooking program, or a more versatile photo-editing and retouching program, like Adobe Photoshop Elements. I strongly recommend Photoshop Elements as a page-creation program as well as for photo retouching and editing. It requires that you use your own creativity, rather than simply relying on predrawn templates and page themes, and isn't that the whole point of doing it?

After you have learned basic computer functions like Open, Save, and Undo, you can transfer these skills to any program you use, including both word processors and image processors. The tools, palettes, and menus included in Elements are very much like those in other programs, and you should leave this chapter knowing, at least in theory, how to use them.

Building Your Scrapbook

The rest of this book takes you through some of the many ways to use your computer to make your scrapbook pages more attractive, more interesting, and more fun. You start with some basic layout and design ideas and go on to make interesting backgrounds. Then you learn how to rescue old pictures that are cracked, stained, or faded. You discover how to use a scanner to bring your old photos into the computer and how to repair the damage they inevitably have. Then you learn about using a digital camera and editing digital photos. I cover cropping and resizing, fixing red eye, and how to remove anything you don't want in the picture, including wild hair, extra inches on the hips, and even your ex-spouse.

After that, the next chapter deals with making good pictures out of bad ones by turning them into "art." For instance, when a photo is out of focus, you can turn it into a pastel drawing, a watercolor painting, or even neon tubing. Then you learn about working with type, including some tricks to make your words stand out on the page. You learn how to use shadows and special effects, and we talk about *journaling*—both how to put your words on the page, and how to write something meaningful.

This part also covers *paperless scrapbooks*—putting your pages on the Web and on a CD or DVD. Web and video scrapbooks can include sounds and movies as well as still pictures. You learn how to add them to your project. You also learn where you can get a free website, and how to set one up.

Happy scrapping!

Page Layout and Design

Just the thought of designing a page from scratch sends many a novice scrapbooker running and screaming. There's no need for panic, though. Simply understanding a few basic concepts makes the whole job easy and fun. In this chapter, you learn about layout and page design. You learn about using layers and templates, and how to add design elements without making clutter. Let's start with layers.

Working in Layers

If you want your pages to have a sense of depth or texture, you probably realize it comes from working in *layers*, adding one piece on top of another. The old-fashioned way is to literally pile up layers of paper on the background sheet. You might, for example, use torn tissue to make an edge around a photo or mount a photo on a piece of double-stick foam tape, so it stands out slightly from the rest of the page. Digitally, layering is even easier.

To really understand layers, think about a cartoon. When Disney Studios turned out its first Mickey Mouse cartoon, *Steamboat Willie*, back in 1928, Mickey was actually created out of about five layers of celluloid, or *cels*, laid over a background, and filmed two or three single frames at a time. Because film runs at 24 frames per second, it took a lot of pieces of celluloid to make Mickey do that happy little dance. But the animators were able to save a lot of time and paint by using one set of cels for his arms, another set for his legs, and one that didn't move as much for his body. That's basically how layers work in photo programs, too. Each thing you add to a page is on a separate transparent layer, so you can slide the photos, text, and frames around until they're in the perfect place. Then, when you save the page, you merge everything so it's all "stuck down" as if you glued it there. Why not leave it in layers? Well, you can, and should, as long as you continue to work on that page. But, just as a lot of pieces of paper and plastic flowers and studs and charms add bulk to a paper page, piling up a lot of layers adds extra bulk to the digital file. If you have plenty of storage space on your hard drive, that's not such a problem, but working with huge files also slows down the computer, and some computers quit in disgust if you ask them to do more than they want to.

The good news about going digital is that layers are easy to create and can be moved around and eventually "stuck down" with a lot less trouble than if you have to glue them in place. When you use Photoshop Elements, your layers appear on a layer palette so you can see what's where, and move it up or down and even apply special effects accordingly. Figure 5.1 shows a typical page I'm working on in Elements, and Figure 5.2 takes a closer look at the Layers palette.

Figure 5.1

Designing great pages is easy when you put each element on a new layer.

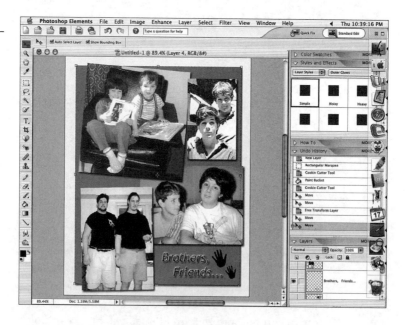

Figure 5.2

Elements has a
logical approach
to layering.

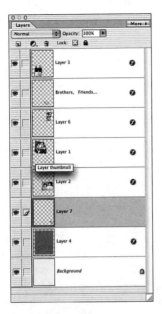

The Layers palette in Photoshop Elements allows you to add or remove layers or rearrange them just by dragging them. As you can see by the Layers palette in Figure 5.2, I have a lot of different layers. Some hold the photos and others the shapes that are behind or in front of them, and there at least two or three more, including the text layer to identify the pictures and an effects layer to add drop shadows behind the frames. Then I'll flatten the image by merging all the layers and watch my file become much smaller. That's especially important if I'm going to put the page on my website. Ever waited for a big file to load from a web page? The page in the figure, even only partially finished, is 24 megabytes. That's a lot of disk space and a lot of download time. If I flatten the image and save it as a JPG, which is a very Web-efficient format, it'll reduce to 46 kilobytes, which downloads in two seconds or less. Better? You better believe it.

It's important for you to understand the uses of the Layers palette and the Layers menu shown in Figure 5.3. Both provide helpful options such as adding a new layer, removing one, and flattening the image. It doesn't matter whether you use the menu or the palette to add a layer, so do whatever's convenient. However, some actions, like merging layers, can only be done from the menu. That's so you won't do it accidentally.

Figure 5.3
Whenever you see
an arrow on a menu,
click it. It leads you
to more menus or
tools.

Figure 5.4 shows a closer look at the Layers palette, with a much less complex page. I've dragged the palette out of its palette bin so you can see it with the picture. I've created a document with three layers. There's a Background layer that has a patterned background; a layer I've painted on, called Layer 1; and a Type layer, which is recognizable by the *T* on the palette. It also has the text I typed as the name of the layer. The open-eye icons to the left of the palette indicate these layers are all visible. If you want to hide a layer, you simply click the icon to remove the eye. The paintbrush icon tells you which of the three layers is currently active. That's important because you can work on only one layer at a time. Anything you do to the active layer doesn't affect the others. If I want to erase part of my drawing and try again, I can do so without erasing the pattern behind the cat. Remember, always check the Layers palette if you "lose" a layer. It's probably just hidden behind another one.

Figure 5.4
To make a layer
active, click on it.

The icons at the top of the palette represent things you can do with a layer. The dog-eared page icon adds a new layer to the stack. The half-black, half-white circle icon adds fill or adjustment layers, which affect only the layer that's active at the time you click on the icon. Drag layers you don't want to use to the trash can icon. The More button at the top of the Layers palette opens a menu that lets you rename layers and merge them, among other useful tasks.

To move a layer on top of another, go to the palette and simply click on one and drag it up or down in the stack. You can also change the transparency of layers so an upper layer appears to be more or less transparent, letting what's below it show through or not, and make them blend together in different ways. Layer blending is best learned by observation and experimentation. To get you started, *Dissolve* gives a speckled effect, and *Normal* is an even mix.

note A *fill layer* is a layer that holds a color or pattern. An *adjustment layer* applies an adjustment—such as a change in brightness or contrast—either to the contents of the previous layer only or to the entire document.

Bitmaps? Vectors? Rasters? Wha'?

All image files can include both raster, or bitmap, images and vector images. (Raster and bitmap are terms used interchangeably.) Let's start at the very beginning, with the bitmap. A *bitmap* is simply a way of describing all the pixels or dots that make up an image on your screen. Think of a map printed on a piece of graph paper. Each little box represents a pixel. Each pixel is identified in a code that tells the computer its precise location and color. When you send a picture to the printer, each bitmap pixel asks for, and gets, the right mix of inks to reproduce the color. Cool, huh? It's what makes computer graphics possible.

Vector images, instead of being described dot-by-dot as bitmap images are, are geometric codes. The computer draws a box, for instance, by being told: Start at this location. Draw a line one pixel thick at 90 degrees for a distance of one inch. Draw a line from that point 180 degrees south for a distance of one inch. And so on, until the whole box is described. This system can describe intricate curves and shapes, too, which is why it's used for type.

In Photoshop Elements you have separate type and shape layers, which are actually vector layers. When you're finished making changes to the vector layer, you can rasterize it to make it a bitmap by choosing Simplify Layer from the Layer menu. It's as if the lines on a vector page were just made of some kind of imaginary string, and until you paste them down, they aren't really there. Rasterizing transforms them from lines back to bitmaps, which is what all computer pictures are.

After type has been simplified in Photoshop Elements, you can't go back and edit it, so you need to check your spelling before you take that final step. If you want to change the typeface or the size again, you *must* do that before you convert it. You can still drag the rasterized type around on the page, independent of the other layers in your document, until you flatten the image, which places everything on the same layer. Another option is to duplicate a type layer and rasterize the duplicate, preserving one type layer in case you want to make changes or use that type in another form within the same document. You can make the duplicate layer invisible, and still know it's there if you need it.

Working with Templates and Grids

The programs specifically dedicated to scrapbooking, such as American Greetings Scrapbooks & More or Art Explosion Scrapbook Factory Deluxe, come with dozens of premade templates, complete with backgrounds, and some designer's ideas as to which decorations are appropriate and where the pictures are to be placed. You can use these to get started, but sooner or later you will stop being satisfied with somebody else's ideas and want to make your own.

If you have a more robust graphics program, such as Photoshop Elements, making your own templates is very easy. I usually start with a colored background, and add a layer dedicated to guidelines, and then use those guidelines as a basis for my layouts. If you turn on the rulers, placing guidelines at specific intervals is easy. Rulers can be turned on and off from the View menu or simply by pressing (⌘-R) [Ctrl+R]. Then use a single pixel pencil to draw straight lines. (Hold the Shift key as you draw to keep the line straight.) When you're done with the guidelines, trash the layer or just hide it by clicking its eye icon.

You can also use a *grid*, which is a pattern of crossed lines like graph paper, that you turn on and off from a menu. In Photoshop Elements, you can show or hide the grid by choosing View, Grid. You can customize the size of the grid by clicking on Edit, clicking on Preferences and selecting Grid, and then entering the measurements you prefer. Grids can be single or double page, and they don't print with the rest of the page, so you can place them wherever you think they'll help you keep things aligned, and not have to worry that they'll show up in the final page.

Figure 5.5 shows an example of a basic layout template, drawn in Elements. If you are consistent with regard to color, type styles, and picture placement, your pages are pretty much guaranteed to work well together. This absolutely does *not* mean you must use exactly the same layout template for each page in your scrapbook. Just make sure some element of the page design—be it colors, type, or photo placement—is consistent from one page to the next.

Figure 5.5
I've placed this grid to divide the page into thirds both horizontally and vertically.

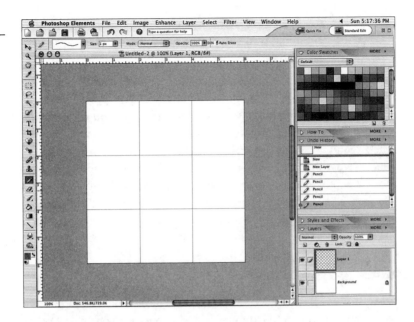

After you open the Preferences dialog box in Photoshop Elements, choose Grid. You'll see a window something like the one shown in Figure 5.6. I suggest you set the gridlines to inches and the division to quarter inches, unless the metric system is used where you live.

You can even adjust the color of the gridlines so they show up against a colored background. If they get in the way, turn them on and off in the View menu.

tip

The Photoshop Elements Preferences dialog box lives on the Edit menu in Windows and Mac OS 9. If you use Mac OS X, it's under the Photoshop Elements menu.

Figure 5.6
The pop-up menus open when you click the arrows.

If you like placing pictures at an angle, use the grid anyway, to help you keep the photos from bumping into each other or running off the page.

Composing a Page

When you are laying out a page, keep in mind that you have several elements to work with. First of all, you have the pictures you're putting on it. Secondly, you have the background you're putting them on. Third, you have type that tells you, at the least, who or what's in the picture and possibly when and why it was taken. Fourth, you have any other *design elements* you want to use, such as blocks of color, lines, frames, and embellishments of all kinds from rubber stamps to charms to ribbons and more. These can be overwhelming if they're not carefully placed. One of the main design points to remember is *don't crowd*. A cluttered page is unattractive and hard to read.

The Importance of White Space

Well, first of all, white space doesn't have to be white. Colored backgrounds are nice, too. But you do need to leave some space on your page. When you fill up a page with text and pictures, it's hard to look at because there are so many elements competing for your attention. *White space*, sometimes called *negative space*, describes the open space between design elements. It can be between words or paragraphs of text. It can be space inside or around a picture, or between the elements of the page. It's easy to concentrate on what you're putting into a page, to the point that you ignore what you ought to leave out.

If the viewer's eye is to flow from one photo or paragraph to another, you need to give it a reason to do so. The reason can be white space. White space is essential for providing spatial relationships between visual items, and actually guides your eye from one point to another. White space doesn't have to be large. Just a generous gutter between text and pictures can make a big difference, as you can see in Figure 5.7. (*Gutter* is a typesetter's term for the space between columns of text.) The page on the left in Figure 5.7 is jammed full of stuff. The same elements, on the right page, have added just a bit of space and there's a noticeable difference in the "viewer-friendliness" of the page.

Figure 5.7

This is a journal-style scrapbook page. It's important that the text be readable.

Eye Leading

The way you place your elements on the page can determine whether they're seen. The reader's natural tendency is to look from top left to bottom right, at least in English-speaking countries and in most of Europe. Therefore, you want to arrange your pictures and text so there's a natural flow from the upper-left side of the page to the bottom right. This is especially important if, as in the example shown in Figure 5.7, there's a lot of text to read. Use the photos to balance the page.

Wide margins also direct the reader's attention to the center of the page. Remember that the wider the columns of type, the more space needed between them. If you have three narrow columns of type, the gutter can be narrower than if there are only two. Also allow ample vertical space between the lines (called leading, it rhymes with sledding, as opposed to eye "leading," which rhymes with pleading) for the sake of legibility. Tightly spaced text darkens the page and makes it less attractive.

tip

Flipping pictures is okay, unless there's somebody wearing a T-shirt with words, or a guy with one earring, or an obvious wedding ring, or a sign or anything similar that readers might notice.

When you use a photo, try not to place it so the subject is looking away from the page. If you have a right-facing subject, place it on the left side of the page. This way he, she, or it appears to be looking at the text, not away from it. If there are no characteristics like type in the photo that gives away the secret, you can flip a picture horizontally to give you more flexibility in the layout. Your reader tends to look in the same direction as the photo subject, and you want to keep the reader's eyes on the page.

The Rule of Thirds

Much to my surprise, when I started laying out scrapbook pages, I discovered that the same principles apply to a page as to a single photo. Make shapes work together within the context of the whole design, be it page or picture. Avoid crowding. Decide on a center of interest, and make it the focal point of the page.

Good photos and good pages have what's called a *center of interest*. In a portrait of a single person, it's the face. In a group of people, there's ideally one who dominates, whereas the rest are subordinate. The dominant one, because of position, size, or placement, is the center of interest. In a landscape or still life, it's the part of the picture to which the viewer's eye is attracted first. Your first step in composing a picture—or a page—is to find the center of interest. Most of the time, it's obvious. It's the dominant feature of the landscape. It's the one yellow flower in the field of red ones. In the world of advertising, it's the widget that goes next to the catalog description, or the house that's for sale. It's the reason why you're taking the picture or making the page. On a page about your child's birthday, it's the child blowing out the candles on the cake.

After you locate or decide upon the center of interest, look for anything that might detract from it. Is there something behind the portrait subject that interferes with him? Does he have a lamp, a window, or some other object in the room that appears to be growing out of his head? If so, change your camera position, or else move him to a more neutral background.

Deer Me!

I once saw a remarkable portrait of the CEO of a large corporation. He apparently liked hunting, and had a trophy deer head mounted and hung on a wall in his office. The photographer who was sent to shoot a portrait for a business magazine was an animal lover, and managed to position the CEO so he appeared to be wearing the deer's antlers. He looked idiotic. (What was *most* remarkable about the picture was that the magazine editor allowed it to run.)

The center of interest generally shouldn't be right in the middle of the page, unless it's the only thing of importance on the page. The center of interest also shouldn't be right at the edge of the page, because this tends to draw the viewer's eye away from everything else, and usually right off the page. It knocks the viewer off balance.

If you analyze a number of successful pages, you'll probably find that in more cases than not, the center of interest falls in one of only four spots. These spots can be defined, and even turned into a rule that artists and designers know as the *rule of thirds*. Quite simply, you divide the frame into thirds, vertically and horizontally, as in Figure 5.8. The four points where the lines intersect are the approximate "best" locations for the center of interest. The ancient Greeks had discovered this, along with many other geometric "rules" for artists and sculptors. They were used in everything from the design of the pyramids in Egypt to the Parthenon to DaVinci's painting of the Last Supper, and are found with astonishing frequency in nature. If you want to learn more, visit http://www.goldennumber.net/.

Like all good rules, it's meant to be broken occasionally. (Think how much better the chocolate cake tastes after a week of dieting.) But if you follow it more often than not, your pages have a greater impact.

Figure 5.8

The rule of thirds applies to any size or shape of page.

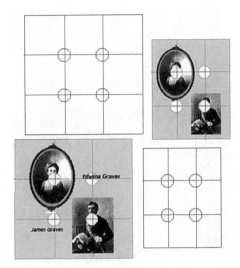

Coherent Pages

The main goal for your scrapbook pages is to be enjoyed and understood. Although it's lots of fun to use exotic fonts and quirky layouts, don't lose sight of the goal. When you have too many gimmicks on a page, your viewers don't bother with it. Limit yourself to a few interesting but legible fonts per document. Make your titles stand out by leaving white space around them—it's better than big black type for attracting attention.

When you are working with facing pages, try to do the two at once, or at least consider how the right-side page relates to the left one as you put it together. Remember to put a strong element such as a large title, a contrasting color block, or a large photo in the upper-left corner of the right page, so the viewer's eye is attracted back up, instead of continuing across the bottom of the right page, and out of the book. Figure 5.9 shows how this might look.

Figure 5.9

Facing pages need to work together.

Design Elements

You might find that, despite your best efforts to follow the rules, your pages still don't quite work the way you want them to. Perhaps they are too formal or too plain. That's when it's time to think about adding more elements to the total design. You can use lines or blocks of color or texture to help with eye leading. A line next to or under a picture really helps to draw your attention to it. In Figure 5.10, I've experimented with a couple of ways to make the square page from Figure 5.8 more interesting.

Figure 5.10

Adding another element makes the page layout more effective.

If there's only one photo on the page, you can put it in the center and maybe add a frame around it, or a block of color behind it, so it's obviously the center of attention. Better yet, try it off-center with a color block, or put some embellishments behind it. Figures 5.11 and 5.12 show a couple of examples.

Figure 5.11

The schoolmarm gets a background of old report cards.

Figure 5.12

The dog looks better a bit off-center. Notice how the color block helps balance the page.

Adding Textures in the Computer

If you look closely at the color version of Figure 5.12, you can see that I added some texture to the colored block. It's very easy to do this in Photoshop Elements. There's a filter called Noise in the filter list. You can remove noise or add it.

Noise, by the way, is not a soundtrack for your pictures, or even a comment on them. *Noise* is a random pattern of single dots or pixels kind of like we used to see on TV, back in the days before cable and satellite, when trying to tune in a distant station. Really bad noise looked like dirty snow. You probably need to remove noise from scans of old or dusty pictures. In this case, to make a textured background, you want to add some noise. You can choose colored or monochromatic (black) dots, and decide just how random the placement is. Photoshop Elements offers you a choice of uniform or Gaussian noise. Gaussian noise is supposedly more random.

There are lots of other ways to add texture to a block of color. Assuming you are doing the whole page on the computer, you can scan pieces of cloth or lace, or even things as common as a paper towel or a piece of interesting textured paper, and apply those, just as you might paste the real item on a page. Photoshop Elements has a filter called Texturizer, which adds texture to a selected object or a page. It's shown in use in Figure 5.14. I've created one texture from its basic Sandstone preset, and another from a texture I loaded from the textures folder called Feathers. You can vary the size and depth of the textures you create, as well as experiment with which way the light strikes them.

Figure 5.13

Choose the amount of noise by using the slider.

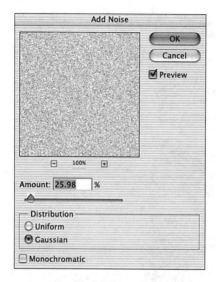

Figure 5.14

In Photoshop Elements, the path to the Texturizer is Filter, Texture, Texturizer.

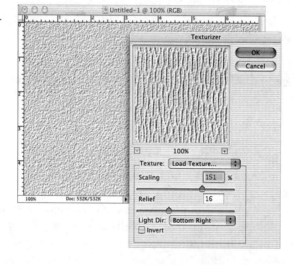

I strongly urge you to experiment with your filters and plug-ins. You can learn a lot just by poking around with them and trying different combinations of filters. Remember, you really can't break the computer by trying new things. If there's not enough memory to do what you want to do, the application might crash. There are at least a dozen other reasons why the computer might crash, and it's almost inevitable that one day, it will. The worst that can happen is that you'll need to restart the computer and start over. For that reason alone, it's important to save your work frequently as you go along. If a program crashes with unsaved work, you *cannot* recover it. Save every time you add something. If possible, and there's usually no reason not to, save in a format that allows you to keep layers active, such as TIFF (`.tif`), or Photoshop (`.psd`). It makes recovering from a crash that much easier. That way, you can resume at least close to where you were, as opposed to having to start from scratch again.

Textural Objects: Ribbons, Fiber, and Fabrics

Don't forget that it's okay to mix "real" stuff with computer-generated pages. A piece of glued-on ribbon or fabric or lace might be just what your page needs to bring it up from good to great. I sometimes outline nature photos in twisted grasses or sisal twine. They work fine, as long as they are stuck down well and the page goes into a page protector sleeve when it's done.

Clip Art for Scrapbookers

Clip art is another element you can, and should, consider when you are designing pages. The term *clip art* comes from the precomputer, even pre–office copier days. Artists, mainly those who worked for newspapers and advertising agencies, subscribed to clip art services, which supplied a book of art every month. The individual pictures included anything from a platter of roast chicken for a grocery ad to a young man on one knee gazing fondly at his girlfriend as he slipped a diamond ring on her finger. These were cut out with scissors and pasted right into the ads, or enlarged or shrunk with a Photostat camera, which made a copy on photo paper.

There are lots of sources for clip art. You can find it for sale in the back pages of computer magazines such as *MacAddict* or *PCWorld*, or on many CDs, including those that accompany certain scrapbooking software. Figure 5.15 shows a single page from the Print Explosion Deluxe catalog.

In this Macintosh-only program from Nova Development, there are 90,000 pieces of clip art, which you can use for any noncommercial purpose. (You're not allowed to resell them or to use them on commercial websites.) There are also a bunch of fonts that work with any Mac graphics or word processing program. There's a very similar collection for Windows users called Art Explosion Scrapbook Factory Deluxe. It has the same font collection and a lot of clip art from the same sources, but selected to be more useful specifically for scrapbooking.

Online Sources

Just for fun, I did a Google search on clip art for scrapbooks. The Google search engine (http://www.google.com) returned 62,500 sources. I didn't investigate more than a few, but here are some to get you started. These also have links to even more art sources. There's tons of stuff out there, if you know where to look.

Figure 5.15

The Print Explosion Deluxe clip art catalog shows everything in very small black-and-white illustrations, but the actual art is in color and can easily be resized as necessary.

- http://scrapbooking.about.com/od/clipart/
- http://www.gatherings.info/capture/clipart.asp
- http://www.countryclipart.com
- http://www.leavesoftime.com/tfree.html

These places have free downloadable clip art and some you have to pay for. If you really like the art and the style of the artist(s), it's worth buying a CD. The typical price is around $10–20 for a full collection, and having a bunch of clips in the same style helps you keep the theme and flow from page to page in your books.

Summary—What You Need to Remember

Pages, whether designed on the computer or with pieces of paper and other scraps, are composed of layers of different elements. Most computer graphics programs allow you to work in layers as you assemble your photos, type, and other page elements.

Using templates and grids helps you keep things in line, or consistently out of line, if that's what you want. You can use predrawn templates that someone else designed or you can invent your own.

Remember to consider the natural tendency of viewers to read a page from upper-left to lower-right, just as they do a page of type. You can make this eye leading work for you by placing important objects in specific places on the page and leaving white space in between them. The best places to put the pictures are at the junction of imaginary lines that divide the page into thirds vertically and horizontally. Don't crowd the page, but remember that a block of a contrasting color can help balance a photo. Color blocks, texture blocks, and lines, properly used, help your page design. Don't be afraid to experiment with the features in your program—you can't really break the computer.

Clip art is readily available and can also be used to maintain a style over the course of many pages. Some clip art comes with most commercial scrapbooking programs, and more is available for sale, or free, on the Internet.

Creating and Using Backgrounds

There's one question scrapbookers have to resolve when going digital for the first time. How far should you go? Should you print the background on the page, or assemble the page from computer printed titles and photos on a preprinted background? Really, you can do it either way. Many printers can print on card stock, either by adjusting the rollers for paper thickness, or by feeding a single sheet of heavy paper or card stock through a slot in the back of the printer. If your printer can't handle the heavy card stock you'd otherwise use, print on regular paper and slide a piece of plain white card into the plastic sleeve behind the printed page. If you're not using sleeves, you can mount the page on card stock as a last resort.

Using Premade Backgrounds

The craft stores have stacks and stacks of different preprinted background pages. Figure 6.1 shows a handful I bought this afternoon at the local Michael's. These cost about 25 cents per sheet, and they come in a wide selection of styles and colors. Backgrounds come in sets with elaborate backgrounds as well as plainer, harmonizing sheets, so you can use a fancy first page and follow up with related but simpler sheets for the following pages. That way, the project hangs together a little better than it would if every page were the same and all screamed Christmas, wedding, or whatever.

Figure 6.1
A modest collection
of preprinted
background papers.

No matter what else you do with the backgrounds, make sure they relate in some way to the photos. However, that doesn't necessarily mean using the same predominant color, as I have in Figure 6.2a. The lilies are a rich yellow, which I duplicated for the background. It doesn't work well because the yellow page overwhelms the flowers. A contrasting panel behind the photo would help, as would a frame around it, or simply choosing a different shade, preferably a lighter one, for the background. In Figure 6.2b, I've added a frame and changed the background. Even in black and white, you can see the difference.

Figure 6.2
A frame around the
photo helps set
it off.

When you have a busy photo like this one, avoid patterned backgrounds. They also detract from the picture. Patterns can work well with portraits because we are mentally accustomed to sorting out human faces from the clutter around them.

tip

In Photoshop Elements, to copy a color from your photo or any other source, click the Eyedropper on the color you want and it becomes the foreground color. To make it the background color, press Option/Alt as you click.

You can buy scrapbooking kits from many sources, both for paper work and for computer scrapbooking. Each set has a title page, a preprinted page with a central color and border as in Figure 6.3, and other embellishments, frames, and borders all related to the same theme. Using these, it's hard for a beginner to go very far wrong. Just remember that the pages of frames and borders are meant to be copied and placed on different pages, not used all together as they're displayed on your screen. The example in Figure 6.3 comes from http://www.princesscrafts.com, a good website for downloading predrawn pages.

Figure 6.3

There's a wide range of formats for seasons, special occasions, and holidays as well as everyday pages. (Example used by permission.)

Personally, I don't like to use that approach to scrapbooking because I want my pages to be something different from everyone else's. Also, it's sometimes easier for me to start from scratch with a couple of Elements shape tools, and put together a page that's just right for the picture. In Figure 6.4, I've done an example of a small square "brag book" page. I took a dark pink background and used one of the shape tools to make a rough edged shape, which I filled with a lighter pink. The black-and-white photo pops right out of the color, especially since I trimmed the top of the photo background out. Then I took a second shape, the kid face, and added it as an accent, filled with a darker pink. (The original shape was frowning, so I selected the mouth and flipped it. "Turn that frown upside down...") Then I added a small banner below the photo with name and age. Done. After I print this page, I may decide to add a silver charm or wire on some baby name beads. Or not. There are no rules when you do it your way.

Figure 6.4

Three Elements shape tools and one photo. Five minutes total, including time to admire it.

Remember that you can always copy elements from a predesigned layout and add them to a blank page you have started from scratch. If you can't draw, this is a good way to pick up some useful art, without being stuck with somebody else's page. Isn't it better to personalize your pages? When you go to cropping parties, you're probably going to see other people's pages using the same backgrounds. Even if yours is better designed and makes better use of the material, it's still obvious that it's not strictly your own invention.

Here's an example of a customized page, based on a purchased one. Working in Photoshop Elements, I copied the little bear and flipped him horizontally so he faced the other way. I filled in the moon with a small brush and the same shade of yellow. Then I used a large, soft-edged brush to fill in the clouds, and added a background layer in the same shade of sky blue as the original. Because they were beneath the cloud and bear layer, the soft edges blended nicely. Finally, I took a star-shaped brush and placed stars where they seemed to want to be, changing the brush sizes occasionally so the stars wouldn't all look the same. The original page is shown in Figure 6.5 and my version is in Figure 6.6. They'll be great as a double page spread for sleeping baby pictures.

Figure 6.5

This is the page I bought...

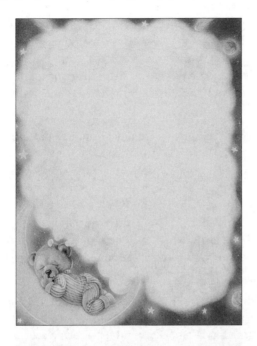

Figure 6.6

...and this is the page I made.

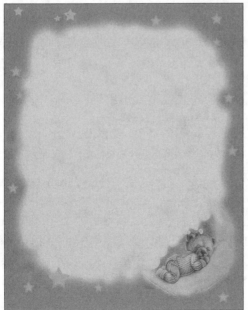

Backgrounds from the Scanner

Your scanner can be a good source of textured backgrounds, too. Try scanning things like paper towels, wrapping paper, torn pieces of Japanese mulberry paper, and even cardboard. You can scan any kind of reasonably flat material including flowers, rice, beans, jelly beans, or any kind of colorful candy. Making a frame of (unwrapped) candy canes would be fun for a Christmas page, and then you've got a treat to enjoy while you're working. Just be sure to clean the scanner glass afterward.

If you don't happen to have a scanner, or don't want to risk putting food in it, you can also lay the stuff out on a sheet of paper or cardstock and photograph it. Try to shoot straight down, as much as possible, so you're not dealing with perspective. When you're out walking around, keep an eye open for natural objects that might make an interesting page. In the fall, especially in New England where I live, the leaves turn wonderful colors, and can make a great background. In the spring, we get asparagus and fiddlehead ferns, which also make a nice accent for a page, especially if you scan them along with a piece of handmade paper or mulberry-textured tissue.

When you go to fabric shops, rummage sales, or yard/garage/tag sales, be on the lookout for interesting pieces of fabric to scan. I bought one hand-woven placemat at a church fair, and scanned it as a background for a recipe collection. It tied everything together nicely. I was also able to change the colors in Photoshop Elements and tint the texture yellow for breakfast foods, light red for meats, blue for chicken or fish dishes, and other colors for cookies, desserts, salads, and veggies.

The only rule to remember when using textured backgrounds is that the texture shouldn't overpower the pictures. If you have a busy photo, with many colors and lots going on, the background needs to be fairly simple. On the other hand, when you are dealing with a page of head-and-shoulders portraits or a bunch of old black-and-white photos (as in Figure 6.7), a textured page or a texture block behind the pictures really does help to make the page more interesting and appealing.

tip

If you have an inkjet printer, read the manual before you go paper shopping. Find out if there are any kinds of paper that are not recommended, and if so, avoid printing on them. Also avoid the handmade papers with twigs, leaves, and flower petals embedded in them. They'll shed little bits of stuff into your printer, and that's not good for it. If you want to use these, scan them or photograph them instead.

Figure 6.7

These textures are supposedly feathers and footprints.

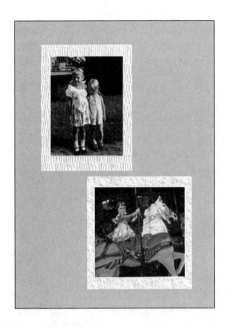

Papers: What's Available

Take a walk down the paper aisle at your favorite scrapbooking store. You will find all of those preprinted pages we've talked about, plus a whole lot more stuff you really need to try. There are lots of textured papers in white and colors. Some are even suitable for running through a printer. You'll also find *Japanese mulberry paper* (which is semi-transparent and has textured bits pressed into it), tissue, vellum, and more. *Vellum* is also a semi-transparent paper, intended to mimic the look of old parchment scrolls.

What you shouldn't use for scrapbooking, or for any kind of inkjet printing, is office copier paper (with one exception that you'll learn about shortly). Why not? The main reason is print quality. Copier paper is intended for quick, cheap copying of documents that are most likely going to be read and thrown away. It's not pure white, so it won't give you true colors from your inkjet inks. It might not be acid and lignin free, so it could affect other parts of your page, such as photos or embellishments. (Refer to Chapter 2, "Traditional Scrapbooking Tools," for more information.) It's more likely to jam than paper designed for the inkjet process, and it just doesn't look or feel as good.

Consider the basis weight of the paper you buy for scrapbooking. *Basis weight* is the standard measurement of an amount of paper. For example, the basis weight is determined by the weight of 500 sheets of 17"×22" paper (the parent size). If a ream of 17"×22" paper weighs 20 pounds, this is called 20 lb. bond paper. Good quality office paper is usually 20–24 lb. bond. Greeting card paper is more like a 60–65 lb. card stock. It's flexible enough to print on easily, but holds a crease well, if you need to fold it. Index card stock is heavier still. It runs from 90 to 150 lb.

Paper whiteness is a measurement of how much light it reflects. Whiter papers reflect more light, and therefore represent bright colors better. What's most important is whether the paper tends toward a bluish-white or a warmer yellowish-white. Bluish-white papers are perceived as cleaner and cooler. The yellowish-white papers give an impression of warmth and humanity. For the best overall color, choose a neutral white.

Photo papers are classified differently, of course. Nothing's ever consistent in the world of printing. Instead of pound weights, they are measured by thickness in millimeters or *mils*. A typical glossy photo paper is somewhere between 8.5 and 10 mils thick.

It's equally important to consider the surface of the paper, along with the way you intend to use it. Epson and Hewlett-Packard (HP) both make a wide variety of papers for inkjet printing. For pages with crisp lines and intense, high-quality color, look for a matte surface, such as HP or Epson Bright White or Premium Inkjet paper. Epson Archival Matte is also excellent for scrapbooking. Kodak and Canon also have a wide selection of papers, but I haven't really experimented with them enough to say they are necessarily better than the other brands.

tip You can buy small sample packs of various kinds of photo-realistic art papers and even printable canvases at http://www.inkjetart.com.

Glossy paper gives more of a photographic look and produces vibrant color, but is susceptible to fingerprints. That's why a heavier weight matte paper might be a better choice for prints that will be handled often. If the prints are going on a page with a page protector, photo glossy paper is great. You can even get fancy edging scissors and give it that "drugstore processing" look. It makes sense to pick up a sample pack of assorted papers, so you can see for yourself what looks and feels right.

You might also discover some other interesting papers. My Epson sample book, shown in Figure 6.8, includes backlight film, canvas, four kinds of artist paper, and even synthetic paper with and without an adhesive backing for outdoor use. Because it's waterproof, synthetic paper also makes a great scrapbook cover, stuck carefully over book-binding boards.

Figure 6.8

This is just one of Epson's sample books.

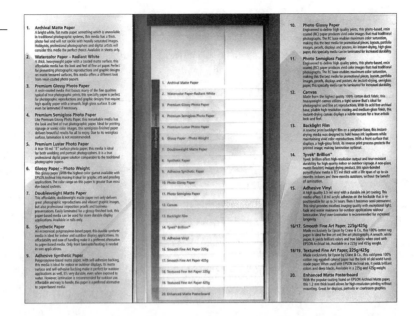

Art papers should be considered when you're printing photos that have had filters applied to make them mimic some other medium. There's something about the texture of watercolor papers and the way they absorb ink that makes your filtered photo art look more like the real thing. I've done photographic "watercolors" that, from a reasonable distance, would fool an expert. The Photoshop filters include some that turn your photos into charcoal or chalk drawings; they look much more real on an appropriate art paper. The Arches, Legion, and Somerset brands are all very good for printing. These papers come in several surfaces. *Smooth* is nearly so, having only a little bit of "tooth" to help hold onto the inks. *Velvet* is, as you might expect, rougher than smooth. It's about halfway between smooth and *textured*, which is the somewhat bumpy surface preferred by many painters. Both photos and digital art look really good on these papers.

There are, of course, other specialty papers, such as iron-on transfers and transparency films. Your computer store or art supply store probably has these too, and they might lead you to think up some interesting uses for them. How about setting a scrapbook title and a photo or some clip art and ironing them onto a piece of fabric for a scrapbook cover? Or turning your favorite pages into t-shirts for your family? Transparencies give you the opportunity to layer type over a photo without damaging the photo itself. You can print frames on them, and cut and stick them over photos for protection. Just be careful to use archival-quality plastics.

HP even has a temporary tattoo paper! You can simply print some clip art on the transfer paper to make a temporary tattoo, paste it on the kids, and then pose them for a photo to go on a page with the same piece of clip art.

When you have small pieces of paper you want to print on, use a temporary adhesive to stick them to a *carrier sheet*, which can be any kind of paper that glides happily through the printer. I admit I keep some cheap copier paper on hand for carriers and to print *proofs* before I attempt to print on something fancy. In this case, the proof is used strictly for positioning, and the paper is thin enough that I can put the fancy paper behind it and use the proof to make sure my type or photo falls in the right place.

Other Materials You Can Print On

Let's start with cloth. Canon has a white cotton fabric that works with any wide-body printer. It measures 9 1/2 by 14 inches, so it's too big for the letter-size printer.

> **tip**
>
> When you work with iron-ons, tattoos, or transparencies, be sure you flip the artwork before you print it. In order to appear correct when ironed or applied, the picture must be backward on the transfer paper. Similarly, if you are printing on transparency film, you want the type and art to read through the film, so the ink is protected from being scratched or rubbed off. Please note, however, that the rules are different for iron-on paper designed for dark fabrics. These are printed on a white page and not flipped before you print.

Epson has a canvas material specifically for wide body printers. The narrowest size available is 24 inches wide on a four-foot roll. Although you probably can't work with it at home, it's worth calling the local copy shop to see whether they have it and can make big prints for you. Imagine a wrap-around cover for a scrapbook, printed on canvas. You could use art and photos from inside pages on the cover, as well as add the title, date, or whatever else you want.

Art supply stores and some computer stores also have canvas and other printable materials from less well-known makers, and you can find even more on the Internet. I have letter size canvas from both Xerox and Labelon. Xerox has an ivory cast and a heavier texture. The Labelon product is coated with bright white on the printable side, and is much more flexible. Both make decent prints. Figure 6.9 and the color section show the same picture printed on both using a standard Epson inkjet printer. As you see in the color version, the colors are definitely "off" in the Xerox canvas, and the canvas texture is more obvious.

Figure 6.9

Labelon on the left;
Xerox on the right.

Be sure to read and follow the instructions when you're working with any "unusual" papers, such as canvas or heavy art papers. Usually, they ask you to insert only one sheet at a time into the printer, as opposed to thinner papers that seem to feed into the printer better if there are at least a half dozen sheets in the tray.

There are presently not metallic inks for laser or inkjet printers, but if you really need three-dimensional gold lettering, you can make a pretty good imitation. First, print the type in a medium gold color, and then go over it with the adhesive and metallic powder rubber stampers use (see Chapter 2 for more information). Finally, fuse it to the paper with a heat gun. The resulting type looks and feels as if you used a thick gold paint.

In Chapter 10, "Adding Text," I'll teach you some tricks to make ordinary type look as if it's set in molten metal, chiseled into bronze, or drawn with a squeeze bottle of mustard.

> **tip**
>
> If you think something metallic-looking might be in order, visit http://www.paperandmore.com to see their line of metallic vellums. They have standard metal colors as well as a collection of shimmering pearl-like colors that are great for wedding or baby pages. They also have card stocks of various kinds and a lot more products, and most important, they are scrapbook savvy, so their products are generally safe to use with most printers.

Summary—What You Need to Remember

Backgrounds are the paper on which you put your memories. That's why paper is important, whether you're pasting or printing on it. Choose the right paper for the job, but be careful about always using preprinted page backgrounds. They are easy and affordable, but your scrapbook could end up looking just like your best friend's or neighbor's, with the same theme but different faces. Anyway, it's just as easy and a lot more creative to make your own.

Keep an eye out for interesting textures you can photograph or scan. Fabrics are good, but so are natural objects like leaves and ferns. A tray full of jelly beans or candies makes an interesting background, as does popcorn, pasta, or anything else of that nature.

Get to know what kinds of papers are available for your printer. Look for paper sample packs in various kinds. Papers come in matte, glossy, and textured surfaces. Use those that are acid and lignin free and avoid plain office copier paper.

Glossy papers make photos look more like the darkroom kind, but they can be damaged by fingerprints. Matte papers are more durable, and are ideal for printing entire pages or journal entries. Art papers and canvases add an interesting depth and texture to pages, but read the instructions before you use them to make sure they are suitable for your printer.

Above all else, remember that backgrounds are the basis for everything else.

Working with Old Photos

If there's just one thing scrapbookers can do better with a computer, it's rescuing old photos. Actually, there are a lot of things computers do better, but I have to admit that taking an old, ripped, cracked, and faded portrait and turning it back into a useable photo is one of my favorite tasks. For one thing, as you get deeply into these old pictures, you begin to get a real sense of who the person was—how he spoke, or how she laughed. And you find family resemblances you might not otherwise have noticed. One of my sons has his grandfather's nose and eyes, and in turn my dad had *his* grandfather's nose and eyes. So, that nice nose has been handed along through five generations.

The first step in working on an old photo is to find a way to get it into the computer. As I mentioned in an earlier chapter, if you don't have a scanner, you can simply take a nice close picture of the photo. Use the macro setting for close focus, if your camera has one. It won't be quite as clear, but it'll work. Scanning is better if you have that option. You could also contact a professional photographer who could do it for you, for a price, or take it to a photo shop or a copy shop such as Kinko's, and have it scanned to a CD-ROM.

Getting a Good Scan

To get the best scan you can, first study the photo. Is there dust on it that you can wipe off with a soft cloth? Is it in black and white or sepia (brown)? (If it's a newer, color photo, set it aside until the end of this chapter and find a really old one to work on.)

Make sure your scanner software is properly installed and working. You need a *scanner driver*. This enables the computer to "drive" the scanner, telling it when to make a low-resolution preview of your photo, when to perform the real scan, and where to put it when you are done with it.

Next, look at the scanner. Do you know how to work it? If not, stop and read at least the first few pages of its manual. Is the glass plate clean and free of scratches? Any dust or hair on the glass will show up in the scan, and it takes time and practice to remove it all. If you can avoid the problem, do so.

No two scanners work exactly alike. Some scan from top to bottom, others from bottom to top. No two scanner software programs are alike, either. But there are a few basics you can apply in just about all cases. First of all, if you are scanning a black-and-white photo, scan it in grayscale, not in color. If the picture is sepia toned, I usually scan it in color, and then remove the sepia later.

If you intend to print the photo, set the scanner resolution to 200dpi, or 300dpi if it's a very small photo. This gives you a larger file, but picks up more detail. Although screen resolution is usually 72 or 96dpi, you should still scan your picture in at a higher quality, even if you know for certain that this picture is only going to go on a web page or CD album. To save file space, you can reduce it to 72 or 96dpi when you're done working on it. Also, remember that the farther the scanning arm has to travel, the longer it takes. If you have a tall, portrait-shaped picture, you can save a minute or so by scanning it sideways and then rotating it in Elements.

Before you settle on a resolution, think about the picture. If the photo you have is very small, scan it at a higher resolution, even as much as 600dpi. You'll pick up more detail that way, and you'll be able to enlarge the picture to a more useful size.

tip If you're taking photos somewhere to be scanned, take as many as you think you'll use for that project. If you do them one at a time, you'll end up paying more and having a handful of CDs with one picture on each.

tip *Sepia* is a brown dye, originally made from squid ink, that is sometimes applied to photos to make them "warmer" toned. Otherwise, the grays sometimes tend to look bluish.

Many scanners include a slide scanning tray and/or a carrier for larger transparencies. If yours doesn't, your local photo shop can make prints from your slides. But if you are lucky enough to have one of these gadgets, you can do the job yourself. Scan slides at a resolution of 200dpi or more, to pick up as much detail as possible. Remember, the inch-high picture was intended to be seen on a four- to five-foot screen, so the detail is there. You can generally expect color slides to need some color adjustment. Kodachrome film is very contrasty. European-made slide films, like Agfa, seem to favor cooler colors than Kodak. So you might want to consider decreasing the contrast or warming up the color, if necessary.

Basic Photo Corrections

Now that you've got the picture into the computer, you're ready to get to work. Let's start by looking at some of the things you can do to fix an old picture that might have faded, yellowed, or been damaged. First, we'll consider a couple of old family photos that need a little bit of adjusting and touching up. We'll run through the steps involved in fixing them and the tools you'll need to know how to use. Finally, I'll take an extremely damaged picture and work through it step-by-step, until it looks like new again.

Figure 7.1 shows the example I'm going to be working on first. This is a pretty good scan of a not-so-great photo, from some time in the late 1930s or early 40s.

Figure 7.1

You can see she's holding something, but you can't tell what. (Photo courtesy of D. Maynard.)

Compared to many of the photos I've worked on, this one's easy. It's in sepia, of course, because that was the style back then, but will probably look just as good or better in grayscale. This picture has mainly dust and focus problems. It can also use a little more contrast, and it needs its corners cropped away. (You'll learn about digital cropping in the next chapter, "Working with Digital Photos.") If you look closely, you can see that someone trimmed this picture into an oval, and someone else tried to make it a rectangle again. Net result—four missing corners.

To begin fixing this picture, I'll use the *Cropping tool* to first crop the borders and remove the edges. The Cropping tool is the one that looks like two overlapping L-shapes. To use it, select the tool and click on the picture. Just drag a box around the part of the picture you want to keep, and then double-click inside the box to confirm the cropping.

Adjusting Levels and Contrast

Now that the picture has been properly cropped, it's time to correct the damage to the image. Set the mode to Grayscale (Image, Mode, Grayscale), which removes any color information the scan picked up. Doing this immediately eliminates the yellow and brown tones. The next step is to improve the contrast. You can do this two ways—with Quick Fix, which is at the top of the Enhance menu; or the way professionals do, by adjusting the levels. The Levels dialog box (Enhance, Adjust Brightness/Contrast, Levels) is shown with the photo in Figure 7.2.

Figure 7.2

The Levels dialog box is actually a histogram that measures all the dark and light pixels in the photo.

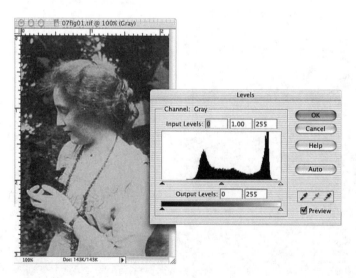

If you took statistics in school, or almost any kind of a science class, this graph should be familiar. It's a *histogram,* and it shows the range of tones in the picture from black to white. If you managed to avoid most math and science classes, as I did, a histogram is simply a display that uses vertical lines to denote the amount of something in a larger something. In this case, it's showing how many pixels in the photo are in each of the 255 shades of gray. With a little experience using histograms, you can easily see what the problem is. There are no real whites or blacks, just a lot of light and middle grays. You need more contrast. To get it, select the empty Eyedropper (it's the one on the right) and click it on the lightest point you can find in the photo. Notice that the white triangle under the histogram jumps over to a spot under where the histogram begins to peak for whiteness. Click the left, black Eyedropper on the darkest point in the picture. Its triangle in the histogram also moves. Now click on the gray, middle triangle under the histogram and slide it back and forth until the picture contrast looks right. Figure 7.3 shows the result. Remember to click OK to make the changes and exit the dialog box.

Figure 7.3

Now you have a better-adjusted photo.

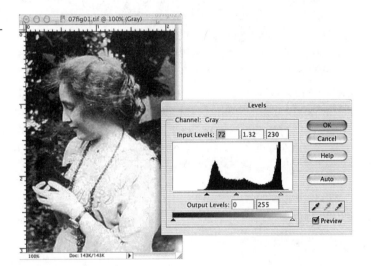

Dodging and Burning

Now it's obvious, as it wasn't before, that she's holding a black kitten. A little dodging and burning will help bring out the details of her dress, and will separate the cat from the background. Dodging and burning are probably quite familiar to anyone who ever worked in a real (nondigital) darkroom. In the photographer's darkroom, *dodging* is accomplished by waving a dodge tool, usually a cardboard circle on a wire, between the projected image from the enlarger and the photographic paper. This blocks some of the light and makes the dodged area lighter when the print is developed. It's also called *holding back* because you effectively hold back the light from reaching the paper. Photoshop Elements's *Dodge tool*, shown in Figure 7.4, looks just like the darkroom version.

Figure 7.4

To me, the Dodge tool always looked like a black lollipop.

The *Burn tool* has the opposite effect of dodging—it darkens the area instead of lightening it. In the darkroom, *burning* is accomplished either by using a piece of cardboard with a hole punched out (the opposite of the Dodge tool) or by blocking the enlarger light with your hand, so the light only reaches the area on the print surface to be burned. The Photoshop Elements Burn tool icon is a hand shaped to pass a small beam of light. Both the Dodge and Burn tools are considered brushes, and you need to select a brush size and shape before you apply them. You can do this on the Tool Options bar at the top of the workspace. Like any other brush, you apply it by holding the mouse button down and dragging it over the area you want to affect. I almost always use a soft-edged brush for dodging and burning. The softness helps hide the fact I've done something to change the picture.

If you are working on a small part of the picture, as we are in this example, it helps to zoom in and make the image bigger, so you can see what you are doing. Use the *Zoom tool* (magnifying glass) to click on the area you want to enlarge. To zoom out again, press the (Option) [Alt] key as you click the tool on the image. Each click takes you a step farther in or out. (See Figure 7.5.)

Figure 7.5

Working at twice the normal size makes it easier to see and fix details.

Click the Dodge tool and look at the Range drop-down menu in the Tool Options bar. As you can see, it gives you three choices:

- Shadows
- Midtones
- Highlights

These options indicate the types of pixels the tool affects. If you want to adjust the shadows, such as making them lighter and leaving the lighter pixels untouched, choose *shadows*. The default option for the Dodge tool is *midtones*. This is a good choice when you want to affect the midtone pixels, or when you are unsure of how to proceed. Select *highlights* when you want to lighten already light-colored areas, leaving the darker areas untouched. For the moment, I'll set it to shadows and use it to lighten the area behind the kitten. After all, he's the real subject of the photo. To see him, refer to Figure 7.5.

I used the Burn tool to bring out the details in her lace collar, and to darken her hair.

Cleaning Up Dust Spots with the Clone Stamp Tool

There are some dust spots you can remove with the *Clone Stamp tool*, which looks and works like a rubber stamp. It copies pieces of the picture and clones them over other places when you click. To use it, you first select a brush size appropriate for what you want to cover. (Option-click) [Alt+click] on the piece of the picture you want to copy, and then click the Clone Stamp tool on the spot you intend to cover. You can use whatever matches.

If *Aligned* is checked in the Tool Options bar, the source point to be duplicated moves with the tool. Say you (Option-click) [Alt+click] to set the source, and then move slightly up and to the right to use the tool. Each time you click, or as you drag the rubber stamp, the source point moves with your mouse to stay exactly the same distance away from the stamp. Conceivably, you can reproduce the entire image if you have enough blank canvas in the working document.

tip When you use the Clone Stamp tool to retouch in Photoshop Elements, always choose a soft-edged brush in a size only slightly larger than the scratch or blemish you're hiding. Retouching is generally easier if you zoom in on the image first.

If you don't choose Aligned, the Clone Stamp tool behaves differently. After you select your reference point and start painting, the duplicate portion of the image expands only while you continue to hold down the mouse button. When you release the mouse button and press it again, you start painting another duplicate image from the same reference point.

For this job, I am using a small soft-edged brush, and copying the adjacent tone. Then I'll use the *Sharpen filter* (Filter, Sharpen) to put things in better focus. Figure 7.6 shows the finished picture.

Figure 7.6

Now you can see the kitten and her new mommy much better.

Other Touches

I'd call this picture finished, although there are a few more things you can do to it. You can bring back the sepia tone by returning the image to RGB color (choose Image, Mode, RGB Color). Then you can apply color variations (Enhance, Adjust Color, Color Variations) and add red and subtract blue until you have a believable sepia. You can also apply the Unsharp Mask filter (Filter, Sharpen, Unsharp Mask) to strengthen the focus. But it looks fine, and it will do very nicely for my friend's genealogy album.

Here's another image in need of some retouching. It looks pretty bad right now, as you can see in Figure 7.7, but it's far from helpless. For this one, we'll use the Clone tool, also called the *Rubber*

tip

Did you ever wonder where those little spots are coming from? Black spots are usually dirt on the photo or on the scanner glass. White spots on the photo were caused by dust or dirt on the negative. The dirt stopped the light from passing through the negative and exposing the print. You can often get rid of black spots by wiping the print and the scanner with a soft cloth and then rescanning. White spots need to be digitally retouched.

Stamp, because that's what it looks like in the toolbox. This tool is extremely useful for removing all kinds of spots and also for filling in backgrounds you want to change. Use the Aligned Mode box in the Tool Options bar at the top of the window to make aligned copies. (Option-click) [Alt+click] on a piece of the picture that's the same shade as what you need to cover. Then position the stamp over the bad spot and click. It's gone. A soft-edged brush works best for most damaged areas, but occasionally you'll need precision. When that happens, use a hard brush. In Figure 7.8, I'm about half done with the Clone tool and it's already much improved.

The Clone tool is probably one of the ones you'll use most in restoring old photos. Be sure to spend some time learning how it works and practicing with it.

Figure 7.7

Notice the brush options on the Tool Options bar. You can adjust the brush (stamp) size as large or small as you want it. Photo courtesy of Kathleen Rudden.

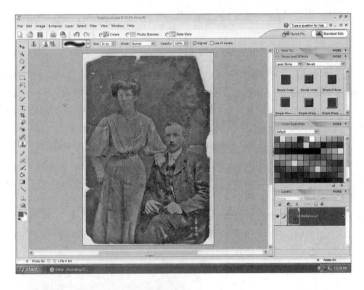

Figure 7.8

I also cropped some ragged and unneeded edges.

Moving Paint—Blurring, Sharpening, and Smudging

Did you ever wonder why artists always have those paint-soaked rags lying around, and why they always have paint on their hands, under their fingernails, and all over their clothes? It's because you don't just paint with a brush; you sometimes paint with your finger, with a piece of cloth, with your elbow, or with some other tool that helps you blend the paint or lighten or darken it just a little bit. You can learn the tricks painters and darkroom technicians have been using ever since their respective art forms were invented. The early cave people knew the value of "hands-on" art. The famous cave paintings at Lascaux were done, literally, by hand, and there are many hand prints on the walls along with the drawings of the bison, horses, and other animals.

Smudges

Smudge is the artist's term for blending two or more colors. In Photoshop Elements, and most other applications that have a similar tool, the *Smudge tool* looks and works like a finger. It's in the same toolbox compartment as the Blur and Sharpen tools. The Smudge tool picks up color from wherever you start to drag it and moves it in the direction in which you drag. Honestly, nothing is simpler. You do, however, have to use the Tool Options bar to set the pressure of your smudging finger. At 100% pressure, the finger simply wipes away the paint. At 50%, it smears it. At 25%, the smear is smaller. Figure 7.9 shows these smudge pressures. Photoshop Elements considers the Smudge tool to be a brush, so you can set the width of the finger by choosing an appropriate brush size in the Tool Options bar.

Figure 7.9

The lighter the pressure, the less you smudge.

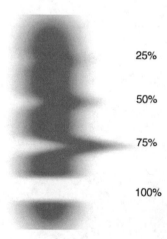

25%

50%

75%

100%

Focus Tools

Now focus your attention on the *Focus tools*. These tools, Blur and Sharpen, are great for touching up an image, fixing tiny flaws, and bringing items into sharper contrast. They can't save a really bad photo, but they can do wonders for one that's just a little bit off. *Sharpen* can bring up the contrast to create the illusion of sharper focus, whereas *Blur* is most useful to rid the background of unwanted clutter and to de-emphasize parts of the picture you don't want viewers to notice.

Sharpening

Sharpening is definitely a useful tool, especially because many of the photos you work on will be fuzzy. The older the picture, the fuzzier it's likely to be. Back then, lenses and cameras just weren't as good. Early photo plates required a long exposure, and it was sometimes difficult to make people stand still for the five to ten seconds it took to make a photograph on a glass plate.

There are two ways to sharpen a picture. The first is the method you used on the cat lady photo—the Sharpen filter. There are actually two Sharpen filters you'll use most: Sharpen and Sharpen More. The latter simply applies twice as much sharpening as the first. You can keep on applying these filters until you are satisfied with the result, or until you realize you have overdone it because the image has a very jagged, pixelated appearance. In Figure 7.10, you can see the result of over sharpening.

The way to sharpen just a small part of a photo is to use the *Sharpen tool*. Select it, and then click and drag it over the area you want to sharpen. If you use it carefully, it can be extremely helpful, but don't overdo it. In Figure 7.11, I have sharpened the woman's face and left the man alone.

Figure 7.10

This kind of sharpening works by increasing the contrast between adjacent pixels.

Figure 7.11

She's been sharpened. He hasn't. It does make a difference.

Blurring

The Blur filter and the Blur tool (which looks like a drop of water in Photoshop Elements) work similarly to Sharpen, except that rather than increasing the contrast between pixels, they lower it slightly. That produces the blur.

You might be wondering why you'd deliberately want to blur something, but there are times when it's a very valuable tool. The *Blur tool*, simply put, creates blurs in images. In other words, it softens or evens out pixel values. It's helpful when you need to separate a person from a busy background, or disguise something that there's no other way to get out of the picture. To use it, select the Blur tool from the toolbox. The Tool Options bar shows you the Blur tool's options. When you are working with the Blur tool, you can temporarily select the Sharpen tool (and vice versa) by pressing (Option) [Alt] on your keyboard. The Use All Layers option only affects the image if your image has more than one layer. In Figure 7.12, I've blurred the background behind the lily, so the photo focuses on the lily and not on the whole bouquet.

Figure 7.12

The first picture is the original. In the second, I've blurred the background, adding instant depth of field.

Color Gallery

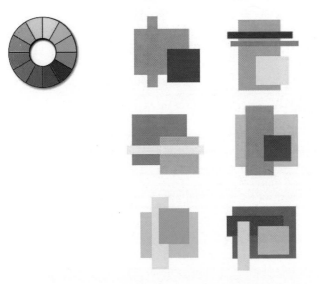

Charles River at Sunset

Looking from Cambridge toward Boston

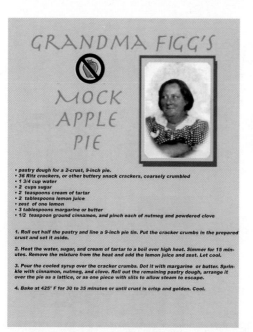

Figure 5.9
Facing pages need to work together.
Chapter 5, page 99

Figure 5.12
The dog looks better a bit off-center. Notice how the color block helps balance the page.
Chapter 5, page 101

Consider the lilies of the field...
They toil not.
Neither do they spin...

Consider the lilies of the field...
They toil not.
Neither do they spin...

Figure 6.2
A frame around the photo will help set it off.
Chapter 6, page 108

Figure 6.9
Labelon on the left, Xerox on the right.
Chapter 6, page 117

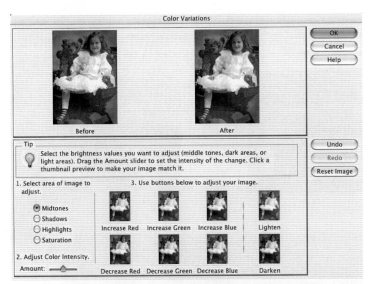

Figure 7.20

You can also use this to turn a photo or line drawing green or purple or whatever color strikes your fancy.

Chapter 7, page 135

Figure 7.21

The final photo, restored to probably better than the original.

Chapter 7, page 136

Figure 7.27
Can this one be saved?
Chapter 7, page 141

Figure 7.29
Better, but not there yet.
Chapter 7, page 142

Figure 7.30
Doing it yourself in Photoshop Elements will give better results.
Chapter 7, page 143

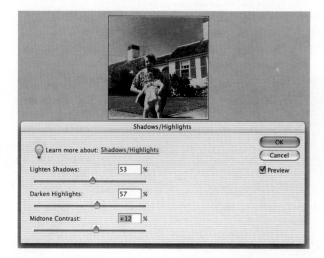

Figure 7.32
Maybe the edited picture is not quite perfect, but considering how much better it is, I'm satisfied.
Chapter 7, page 144

Figure 8.1
Look for variety in your scenery shots as I did in these pictures from Nevada. **Chapter 8, page 147**

In the United States
there is more space
where nobody is than
where anybody is.
That is what makes
America what it is.

Valley of Fire State Park

In the desert
a fountain is
springing,
In the wide waste
there still is a tree;
And a bird in the
solitude...

Figure 8.2

This is Red Rock Canyon, fifteen minutes from downtown Las Vegas, and a world away.

Chapter 8, page 148

Figure 8.14

You can see we're on the same side of the fence.

Chapter 8, page 158

Figure 8.16

The cage is still there, but it's not the first thing you see.

Chapter 8, page 159

Figure 8.17
Notice how the three animals seem to focus on each other, leading your eye around the page. **Chapter 8, page 160**

Figure 8.21

You don't need to understand the physics of color to know what looks right.
Chapter 8, page 163

Figure 8.29

He's really a nice cat, not as evil as he looks here.
Chapter 8, page 168

Figure 8.31

Paint over it as much as you like with Photoshop Elements's Red Eye Removal tool, but it won't get any darker. **Chapter 8, page 169**

Figure 9.5
Photographers call this light "open overcast."
Chapter 9, page 181

Figure 9.7
The dry brush filter is a good way to make a watercolor with lots of detail.
Chapter 9, page 183

Figure 9.8
The original photo is on the left, the dry brush version on the right.
Chapter 9, page 183

Figure 9.10

Turning one of your photos into an oil painting lends an interesting effect to your scrapbook pages. **Chapter 9, page 186**

Figure 9.15

Like the underpainting filter, rough pastels apply a texture to the photo. **Chapter 9, page 189**

Figure 9.17

Notice how Find Edges picks up the detail of the sidewalk and the soda can collection. **Chapter 9, page 190**

Figure 9.18

Some of the color remains, but the background goes black. **Chapter 9, page 191**

Figure 9.22

This was done with Posterize set to four levels. **Chapter 9, page 194**

Figure 9.23

No animals were harmed in making this page (unless you count injured dignity). Photo art courtesy of Judy Blair. **Chapter 9, page 195**

Our Wedding

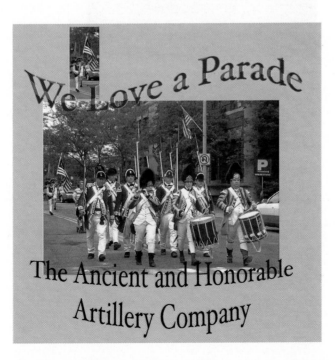

Appendix A.3

Without the feathers, it's just another bird.

Appendix A, page 249

Appendix A.4

Soon, I will have a useful and pretty souvenir.

Appendix A, page 251

Appendix A.6

The Butterfly box.

Appendix A, page 253

Removing Dust and Scratches

If you are using Photoshop Elements, cleaning up dust is easy with the Despeckle filter and the Dust and Scratches filter, both found under Filter, Noise. Use Despeckle if all the spots are tiny, and try Dust and Scratches on the larger ones. In my sample photo in Figure 7.13, you can see that it's mostly removed the large white scratch on the man's hat as well as all of the smaller bits of dust and dirt. Experiment with the sliders until you find a setting that works, but be careful. "Over-dusting" removes sharpness, too.

Figure 7.13

The Dust and Scratches filter allows you to decide for yourself how much to remove.

Rescuing a Badly Damaged Photo

Now, let's take a look at a picture that really needs some work. In Figure 7.14, and in the color section, you can see this picture of a little girl, taken about 1908. It was printed on a heavy paper which cracked, and suffered some damage in an oval frame. Can I save it? Of course I can. It's my mother, so I'd better do a good job, too.

First, I'll convert it to grayscale to get rid of the sepia (choose Image, Mode, Grayscale). Figure 7.15 shows how easily this is done in Photoshop Elements.

Figure 7.14

The photo has some bad damage, but it's all fixable.

Figure 7.15

Convert to grayscale because it's much easier to match grays than sepia tones.

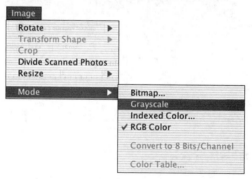

Now we're ready to start repairs. The first step with this picture, and with most of the ones you'll be working with, is to crop it. Anything you can remove doesn't have to be retouched. I can't crop too tightly because she fills out the frame pretty well, but I can get rid of some of the edges and one big spot. Figure 7.16 shows the cropping frame in use. Just drag the corners of the cropping frame until you're satisfied with the crop, and double-click inside it to confirm it.

Figure 7.16

Cropping saves some retouching time and usually improves the composition, too.

The next step is to improve the contrast in the photo. It's good to do this now so that when you start moving pieces of her dress and the background to cover the cracks, you won't have a problem making them blend in. In Photoshop Elements, the quickest way to fix the contrast is to use Levels, as we did before. Other programs might have other ways of adjusting contrast, so check the help screen or the manual if you aren't sure how to proceed. Figure 7.17 shows the result of this step.

Figure 7.17

It's looking much better already.

By increasing the contrast, you saved yourself some work. The next step is to work with the Clone Stamp tool, to rubber stamp over the cracks. Figure 7.18 shows a closer look at this process. Using a fairly small, soft-edged brush, with Aligned checked in the Tool Options bar, you can stamp the areas next to the bad crack over her face and fill it in. I also filled in the missing corner of the picture.

Figure 7.18
You need lots of patience to do this well.

From here on, it's just a question of more stamping to cover the rest of the cracks and corners. When you have delicate areas to fix, such as faces, enlarge the picture as much as you can. Most graphics programs have a Zoom tool, which enables you to move in and out on the picture as you're working. Usually, the icon looks like a magnifying glass. Click it to zoom in, and (Option-click) [Alt+click] it to zoom out. In Figure 7.18, I zoomed in to work on the crack on her face. In Figure 7.19, I zoomed out again to look at the whole picture.

The Clone Stamp tool took care of all the spots and other damage. I used a small brush to complete the toe of her shoe. But I think I'll put back the sepia. In Photoshop Elements, the easy way to do this is to reconvert the photo mode to RGB color (choose Image, Mode, RGB Color), and then use the Color Variations dialog box (Enhance, Adjust Color, Color Variations) to first add red and then decrease blue, which gives you a nice believable sepia tone. Be sure to see this in color in Figures 7.20 and 7.21.

Figure 7.19
It's pretty close to
done now.

Figure 7.20
You can also use this
to turn a photo or
line drawing green,
purple, or whatever
color strikes your
fancy.

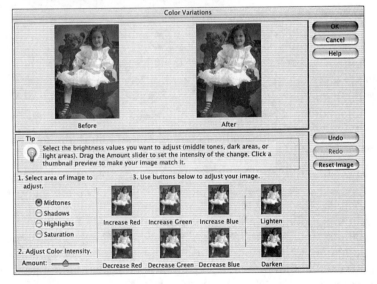

So, here it is, as good as it's ever going to be and pretty good indeed for a picture nearly 100 years old. That looks like one of the very early Steiff teddy bears.

By the way, most graphics programs have some way of reapplying sepia. Another easy way to do it in Photoshop Elements is to use the Hue/Saturation sliders to adjust the color to whatever looks right to you.

Figure 7.21

The final photo, restored to probably better than the original.

Vignetting a Picture

I can still take this one step further, if I want, by converting it back to the oval format it was in originally. But I don't think I want to do that to this particular photo since I've already cropped it tight. Instead, let's take a different portrait and turn it from a rectangle into an oval. This process is called *vignetting*, and it's a very common format for old pictures. The main reason it was used so often in the early days of photography is that the lenses weren't very good. Only the center part of the lens produced a sharp picture. The edges kind of fuzzed and faded out.

On the left in Figure 7.22 is the original photo. It's pretty awful, but Elements Quick Fix, located on the toolbar, and shown in use here, gives us a head start on fixing it.

If you look carefully at Figure 7.23, you can see the improvement in the picture, as well as the selection tool I'm using. The tool is an Ellipse Marquee, chosen by clicking Fixed Aspect Ratio in the Tool Options bar, and setting the ratio to 3:2. I've drawn an oval frame by dragging the tool across her, in the process trimming away the forearms worthy of Popeye the Sailor, and I've also feathered the selection by 20 pixels. The effect of this is to soften the edge of the oval so it looks like it's fading away. The amount of feathering can be determined before or after placing the selection marquee. If you don't like what you've chosen, undo, change the setting, and try again.

Figure 7.22

Nice lady, lousy picture. (Photo courtesy of Peggy Ogan.)

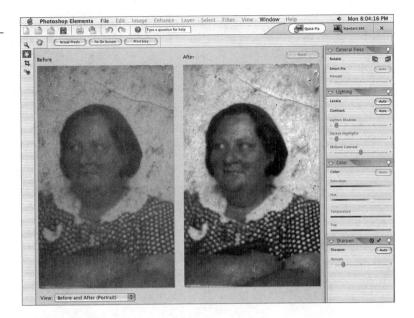

Figure 7.23

The middle is selected.

Because I've selected the middle of the picture, and I want to remove the edge, I need to *invert* the selection (choose Select, Inverse). This simply shifts the "working" part of the selection marquee from the middle to the outer part of the picture. Instead of just the oval, you can now see the corners of the picture selected, too. After that part of the picture is surrounded by the selection marquee, either press the Delete key, or press Ctrl+X to trim it.

This photo still needs some clean up and despotting, but it's much improved. The final version, in Figure 7.24, has also had the contrast adjusted. There's something about vignetted photos that always reminds me of my mother's and grandmother's prized cameo brooches. A good setting for a vignetted portrait might be to simulate a silver or gold frame from a brooch. Of course, if you've done the same thing to a portrait of a man, the delicate look won't do. Instead, perhaps a dark oval frame that looks like wood.

Figure 7.24

Even without a frame, she looks much better, and thinner too.

If you wanted to put a frame around this photo, there are several ways to do it. You can find a frame in a clip art collection and stretch or shrink it to fit. If you have a frame-generating plug-in like Auto FX Photo/Graphic Edges, you can use that. Otherwise, make a new layer, and drag an oval selection around the photo. If it's not quite where you want it, click the edge and drag it until it's centered on the photo. When the oval is properly placed, select Edit, Stroke, or right-click in the selection and choose Stroke from the pop-up menu. Enter a number of pixels to create a wide or narrow frame and decide whether it will draw inside, outside, or centered on your oval selection. Before you Stroke the selection, be sure the Feather is set to 0, unless you want a fuzzy frame. You can then go ahead and have some fun with it. Using the Layer Styles window (Window, Layer Styles), as shown in Figure 7.25, I chose Wow Chrome Dark from the Wow Chrome effects. Actually, I tried a couple of others first, but liked this one best.

Figure 7.25

The Wow Effects are presets that combine several effects to make a complex one. They definitely add some wow to your pages.

Photo Tinting

Years ago, before color film was readily available, it was common to see *hand-tinted photos*. These had been painstakingly overpainted with thinned-out special paints to add a pale suggestion of color to the picture. The Photoshop Elements brushes are well suited for re-creating the look of a hand-colored photograph. You can even do the whole Ted Turner routine and colorize stills from your favorite Marx Brothers movie or Bogart classic. (You can find lots of movie stills and movie star pictures on the Web to practice on. There might be copyright issues on these, so don't try to sell them. You can use them safely in a personal scrapbook.)

After you have cleaned up the image you want to hand-tint, change the image mode to RGB color. Make a new layer and set the layer opacity to between 10% and 30% in the Layers palette. Select the Brush tool, set the Brush opacity to 80% in the Tool Options bar, and paint your tints. Alternatively, leave the layer at 100% opacity, change the blending mode to color in the Tool Options bar, and paint away! Always use a new layer for each color in case you make mistakes.

If you have large, uncomplicated areas to tint, use one of the Selection tools, such as the Lasso or the Magic Wand, to select the area. Select a foreground color and choose Fill from the Edit menu; a dialog box will appear as shown in Figure 7.26.

Set the Opacity to about 25% and choose Multiply from the Blending Mode menu. Do *not* check Preserve Transparency because your fill effect won't show up if you do.

Set Foreground Color on the Use pop-up menu. Click OK to fill all the selected areas with your chosen color at that opacity. If it's not enough, either reopen the Fill dialog box and apply it again, or undo it and set a higher percentage. If it's too much, undo and set a lower percentage.

Figure 7.26
Use Fill for large areas. It's faster and smoother than painting. (Photo courtesy of D. Maynard.)

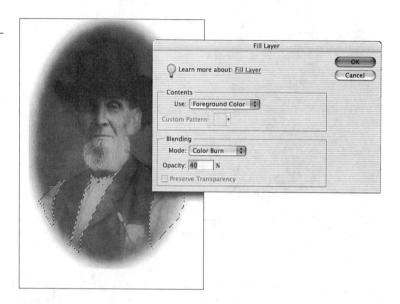

Continue selecting areas and coloring them until you're done. Flesh tones can be tricky. Caucasians tend to look either too pink or too yellow when you try to guess at a flesh tone. My suggestion is to do your best, and then choose Enhance, Adjust Color, Color Variations and tweak the adjustments until the skin color looks right. Remember that you can adjust individual layers, as long as you haven't already flattened them.

Correcting Off-Color Photos

Old color photos are sometimes more difficult to repair than old black-and-white ones. The dyes used in the color printing process can either fade or darken. Along with the other kinds of damage you have already seen, it makes some pictures very difficult to rescue. Relatively recent photos, on the other hand, don't need much correction and usually aren't ripped and stained the way the really old black-and-white ones are. Pictures printed after 1950 or thereabouts just don't get brittle the way the older ones do. First, the pictures aren't as old, so they are somewhat less likely to be physically damaged. The paper tends to be heavier, and being gloss coated, is sturdier and less prone to tearing or folding. So instead of just doing damage control, you can actually improve the pictures.

The single biggest problem I've seen with color photos from the late 40s and 50s is *color cast*, or in its more severe form, *color shift*. When this happens, the entire photo can take on what looks like an overdose of a single color, often pink or purple, but any color can be affected. It's generally blamed on heat or exposure to sunlight, but having seen it happen to pictures that were tucked away in an album or used as a bookmark, I don't think that's necessarily the case. The dyes used back then just weren't stable. Bad processing or letting the film sit in the camera outdoors on a warm day were enough to throw off the color, perhaps not immediately, but as the photos aged.

Of course, bad things can happen to recent pictures, too. The sun ducks behind a cloud just as you shoot, and the colors look washed out. The flash doesn't go off as expected. Nothing is immune to spilled drinks, dog/cat/kid damage, and all the other perils of daily life.

You can't save them all. Some are just too far gone, or the data (color and detail) was never there in the first place. But, with a good graphics program, you can pull off some pretty amazing rescues.

Correcting Color Cast

Several of the available photo-editing programs make color-cast correction pretty nearly automatic. Figure 7.27 shows an old photo that's so badly yellowed, it's almost brown. Be sure to see this example in the color plate section.

Figure 7.27
Can this one be saved?

Using Photoshop Elements, let's work through this photo step-by-step. First of all it needs to be cropped. Drag the Crop tool until you have enclosed the part of the photo you want to keep, and double-click inside the box to complete the action. Getting rid of unnecessary edge clutter also helps. Let's keep a little of the white border, though, until you decide how you want to use it on a scrapbook page. To start improving the color, choose Enhance, Adjust Color, Remove Color Cast. Figure 7.28 shows its very simple dialog box. This tool evaluates the amount of color in what ought to be a black or white pixel. It then applies the same amount of the opposite color (from the color wheel) to cancel out the overdone one. In this case, the color cast is yellow, so Elements adds an equal amount of blue. If the color cast turned the picture red, it adds cyan. If the cast is green, it adds magenta, and so on.

Figure 7.28

Try to find the darkest black or the whitest white.

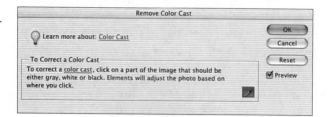

To judge the "correctness" of the correction, find part of the picture that's critical, color-wise. Flesh tones are always a good benchmark. I clicked on several areas I thought should be white, and most seemed to make things worse instead of better. When I tried the baby's dress, though, the flesh tones looked right, even though the picture still needs a lot of work. Figure 7.29, and the color plate, show this step.

Figure 7.29

Better, but not there yet.

Using Fill Flash

Even though the picture was shot in bright sun, there are shadows on both faces. After all, it's the faces that are the most important part of the photo. Choose Enhance, Adjust Lighting, Shadows/Highlights to access the dialog box shown in Figure 7.30. As you can see, I have just moved the sliders a little, to lighten the shadows in the picture and increase the overall contrast a small amount.

Figure 7.30

If the photographer had used a fill flash, you wouldn't need this step.

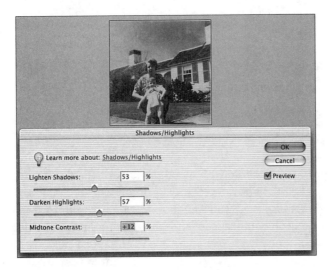

Selective Color Adjustments

Nothing you've done so far has had an effect on the sky. It's still brown, and the only way you can turn it blue is to select it and force the change. So that's what you'll do. You can select the sky with either the Magic Wand or the Lasso tool, or a combination of both. Because this photo has a number of places where the trees or other objects stick into the sky area, these are best selected with the Magic Wand. As long as you hold the Shift key down, you can keep on adding to your selection. If you select a piece you don't want, immediately undo (just once) and the rest of the selection remains selected. With the entire sky selected, you can open the Hue/Saturation dialog box shown in Figure 7.31 (Enhance, Adjust Color, Adjust Hue/Saturation) and make the sky as blue as you want it. In this case, because the rest of the colors are actually quite subtle, I'll resist the urge to improve the weather and go with a pale blue.

That worked so well, and looks so good, I'll do the same thing with the grass, turning it green instead of blue, of course. Figure 7.32 shows the final image, but you really need to go to the color plate section and compare it to what we started with.

Figure 7.31

"Blue skies, smilin' at me…"

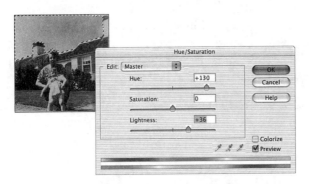

Figure 7.32

Maybe it's not quite perfect, but considering how much better it is, I'm satisfied.

That shows what you can do with a bad picture and good software. There are very few photos that can't be saved one way or another. If the color is really bad, and the photo is otherwise clear and well focused, you can convert it to black and white and hand-tint it. You can also convert it to sepia, and make the page surrounding it sort of moody and nostalgic, as long as the clothing or other surroundings won't give away your secret. If they do, and you still want to use that trick, enlarge the picture and vignette it so you only see the face.

Summary—What You Need to Remember

First of all, you need the right tools for retouching your pictures. That means a good graphics program. Adobe Photoshop Elements 3 is the best I've found.

The steps in rescuing an old damaged photo are easy. First, make a good, clean scan. If the picture is in sepia, convert it to grayscale. Crop away anything that doesn't need to be there. Then adjust the contrast. Use the Burn tool to darken areas that are too light, and the Dodge tool to lighten dark places. Use the Clone Stamp tool to cover dust spots, cracks, and stains. You might even have to paint in missing parts. Finally, if you want, you can replace the sepia tint.

Vignetting isolates the center of the picture so it seems to fade to white. It can make a recent photo look old, if that's what you want, or hide a bad background. You can also make a grayscale photo more interesting and give it that 1930s look by hand-tinting it. Remember to work in layers.

Color correction is often needed when you work with old color pictures. You'll generally have better results when you do it yourself rather that relying on Quick Fix or even Remove Color Cast. Think of these as jumping off places for your work, rather than the complete fix.

Working with Digital Photos

In the last chapter, you worked with scanned images. In this one, you're primarily using pictures from a digital camera. And anyway, as soon as a picture is in the computer, it's within the digital realm. So even if you don't have a digital camera, there's a lot of helpful information coming. Don't skip ahead. In this chapter, you learn about retouching and color correction, as well as cropping and resizing your pictures. You learn how to repair the dreaded red eye, and how to remove things—even people—that clutter up the picture.

Shooting for Scrapbook Pages

With today's automatic "point-and-shoot" cameras, there's not that much that can go wrong, technically anyway. If you wait for the camera to find its focus, which it generally indicates with a little green light, and you hold it steady, you're going to have a reasonably sharp picture. If the subject needs more light, the camera indicates you need to turn on the flash, decides how bright the flash needs to be, and makes it happen. Nevertheless, you really need to sit down with your camera and manual and learn all the buttons and menus. It's not difficult, and you'll take much better pictures when you know what the camera can do. Be sure to keep the manual handy to refer to when you have questions. You can also find help at the camera maker's website.

Of course, there are things you just can't do with any average camera, digital or otherwise. Let's say you're sitting in the nosebleed section at a hockey game. You really want a photo of your favorite player, so you pull out your digital camera. It's kind of dark where you're sitting, so you activate the flash. You aim. You shoot. You *don't* score. Well, you might be able to tell which speck on the ice is him—or her— but you won't get much of a shot. Here's why. First of all, you're too far away. A low-end camera (say $400 or less) doesn't have a good enough lens or good enough resolution to let you enlarge the photo enough to see your player. Even if you have a more expensive camera, with a higher resolution and a zoom lens, you're still not going to get much. For a meaningful picture, get close. Talk your way down the aisle to the barrier, but stand a few steps back so you can shoot over the Plexiglas. You want to see people, not scarred plastic. Zoom in as much as you can. Aim the camera a little bit ahead of the skater. Remember, they move fast. With many cameras, there's a short delay between the button press and the actual shot. This way, he will skate through the picture, not out of it. Also, don't use the flash. It's effective only to a distance of 10 feet or so. After that, it's useless and throws off the automatic exposure settings.

That's kind of a far-fetched example, but the point is, unless you're shooting the scenery, come close. Generally, it's the close photos that look and work better on your scrapbook pages. You want to see faces. Of course, variety is good, too. Let's say you have a kid who likes hanging by her knees from the monkey bars. For your scrapbook page, you can take a shot that shows her upside down, full length, and then you need to move in and get one of just her red face and hair hanging upside down. Much more interesting than just the single shot.

Even when you are shooting scenery, as I was last spring in Nevada, look for variety in your shots. Here's a page I put together about the Valley of Fire State Park (see Figure 8.1). As you can see, I have a long scenery shot, a mid-shot, and a close-up. These three, plus a few words of description, are all I need to convey my own sense of what it was like to be there in this very foreign place. Where I live, the ground is flat and all the rocks are gray.

When people are in the picture, try to have them doing something other than just standing there. We've all seen the vacation pictures friends and neighbors bring home, the ones with the narration that goes something like "This is me in front of the Eiffel Tower. This is Fred in front of the Eiffel Tower. This is me in front of the hotel." And so on, until we're looking for excuses to escape. The people in the pictures are usually hot, tired, and cross, and don't seem very happy to be there. When you shoot photos of people, try to catch them at their best, not at their worst. Let them sit when there's something to sit on. Or let them lean against a railing, tree, or whatever. If I had to pose my kids with the Eiffel Tower, I'd have them turn around and look up at it, rather than at the camera, and then crawl around until I found an angle that shows their faces and as much as possible of the structure.

Figure 8.1

Be sure to see this figure in the color section.

In the United States there is more space where nobody is than where anybody is. That is what makes America what it is.

Valley of Fire State Park

In the desert
a fountain is
springing,
In the wide waste
there still is a tree,
And a bird in the
solitude...

Figure 8.2 shows another piece of scenery. In this one, and you have to either take my word for it or jump over to the color section to look at it, the point of the photo is that the tree branches are exactly the same color as the rocks off in the distance. I shot this in late afternoon, and the low angle of the sun lit up the tree very nicely. What I like about this photo, aside from the color, is that there's something close as well as something far away. This difference adds *perspective* to the picture, and you can get a better sense of how high the rocks are, and how small the tree is.

Of course, there are exceptions to the "get close" rule. There are exceptions to every rule. Zooming in on the Grand Canyon, for example, misses the point, which is how enormous it is. Suppose you are trying to get a shot of the Grand Canyon that expresses how big it is. You're standing at the railing of one of the many scenic overlooks, staring downward a mile or so to the canyon bottom, and across to the other end of the canyon. It's a great view, but a lousy picture. Why? Well, when you're standing there, you can feel the space around you. You can look down at your feet, and then keep looking down and outward just a little, and the next horizontal surface is a long way down. If you're like me, you find yourself hanging onto the fence. If the picture is going to work, you need to find a way to provide some sense of "out there, back here." In other words, perspective.

Figure 8.2

This is Red Rock Canyon, 15 minutes from downtown Las Vegas, and a world away.

When I was looking for the right shot, I got lucky. A tree was kind of hanging out into space, just at the edge of the overlook. I moved over a few feet, got a branch from the tree in the corner of the picture and there it was, the difference that made the picture work. The branch was a little out of focus, but that just added to the sensation. One of the great benefits to digital cameras in this situation is that you're not wasting film, so you can keep shooting until you get the perfect picture.

There are a few things digital cameras do very well. One of these is shooting in low-light conditions. Cameras that use film use one roll at a time, so you're stuck with the same kind of film all day until you use it up. There are "fast" films for low-light conditions and "slow" films for bright sunshine. When the light changes, you might as well put the camera back in its bag. A digital camera can adapt to the changes in light. You can go from dark to light, from indoors to outdoors, with only a couple of seconds to let the camera (and your eyes) adjust. Even when a photo looks dark, as the one in Figure 8.3 does, there's usually enough detail in it that you can save it.

tip That weird pattern on the shirt of the man with his back to the camera is called moiré. It was present in the original photo, which I imported to the computer at 300dpi resolution. To get rid of it, I tried changing the resolution, using Image, Size, Resize Image. At 600dpi, it was better, but not perfect. At 1,200dpi, it was just right. But that file is too big to work with. So I saved it at 1,200dpi, and then reduced it again to 200. Still perfect, and now workable.

Figure 8.3

The lighting was terrible, but my husband was autographing his newest book and I wanted a picture.

I didn't want to call attention to myself by using the flash, although it would have been helpful in this situation. So, I stood as still as I could, braced my elbows on my ribs to keep the camera steady, and took the picture. It's kind of dark, as you can tell at a glance, but there's plenty of detail in the shadows. A photo like this is easy to fix. Even though you should always try for the best possible photo, sometimes conditions are against you. Using a digital camera gives you a big advantage. Digital photos are much easier to correct.

All this photo really needs is an increase in the brightness and contrast. (As you might remember, we talked about this in the last chapter also.) In Photoshop Elements, these two sliders are located in the same dialog box. From the Enhance menu, choose Enhance, Adjust Brightness/Contrast and move the sliders until the picture looks right, as I have done in Figure 8.4.

Figure 8.4

Now it's good enough for the family scrapbook.

A Better Crop of Pictures

Nobody takes good pictures every time, not even the pros. One of the advantages of working with a digital camera and computer is that you're not wasting film and paper, never mind the cost of processing. You can simply throw away the unwanted photos. Just select them from the batch you've downloaded from the camera to the computer, and drag them to the trash bin or recycle bin on your computer's desktop. And say good-bye…. But, if you're like me and hate to throw anything away, take a second look at the pictures before you trash them. There might be something good in there.

The picture might be a candidate for what I call selective cropping. Two friends of mine run an antiques/curiosities shop called Oldies, in Newburyport, Massachusetts. If you're ever up that way, it's a wonderful source of scrapbook ephemera, among other things. I've found Civil War medals, battle ribbons, old photos, odd bits of lace, as well as valuable antiques, and just plain cool stuff. Well worth a visit, but I digress….

Figure 8.5 is a shot of its parking lot. There's also a huge shed, with several tons more of the same. I took the picture because the scene was colorful, but I was too far away. There's too much to look at and nothing to see. But I think with the help of the cropping tool, I can find some good pictures in here.

Fortunately, this was taken with a high-resolution (5.1-megapixel) camera, so I can cut up pieces of it (figuratively, of course) and still have a good-quality photo. If you're going to enlarge a picture, as is the case here, always try to work with the best-quality image you can.

Figure 8.5

Joyce, I told you I'd put you in a book.

Beware of Lossy Compression

There's a file format called *JPEG*, or sometimes *JPG*. It's a very common and useful format, developed by and named after a bunch of photo experts who called themselves the Joint Photographic Experts Group (or JPEG). They developed this file format to use with photographs and the Internet. Photos, as you'll soon learn, can be very large files, especially with today's high-resolution digital cameras. Back in the good old days, maybe five years ago, average people didn't have high-speed cable connections to the Web. They often had dial-up modems, and they ran slowly. It often took several minutes to download a small picture. A big one took much longer. The only graphics file format was called GIF, or Graphics Interchange Format. It had a limit of 256 colors, so photos were blotchy looking and uneven. Not very good. The experts stepped in and developed a new way to compress photo files. It allowed millions of colors rather than the GIF's 256, and it shrank huge files into little ones, with very little quality loss—the first time you applied it. Of course, if you saved the same file as a JPEG again, the file went through the same file-compression process again, and was shrunk down more. After several saves, you often don't know what you were looking at. That's why JPEGs are also called *lossy compression* because you lose some of the color detail each time you save them. The worst part of this is that there's no going back. After an image has degraded, it's gone. Resaving it at a higher quality, or in another format, won't help. The picture data has been erased.

The main thing to remember about cropping is that, just as if you were doing it with scissors, after you cut something up and save the smaller piece, the big one's gone. What does that mean? It means work on a *copy* of the picture. Always save the original. When I download photos to the computer from my digital camera, before I even start to play with them, I make a CD-ROM of the entire folder. So should you. That way, you'll always have the originals to go back to. It's a very cheap form of protection. If you don't have a CD burner, you can designate a folder on your hard drive for the original picture files. Of course, hard drives can crash. I always figure nothing's really saved unless it's in two unrelated places. A second copy on the same hard drive won't help if the drive dies. Consider buying a CD writer or a Zip disk drive if you don't have a second means of storage. (Zip disks are a higher-capacity version of the now old-fashioned floppy disks folks depended on for years. Removable, reliable, and cheap.)

Artists often use a cardboard tool called a *cropping frame* to help work out a composition. It's simply two L-shaped pieces of heavy paper or cardstock. (See Figure 8.6.) You can use them to improvise differently shaped frames. Some pictures are square, some are rectangles. Some demand to be tall and thin or short and wide. Cropping frames help you see the proper shape of the picture. It's no coincidence that the cropping tool in every graphics program I've seen is shaped like the frame.

Figure 8.6

I've made a print of this picture and am using a cropping frame on it.

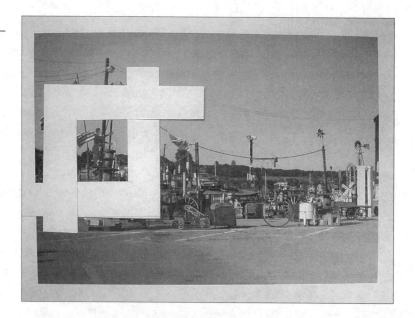

Using a cropping frame is a really good way to train your eye to pick out the best parts of a picture. I strongly recommend you make one and try it, either on your own photos or on pictures from a magazine. You'll be amazed at how different things look when you train yourself to see selectively.

You crop on the computer by using a *Cropping tool* that drags a frame across your picture. You drag the sides or corners of the frame until it fits exactly around the part of the picture you want to keep, and then click inside the frame to make everything else disappear. Photoshop Elements makes cropping especially easy because it darkens the part of the picture you're removing, making it much easier to see exactly what you've got. Figure 8.7 shows an example.

Something new in Elements 3 is the *Cookie Cutter tool*. It allows you to crop a picture using a shape, rather than just a rectangle. To use it, select the tool from the toolbox (it looks like a heart) or press its shortcut key, Q. Then select the shape you want from the drop-down panel on the Tool Options bar. Click and drag the mouse over the picture until the shape includes just the part of the photo you want. When you release the mouse button, you'll see the cropped area inside the cropping frame, as in Figure 8.8. The little squares at the sides and corners of the frame are called *handles*, and as with all the Cropping tools, you drag them until the frame fits the part of the picture you want. Try experimenting with both standard and cookie cutter cropping. Photos in appropriate shapes can really add pizzazz to a page. Take a fresh look at some of your old photos and see what you can find in them.

Figure 8.7

There might be a dozen pictures inside this one photo. The trick is finding them.

Figure 8.8

Yes, I love cats.

About Face! Flipping Images

Most portraits seem to have the subject facing the camera. That's a good thing. You can see the face clearly. But, if you have someone who is looking off in another direction, you might also have a design problem. Our natural tendency, when we see someone else looking at something, is to look at it, too. As discussed in Chapter 5, "Page Layout and Design," if you put a picture on a page that has someone looking away, you need to place it so she is looking into the page, not away from it. Otherwise, anyone looking at the scrapbook immediately looks off in the same direction as the subject, and might not pay attention to the rest of the page. Because the point is to communicate, you have to bring the viewer's eye to the words you want him to read.

You have two options. You can arrange the page so the subject is looking at it, or flip the picture to make her look at it instead of away. Figure 8.9 is a quickie example I threw together to show what happens when the picture faces the wrong way and the right way.

Figure 8.9

Having the subject face the print makes you more likely to read it.

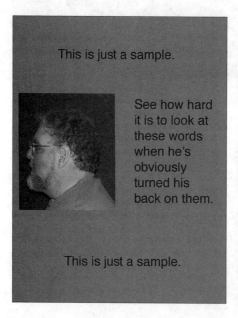

This is just a sample.

See how hard it is to look at these words when he's obviously turned his back on them.

This is just a sample.

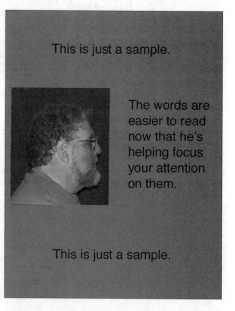

This is just a sample.

The words are easier to read now that he's helping focus your attention on them.

This is just a sample.

The solution is simple. Flip the picture so the subject faces the right way. Some photos, of course, can't be flipped. If there are readable words, like a team name on a T-shirt, or a sign in the background, you're probably stuck. If you can't flip the picture, change the layout or put it on an opposite facing page. To flip a photo, or a single layer, open the Image, Rotate menu, and select the flip or rotation you need.

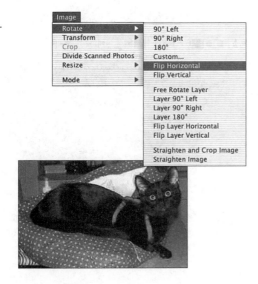

Figure 8.10

You'll probably recognize the cookie cutter kitten from Figure 8.8. Now he's facing the other way.

Resizing

Pictures are almost always either too big or too small for the layout. The nice thing—well, one of the many nice things—about using the digital camera and computer is that you aren't stuck with a wallet-size print, or a 4×5", or whatever format your film camera used.

Digital graphics programs, such as Photoshop Elements, make it easy to change the size of the picture, or of anything in it. If you have one of the current multi-megapixel cameras, your picture can easily be 14×17 inches or more. That's not going to fit on a scrapbook page. So you have to make the picture smaller. In Photoshop Elements, the easy way to do this is to use a dialog box called *Image Size*. Choose Resize from the Image menu. As you can see in Figure 8.11, the current size of the picture is about 8 1/2×6 1/2 inches. That's too big for the page I want to put it on. The space I have is just about three inches wide.

All I need to do is make sure that the *Constrain Proportions* check box is checked, and enter the new width in the Document Size area. The computer does the arithmetic and scales down the picture to the right size. Constrain Proportions means the ratio between height and width stays the same, no matter how the numbers change.

Figure 8.11

Shrinking a photo is
never a problem.
(Photo by Naomi
Rose.)

You can always shrink a digital picture because you
have lots of pixels worth of data. If you happen to
have a small picture you want to make very big,
you might not have enough data. In that case,
you see the individual pixels as little squares. For
scrapbooking, it's less common to have to make a
photo larger, but you can do it if you have
enough *resolution*. By resolution I mean dots or
pixels per inch. (See Chapter 3, "Digital Tools:
Hardware," for an in-depth explanation of resolution.) Put simply, more dots mean better resolution. To enlarge a picture, the program has to take a

tip If you enlarge an image
by resampling it and it
looks fuzzy to you, try the
Unsharp Mask filter in Photoshop
Elements to bring it back. Choose
Filter, Sharpen, Unsharp Mask to
access this filter.

sample of the pixels in each area of the picture and find their average color, and
then stick in more dots of the average color between the two sampled ones. If you
overdo it, the image becomes fuzzy, as in Figure 8.12.

Figure 8.12

This photo was extremely sharp when small. Over-enlarging caused fuzziness and outlines around the branches.

You can also *resize* a selected object. This is very helpful when you place a picture on a page, and then realize it's too big or not big enough. To resize a picture, first select the object or piece of an image to be resized. Use whichever selection tool is most convenient. With the Selection Marquee active, choose Image, Transform, Free Transform. You can also right-click in the selection (Ctrl-click on the Mac) and choose Free Transform from the context menu. This places a *cropping box* around your selected object. See the example in Figure 8.13. Drag any of the *corner handles* on the box to change the size of the image while holding down the Shift key to maintain its proportions. If you drag the *side handles* of the box, you'll stretch the selection's height or width accordingly.

Figure 8.13

Don't forget to hold down the Shift key as you drag, otherwise you distort the picture.

Canada's
Coast Guards

Blurring Backgrounds

How many times have you seen a good picture spoiled by a bad background? If you have the right editing tools available, you can get rid of it. Here's a picture I shot in Florida at a wonderful place called Big Cat Rescue, (http://www.bigcatrescue.org). The subject, a Siberian Lynx named Natasha, is kept in an enclosure, but as you can see in Figure 8.14, I was allowed to go in and visit with her.

Figure 8.14

You can see we're on the same side of the fence.

I'm sure Natasha doesn't like the fence any more than I do, so let's get rid of it. There are several ways you can do it. The most effective, and most tedious, is to use the Clone Stamp tool and simply copy over all the lines with more grass and sand. That would take a while. The quicker and easier alternative is to select pieces of the background and blur them, as I'm doing in Figure 8.15. I can adjust the amount of blur I add until the fence practically disappears. If I do a good job of selecting the area around the cat, I don't risk blurring her.

tip

In any of these dialog boxes, click on the piece of the picture in the window to slide it around so you can see the part of the image you need to adjust.

There's a *Blur tool* in Photoshop Elements. It's useful for blending small areas, but way too much work when you have something as big as the fence to remove. Working with the Gaussian Blur filter, the Blur tool, and a little bit of cloning, I've managed to de-emphasize the fence. Figure 8.16 shows the finished portrait, all ready for a big cat page. Be sure to see the before and after shots in the color section.

Figure 8.15

Adjust the Gaussian Blur slider until the selection is blurred enough to hide the fence, but not enough to stand out from the rest of the picture.

Figure 8.16

The cage is still there, but it's not the first thing you see.

Anything that distracts you from the subject of the picture is worth the time it takes to get rid of it. Instead of blurring the fence, I could simply have traced around the cat with a Selection tool and cut her out from the background. In Figure 8.17, I've done exactly that, and put her on a page with a couple of her friends. Please take a look at this page in color, too.

Figure 8.17

Notice how the three animals seem to focus on each other, leading your eye around the page.

There might be many times when the Blur tool comes in handy. It's good for hiding signs you don't want read and for removing details that don't help the picture communicate, or otherwise don't need to be there. It's always better to avoid the clutter when you shoot the picture, but sometimes you can't or don't want to take the time. In the digital world, you don't have to clean up the yard or sweep the floor until you're ready to do something with the picture.

Standouts

Remember that baby from Chapter 3—the one bouncing out of her chair? I promised I'd show you the trick for removing part of a background. I just used it again on the lynx, and here's how it works. Use the Selection Brush. It's the brush with a dotted circle around the tip, at the bottom of the Selection tool section of the toolbox. Set the Tool Options bar pop-up menu to Mask, choose an appropriate brush size, and paint over the area you want to keep. Using a small brush for the edges and a wide one to fill might make the job easier. (See Figure 8.18.) When you've masked the subject, go to the Select menu and choose Inverse, or type (⌘-Shift-I) [Ctrl+Shift+I] to invert the selection. Now, you have only the masked part selected.

Figure 8.18

You don't need to mask everything, just the part that sticks up.

Press and hold the Shift key, and drag a Selection Marquee around the part of the picture (in addition to the masked part) you want to keep. Figure 8.19 shows this step.

Figure 8.19

Pressing the Shift key lets you add to your original selection.

Now you have a choice; you can either cut and paste the selected object plus lower background to a new page, or invert the selection again, so only the unwanted top is selected, and delete it. Figure 8.20 shows the latter result.

Figure 8.20

The checkered background shows there's nothing visible now on that part of the layer.

Applying Color Correction

The last chapter talked about color shift as one of the things that can go wrong with an old picture. Well, new pictures aren't completely immune. If you shoot photos indoors with ordinary room light, you'll often find they look too yellow or brown. Or if you're spending a day at the beach or skiing in bright sun and snow, all your photos look sort of blue. I could give you a whole lecture on the physics and color temperature of light, but you really don't need to know it.

tip

If you're interested, photographers rate the color of sunlight as 5,300 Kelvin, and ordinary Tungsten light as 3,400 Kelvin. A candle is about 1,000 Kelvin. Higher numbers are brighter, and therefore more blue.

Keeping it simple, have you ever noticed how a white T-shirt that looks really dazzling white in bright noontime sun can look sort of dingy at night in, say, the living room? That's because daylight is a very bright light with a bluish tinge to it. Just like the bluing Grandma used to put in her white laundry, it brightens whites. *Incandescent light*, however, the kind you get from a basic light bulb, isn't as bright. It has a sort of yellow tinge, and it makes colors look warm instead of cool like the blue sunlight. The camera records what it sees. If the shirt looks blue-white, fine. If it looks yellow-white, also fine. That's what it looks like. But we humans are apt to notice if the colors aren't what we think of as "right."

The color we are most familiar with, and the one that's hardest to describe, is human skin. We humans come in flavors from vanilla to coffee to chocolate to licorice. But we know when skin tones are right and when they aren't. So, if there are people in the picture, use them as your benchmark. You know what their skin is supposed to look like, and if it's too green or too purple or too orange, you can fix it with your favorite photo-editing program.

Because I am sometimes rather lazy, I really like Photoshop Elements for color correction. All you need to do is choose Enhance, Adjust Color, Color Variations to bring up the dialog box in Figure 8.21. Then you choose the example that looks most right. You can adjust the amount of color change and whether it's applied to shadows, highlights, or midtones. You can also lighten or darken a photo as needed, and compare the changed photo against the original as you work on it.

Figure 8.21

You don't need to understand the physics of color to know what looks right.

A more complicated way to adjust color if you're working in Photoshop Elements is to use the Hue/Saturation dialog box, shown in Figure 8.22. Choose Enhance, Adjust Color, Hue/Saturation to access it. This dialog box lets you adjust either the entire color spectrum in the photo or a single color. Use the sliders to adjust the hue, saturation, and brightness as needed, after making sure that Preview is checked so you can see the results of your actions on the image in the workspace window. The pop-up menu lets you choose *Master*, which controls all the colors at once, or a single color channel (that is, red, green, blue, magenta, and so on). This is more suited to making dramatic color changes, turning leaves from green to red, and so on.

Figure 8.22

This dialog box can be your best friend.

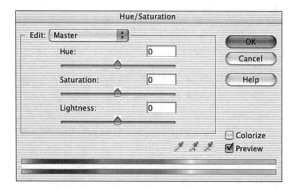

Correcting Perspective

When you're looking up at a tall building from street level, you're not usually conscious of the sides of the building slanting in toward the top, but you see it all the time in pictures. It's a kind of distortion caused by the lens, and it's easy to fix if you have Photoshop Elements. In Figure 8.23, you can see a picture I shot on a trip a few years ago. The building appears to be leaning backward, but in reality it wasn't.

To fix this, I need to stretch the top of the picture out so the edge of the building is vertical. First, I add a layer and draw a vertical line in an easy-to-see color. The Pencil tool, set to one pixel wide, is fine for this. If you hold down the Shift key as you drag, the line is constrained to vertical, horizontal, or a 45° angle. The line acts as a guide to show you when you've stretched the building far enough.

Figure 8.23

It's old but it's not ready to collapse yet.

From the Image menu, choose Image, Transform, Perspective. It places a cropping box around the picture, and then you simply drag the top handles outward until the wall is straight, as in Figure 8.24. Effectively, it has stretched the top of the picture and cropped away the excess. Then, you simply trash the layer with the guideline, and you have a perfect picture.

Figure 8.24

You might use this feature to straighten the Leaning Tower of Pisa, too.

Removing Unwanted Items or People

One of the tricks I've found most useful over the years has been the capability to rearrange people or other objects in a picture. Sometimes there's someone who worked her way into the group shot and isn't part of the group, or maybe it's a former spouse whom you don't want in the family album anymore. Or your teenager's significant other with the spiked green hair and nose ring. Maybe you can't make them go away in real life, but you can usually do it digitally.

Here's one of my favorite examples—three happy couples out for a night on the town. Only problem is, one of the ladies is not the wife of the gentleman she's with. Can we make a "safe" version of this picture? Take a close look at the people in Figure 8.25. The one who's got to leave is the third from the left. But the background is very plain, so this will be easy.

Figure 8.25

His wife would not
like to see him out
with his secretary.

The first step is to draw a rectangle that covers as much as possible of her, and not much else. See Figure 8.26.

In Figure 8.27, I've cut away most of the lady, and slid the right side of the photo over to cover the hole. The next step is to use the Clone Stamp tool to copy the background color to hide what remains of her.

Figure 8.26

Now that she's
selected, I can cut
her out and move
the pieces together.

It's easy to do this when the background is as simple as this one. If you can't match the background, consider replacing the unwanted person with someone else. If I'd had a photo of the guy's wife, I could have put her head on the other body. Or I could have replaced her with some movie star from the same era; judging by the clothes, Marilyn Monroe would have fit in nicely. Figure 8.28 shows the final result.

Figure 8.27

Some cloning and he's home free.

Figure 8.28

It's as if she was never there.

Little Touches Mean a Lot

What we just did was a kind of large-scale retouching. I sometimes think that kind is easier than the little bits of things I have to do to make an ordinary snapshot look good. But retouching is worthwhile, and that makes up for the extra effort. There are lots of reasons to retouch a photo. Professionals do it all the time, and that's why the models on magazine covers look so perfect. It's not that they really *are* flawless. Someone has spent time covering up the tiny skin bumps and lines, and painting out the flyaway hair, and possibly doing some other tricks as well.

Fixing Red Eye

Let's start with something that plagues most amateur photographers—*red eye*. You've seen it, those glowing "devil eyes" in an otherwise great photo. People and Siamese cats get red eye. Figure 8.29 shows a particularly bad example. Other animals, the brown-eyed ones, are more likely to show green eye or yellow eye, but the cure for all is the same.

The strange eye color is caused by light reflecting off the back of the subject's eyes. It's worst when you're taking flash pictures in an otherwise dimly lit place because the pupil (the black part of the eye) is wide open in low-light conditions.

Figure 8.29

He's really a nice cat; not as evil as he looks here.

The easiest way to cure red eye is to prevent it in the first place. Most cameras with on-board flash, both digital and film cameras, have an *anti-red eye flash mode*. It uses one or more quick preflashes to close down the subject's pupils before the main flash goes off. The intention is to narrow the pupil enough to miss the camera lens entirely. It's usually at least partly successful.

The second way to avoid red eye is to increase the *ambient light*. Turn on all the room lights, rather than relying on the flash. Brighter lights narrow your subject's pupils and also allow the use of a dimmer flash setting to dim the reflex.

A less common problem is alcohol and drugs, although certainly alcohol and its results have affected a great many wedding pictures. Both alcohol and narcotics further dilate the user's pupils, and that makes red eye even worse. Besides, there's nothing attractive about being blotto. If that's what's going on, don't take the picture.

Try having your subjects look a few degrees away from the lens. If you know you've got a red eye problem, start by having the subject look at your shoulder instead of the camera, and increase the head turn if necessary. Get closer to your subject to widen the flash-subject-lens angle and thereby avoid the reflection. The longer the camera-subject distance, the greater the lens-flash distance must be to avoid red eye.

None of these methods is 100% effective, of course, so you'll eventually have to tackle red eye reduction yourself. Some scrapbooking programs, as well as the major graphics programs, have some form of red eye removal. Photoshop Elements has a *Red Eye Removal tool*, shown in the toolbox in Figure 8.30.

Figure 8.30

When you select this tool, the dot in the center of the eye turns red.

The good news about this tool is that it has been vastly improved in Elements 3. The bad news is that now it *only* works on red eye that's red or orange. You can't use it on the dog's green eye, or any other strangely colored flash reflection. However, nothing could be much easier than banishing red eye. Click once on each red pupil. If the resulting black isn't dark enough, click again. It may take a few seconds to make the change, even on a fast computer.

Figure 8.31

Be aware that this tool only works on round red areas. It does nothing for other eye colors.

There's another way to do it, of course. Instead of using the Red Eye Removal tool, use the Magic Wand tool to select the red, green, or whatever colored part of the eyes, and then paint in a color that darkens them properly. I usually look for a color on the person or animal that I can copy with the Eyedropper. If the color's already present in the picture, it seems to look more natural. Be careful not to cover the white highlights from the reflected flash. Those are called *catchlights,* and they make the photo look more natural. Figure 8.32 shows a close-up of this procedure. See it in the color section, too.

Figure 8.32
Leave the catchlights where they are.

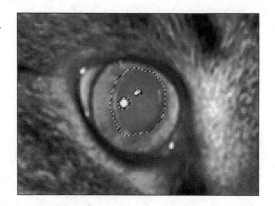

Eliminating Skin Problems

Even the best of the professional models and actresses have an occasional bad hair or bad skin day. Even on a good day, they might have a minor flaw or two. But you don't see those because they're retouched. Most professional graphic artists and retouchers use Photoshop, but you can use the same tools and techniques in Photoshop Elements.

Here's a fairly typical portrait. (See Figure 8.33, also in the color section.) It has a little bit of red eye, stray hair scattered across the guy's forehead, a few red spots, and he really needs a shave. Also there's dirt on the background, and a light switch that adds nothing to the picture. We'll fix this photo step-by-step in Photoshop Elements.

First, we'll do the background. In Figure 8.34, I've dragged a Rectangular Selection Marquee over a matching section of the wall, a little bigger than the light switch,

tip

When you feather something, you are making the edges soft so they appear to fade out. The number of pixels refers to the distance from the unfeathered part of the object or selection until its edges disappear. Feathering can make something you have added to a photo, in this case, a copy of the clean background, blend in better.

and feathered the selection by six pixels (found on the Select menu). The next step is to copy it and paste it. The selection appears on a new layer. I might also need to drag it to place it over the object I am hiding.

Figure 8.33

It's not bad, but it could be better.

Figure 8.34

The Feather command is on the Select menu.

The Clone Stamp tool, or rubber stamp, is ideal for fixing hair and skin problems. Just find a clean bit of skin the same color and start stamping. In Figure 8.35, you can see a close-up view of the man before and after I cleaned up his face and enhanced his beard. It really only a takes a couple of minutes to do this kind of repair, and it makes a big difference to the people in the pictures, who might look at the scrapbooks in 30 years and not groan.

Figure 8.35

I even neatened up his shaggy eyebrows.

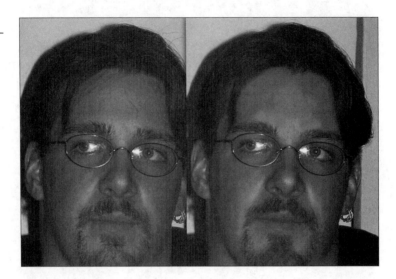

Going on a Digital Diet

What about those extra pounds we all put on as we get older? Can anything be done about those? The answer depends on a lot of factors, but mainly on what's in the background of the picture. In Figure 8.36, I caught a couple of girls spending the day at the beach. The photo isn't very flattering, I'm afraid. But we can help it a little.

As you can see in the figure, I've already used the Lasso and Magic Wand tools to select both women. My next step, which you can see in Figure 8.37, is to copy them onto a new layer. Then I can drag a Transform box around them, and drag the box handles to make them taller and thinner.

Figure 8.36

Bathing beauties at a local beach.

Figure 8.37

They're not overweight, they're under tall.

Now, I can make that layer invisible. (You do this in Photoshop Elements by clicking on the eye icon to close it.) Then I simply rubber stamp the background to cover the edges of the girls that stick out from behind their new shapes. When that's done,

I make the layer with the cutout girls visible again, and after making sure I've matched the background behind them, I move the shadows down to line up with their feet. I then merge all the layers by clicking the More button in the Layers Palette and choosing Merge Visible or Flatten Image. See the final photo in Figure 8.38. They're looking a lot better now.

Figure 8.38
All that swimming is paying off. They've lost several inches each.

As you can see from these simple tricks, reality is what you choose to make it. Your teenager won't want to be reminded of her spotty face the night of the senior prom, but she will love the picture of herself and her boyfriend all dressed up if you just clean it up a little. Similarly, if Dad or Grandpa are sensitive about their receding hairlines, put a little back. They'll never hesitate to pose for pictures again, because you take such *good* ones.

How Much Change Is Enough?

There's a sort of moral question at stake when you're retouching photos. Is it right to do it in the first place, and how far should you go?

You can take people out of the places they've been, or put them into places or situations they haven't been in. You can turn that can of beer in the politician's hand into a harmless can of soda, or vice-versa, depending on your party affiliation. The question is not "can you," but "should you?"

There are certainly some ethical questions to be addressed if you're altering photographs for public display. It really depends on how the picture is to be used. Reputable newspapers and magazines tend to have strict guidelines about photo manipulation. The general rule seems to be that, if a change affects the content of the photo rather than its appearance, you can't do it. You can lighten a too-dark picture of the politician, but you can't change the soda can in his hand into a beer can (or beer into soda). That constitutes a change in content.

On the other hand, your scrapbooks are for your own use and pleasure, and to hand on to your kids and grandkids, or other family and friends. You want the people in them to look good because that's how you'll remember them.

Editing a picture to improve the composition seems entirely reasonable, if it's a picture for your own use, but this is precisely what got the esteemed *National Geographic* magazine in trouble some years ago. They were doing a piece on Egypt and sent a photographer to get pictures of the pyramids. The art director studied the pictures and decided the composition would be better if he moved one of the pyramids closer to the next. As soon as the issue was published, astute readers began calling and writing to the magazine to complain. An apology appeared in the following issue, but simply knowing that the manipulation was possible waved a red flag for many people, both inside and outside the publishing industry. The question has been debated ever since. How much change is okay? How much is too much?

It's clear that you can't always believe what you see. The supermarket tabloids frequently feature pictures that stretch the bounds of believability. Remember the one of the President shaking hands with the space alien? Or Bigfoot carrying off the scantily clad woman? (Why was she dressed like that in the snow anyway?) When a fashion model is having a bad hair day or her face breaks out, retouching is required and expected. Where do you draw the line?

To me, it depends on what's being done and its effect on communication. If it makes a better picture, it's worth doing. When I can make somebody look better than they did when I shot the picture, I'm happy to do so. If it changes the meaning of the photo, particularly in a way that might get me sued, I don't do it. Can anyone's reputation be harmed by it? Don't do it. If there's somebody you don't much like, take him out of the picture. But don't decorate him with zits and messy hair. That's just mean.

Summary—What You Need to Remember

The best way to have good color pictures for your scrapbook pages is to think about what you're shooting. Come in close to the subject, whether it's a person, a flower, or an animal. If you can't get too close physically, use a camera with a zoom lens to make the picture look like you're closer. If you're shooting distant scenery, find a tree or rock or something close by that you can use to give perspective. Otherwise, you can't tell whether something's far away or just small.

When you start to edit a photo, always work on a copy and keep the original untouched. Storing your raw photos on CD-ROMs guarantees that you can go back to them whenever you want.

Color photos and even digital photos can get just as messed up as the old black-and-white ones. Cropping can help by recomposing a cluttered picture or removing unnecessary objects. To make a picture fit a page layout, you can resize it and even flip it so the subject faces into the page instead of away from it. Blurring interfering backgrounds makes them less annoying and adds emphasis to the subject.

Color correction is sometimes necessary, even when you use a digital camera. Skin tones can look wrong, especially under indoor lighting. Some light turns things blue, some turns it orange, and color balancing corrects the off-colors.

Retouching can remove anything from a pimple to a person. The Clone Stamp tool makes it easy to cover up whatever you need to hide. There's no reason not to make your family and friends look good in their photos. It's simple and fun when you have the right tools.

Turning a Photo into Art

If there's only one reason to invest in Photoshop Elements, it's this one. The Elements filters and a few simple techniques I'll show you in this chapter let you turn any picture, even the bad ones, into a work of art. I think you'll find, when you flip through the examples on these pages and in the color section, that you will really want to add this extra dimension to your scrapbook pages.

Many of the tricks you're going to do rely on what are called *filters* or *plug-ins*. They are subprograms that "plug in" to the graphics software to add functionality—such as importing, exporting, special effects, graphics filters, and other options. Filters are a type of plug-in that allow you to apply many types of visual effects to images within photo-editing software. You can use different filters to change the lighting, add three-dimensional effects, or even make the image look like a mosaic tile surface. Photoshop Elements filters appear in the Filter menu. All of the filters I'm using in this chapter are included in the program. There are many others you can find and buy online or at your local computer store. Photoshop Elements comes with about 100 filters. Not all of them are right for scrapbooking, but many can turn even a bad photo into a work of art you'll be proud to display. I also like to use a filtered photo as a page background. You will learn how to do this at the end of the chapter.

Photoshop Elements gives you two ways to select filters. You can choose them directly from the Filter menu, or you can use the Filter Gallery. I recommend using the Gallery while you're learning what filters can do.

Figure 9.1 shows the Filter Gallery. Choose from the filters displayed in the Palette windows to see them applied to your own photo.

tip

Filters take a long time to apply because they are very math intensive. The computer has to do calculations to apply the effect to each pixel. One way to speed this up is to add more RAM to the computer. Another, cheaper way is to tell the software to use more of the RAM in your computer, or to allocate memory. In Photoshop Elements, choose Edit, Preferences, Memory and Image Cache (Windows) or Photoshop Elements, Preferences, Memory and Image Cache (Mac) and increase the percentage in the Memory Usage box. Keep in mind that you have to quit the program and restart it for these changes to take effect.

Figure 9.1

The Filter Gallery shows the effects of the filters on a generic picture of an apple. (Photo by Mohammad Reza Ali Akbari.)

Applying Filters and Effects

Most filters and effects have variable settings that you apply via a dialog box. In Figure 9.2, you can see the dialog box for Elements's Angled Strokes effect. Use these settings to determine what direction the strokes run. Setting this slider midway gives you an equal amount of strokes from the left and right, while pushing it toward the right or left provides a greater number of strokes from that direction. You can also set the stroke length from 1 to 50, and adjust the sharpness of the individual strokes on a scale from 1 to 10.

Figure 9.2

The Preview window shows you the filter applied to the picture, but it's not really applied until you click OK.

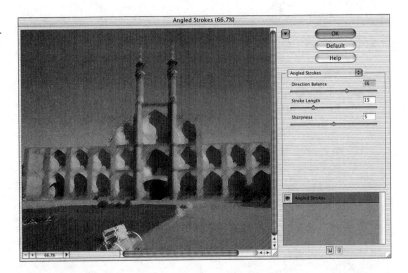

The Photoshop Elements Filter Gallery shows you a great many filters applied to the same picture. But there are other useful filters that don't appear in the gallery list because they don't make radical changes in your pictures, or because they serve special purposes, like the Sharpen and Blur filter sets or the Render filters. For these, you'll have to use the Filter menu shown in Figure 9.3.

Before we move on, there are several features in the Filter Gallery dialog box you should be aware of. The first is the arrow beside the list of filter folders. When it points up, as in Figure 9.4, you can see the list, and open any of the folders by clicking them. But you only see a slice of your image. Clicking the arrow temporarily turns it the other way, closing the panel and showing more of your picture. The second important feature is the pair of icons at the bottom right of the dialog box. The icon that looks like a new page or a new layer is, in fact, a new effects layer. Clicking this button lets you add a second effect (or a third, or as many as you need) on top of the first. You can also use it to apply the same effect twice, making it stronger. Clicking the eye icon next to the filter toggles its visibility on and off. If you decide you don't want the filter you've applied, drag it to the little trash icon.

The effect disappears immediately. You can also drag the filter layers, just as you would regular layers in the Layer palette, to change the order in which filter effects are applied. The last filter you apply will always be the predominant one, but the filters beneath it also have an effect on the picture.

Figure 9.3

Be sure to look at the Adjustments submenu. It has some very useful tools, like Posterize and Photo Filter.

Figure 9.4

This is a good way to experiment with filters.

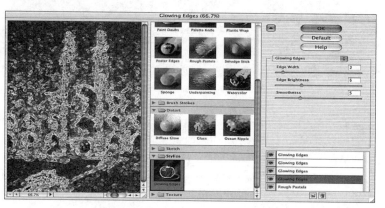

I've been thinking about a scrapbook of all of my lighthouse photos, as I've probably got close to fifty I've shot down the Atlantic coast from Nova Scotia to Key West. But some of the photos aren't very good. Let's take one, and see what we can do with it in Photoshop Elements. Figure 9.5 shows the photo I'll be working on. (It's also in the color section, along with some of its variations.) This is a shot I took several years ago at Portland Head Light in Maine. It's not a really bad picture, but it was a dull day, and the light was diffused and shadowless, making a dull photo.

Figure 9.5
Photographers call
this light "open
overcast."

Figure 9.5
Photographers call
this light "open
overcast."

Faking Watercolor Painting

Artists who work in other media have a great deal of respect for those who can
paint with watercolors. It's arguably the most difficult medium because you have to
work quickly, before the paint dries. But you also have to avoid working with your
paint or paper being too wet, otherwise you'll end up with nothing but a puddle.
Digital paint is, of course, much neater to work with. It doesn't get under your fingernails or leave a mess to clean up. And if you take your picture a step too far, you
can always undo it.

Photoshop Elements has one specific *Watercolor filter* (choose Filter, Artistic,
Watercolor). It gives you one style of watercolor, kind of dark and blotchy. There are
ways to make this filter work better, and there are other filters that also create
watercolors in other styles, but let's start with the official one. You can see its dialog
box in Figure 9.6.

The Watercolor filter, like most filters, has a dialog box with several options. You
can set the brush detail, shadow intensity, and texture. *Brush detail* ranges from 1 to
14, with greater detail at the high end of the scale. *Shadow intensity* can be set from
0 to 10, again with much deeper shadows as the numbers get bigger. *Texture* ranges
from 1 to 3, but there's not a great deal of difference between the settings.

Figure 9.6
Use the plus and minus symbols to change the magnification of the view in the dialog box.

As with several other Photoshop Elements filters, you can end up with a muddy mess if you overdo the shadow settings. The filters have a tendency to darken a picture anyway, so if you intensify the shadows or add extra texture, the result is a lot of black on the screen. I'm actually quite pleased with the way this came out as a watercolor. You can see it in the color section.

Of course, there's more than one way to paint a picture. *Dry Brush* is a watercolor technique that, as the name suggests, uses less water and more pure pigment. It's good for detail, and doesn't darken the picture the way the watercolor filter does. In Figure 9.7, I have applied it with a brush size set to 5, brush detail set to 9, and texture of 3. Because this is so close to the look I wanted, I spent an extra minute with the Sponge and Dodge tools, lightening the bushes, painting in some wild roses, and adding a little extra color to the rocks. Remember, just because you used one tool doesn't mean you can't go on and use others. The point is not to master perfect technique with only one kind of filter, but to make a picture that pleases you, no matter *what* you have to do to get there.

Using the Dry Brush filter on a portrait can be very interesting. When lightly applied with the least radical settings, it softens the details just enough to hide lines and flaws without looking fake. Here it is, with a before and after in Figure 9.8. My settings were as follows: a brush size of 2, brush detail set to 10, and texture of 1.

Figure 9.7
The Dry Brush filter is a good way to make a watercolor with lots of detail.

Figure 9.8
The original photo is on the left; the Dry Brush version on the right.

The only way to learn what these filters do to a particular picture is to try them. Experimenting with the filters is fun, and it's the best way to master them. After you have used them a few times, you'll begin to learn the differences between Brush Size and Brush Detail. You'll know how to get a fuzzy effect, like I did in the previous portrait, or how to get a smooth, almost plastic, look from the same filter by using the opposite settings. Hint: Work with the Brush Detail settings.

Simulating Oil Painting

There are, of course, a great many styles of oil painting, from the Norman Rockwell or more recent Thomas Kincaid style of very realistic brush drawings, to big splashy abstract swoops of color. My own favorite school of painting is the Impressionists. I like soft, slightly fuzzy, but colorful paintings. Monet is my favorite artist, so let's turn the lighthouse into an imitation Monet.

Traditional painters begin a new canvas by creating an *underpainting*, which lays out the scene with a big brush in blocks of color showing little or no detail. After they have the basic underpainting done, the artists go back with smaller brushes and add detail.

In Figure 9.9, I'm applying the Underpainting filter to the lighthouse photo. Unlike some of the other filters that give you only a few adjustments, this dialog box includes textures that can be reset. The defaults are burlap, brick, canvas, and sandstone, but you can also load in any grayscale texture and use it instead. The textures can be scaled by size, and also by relief (or "lumpiness"), and you can decide where to have the light strike them.

tip

If you like the general effect of the filter but it's too dark, go back and lighten the picture before you apply the filter. In case you need to undo more than one step, remember that Photoshop Elements has an Undo History palette that lists your previous steps. Click on an earlier step to revert to that stage of your work.

To create your own texture you can load into a Photoshop Elements document, follow these steps. Create a New document, any size, set to grayscale (not color). Draw with different tools—brush, pencil, shapes, lines, and so on—and remember that high contrast works best to create texture, so draw in black on a white background. When you are done, save the file as a .psd file on your computer someplace where you'll know to look for it, perhaps in a folder named My Textures. Then you can load your custom-made textures whenever you want to use them with a filter in Photoshop Elements. Scanning textured paper or cloth works well, too. Save texture scans in the same way (high contrast, in grayscale).

Figure 9.9

I like painting on sandstone. The default canvas is too rough.

The underpainting only takes one click. (You can see this step completed in the color section.) It's now time to actually pick up a brush and start painting. For this, I use a very small, hard-edged brush, and select colors either from the Swatches palette, or with the Eyedropper tool. Pressing the (Option) [Alt] key while any brush tool is active temporarily converts it to an Eyedropper for quick color selection.

In Figure 9.10, I've been working with the brush for a while, putting back detail and straight lines where the filter has softened the edges too much. If you have trouble drawing straight lines, try this trick. Press the Shift key while clicking the brush at the point where you want the line to start. Move the mouse to the point where you want it to end, and press Shift-click again. The line is drawn between the two points. You can also constrain a line to the vertical or horizontal by holding the Shift key down as you drag the mouse.

When you're overpainting, always do so on a new layer. That way, if you make a mistake, you can erase it without harming the picture. If you're not sure about the colors you're using, keep each one on a separate layer so you can correct them later.

Figure 9.11 shows my semi-finished oil painting. As you can see, it's different from the watercolor version.

Figure 9.10

Be sure to see these in the color section.

Figure 9.11

There's more work to be done, but it's starting to look like a painting.

Creating Line Art

Suppose, instead of painting, you wanted to try to turn the photo into a drawing? Photoshop Elements has a *Graphic Pen filter* (choose Filter, Sketch, Graphic Pen) that does the job very nicely. It uses the foreground color as the drawing medium and the background color, appropriately enough, as the background. You can set these two colors to anything you like, but I think the pen works best with black ink and a white or off-white background. I usually set the Light/Dark balance on this filter to 50%, so it's neither too light nor too dark. Stroke Length, the only other setting to alter in the filter dialog box, is a matter of personal taste, and what looks good with the picture. For this one (Figure 9.12), I chose the highest setting, 15, because I wanted dense blacks in the dark parts of the picture. I also tried it with a stroke length of 1, and discovered an interesting stippled effect, which you can see in Figure 9.13. To get this filter setting to work without having the picture look like a storm of black snow, I had to increase the brightness and contrast. You might often find that you need to adjust a picture before you filter it, and quite often have some cleaning up to do afterward.

Figure 9.12

This one has long strokes. The next example has short strokes.

Figure 9.13

I guess it's just a matter of "different strokes for different folks."

I'm sure you'll agree that these are interesting effects, but you might wonder about their use in a scrapbook. Suppose I took the previous example and instead of using black and off-white, I set the foreground and background colors to two shades of gray, keeping the darker one still fairly light. I could then use it as a page background, setting type for a title page or perhaps a quotation over it.

Figure 9.14

Make sure your lettering is legible over the background.

Photoshop Elements has a very good selection of drawing tools in addition to the Graphic Pen filter. You can draw with chalks, charcoal, colored pencils, pastels, Japanese brush painting (called sumi-e), Conté crayon, and even a sponge. One of my very favorite filters is called Rough Pastels. In Figure 9.15, I've applied it to the lighthouse. This is a filter that looks good with every photo I've ever tried it on.

Figure 9.15

Like the Underpainting filter, Rough Pastels applies a texture to the photo.

If you have a complex photo with a lot of details, you can really have some fun with some of the Photoshop Elements Stylize filters. Figure 9.16 shows a picture I shot in New York City. As you can see, it has a lot going on; all those cans of soda, and water bottles, and the signs…. It's a very busy picture, which makes it a good choice for the *edge filters*: Find Edges, Glowing Edges, and Trace Contour. They're located on the Filter, Stylize menu. These three effects sound as if they look alike, and actually they do look somewhat alike, with Glowing Edges and Find Edges being much more dramatic than Trace Contour.

The *Find Edges filter* removes most of the colors from the object and replaces them with lines around every edge contour. The color of the lines depends on the value at that point on the original object, with lightest points in yellow, scaling through to the darkest points, which appear in purple. The picture looks like a rather delicate-colored pencil drawing of itself. Find Edges works best, naturally, on photos that have a lot of detail for the filter to find. Find Edges sometimes becomes more interesting if you apply it more than once to the same picture. If you apply it once and don't like the result, try it again before you move on to a different filter, or increase the contrast in the original photo before you try again. Touching up areas afterward with the Sponge tool can bring out colors you hardly knew were there. This filter, applied to the right picture, can make a really outstanding page background or bit of art embellishment.

Figure 9.16

In the Big Apple, you're never far from a hot dog.

Figure 9.17

Notice how Find Edges picks up the detail of the sidewalk and the soda can collection.

Unfortunately, you cannot set the sensitivity of the Find Edges filter. In practical terms, this means you have to prepare the picture before you trace it. Begin by running the Despeckle filter (in the Noise filter submenu) so that Photoshop Elements won't attempt to circle every piece of dust in the background. If you don't want the background to show, select and delete it, or select your object and copy it to a separate layer. You can lower the opacity of each separate layer too. Using this filter with different layer blending modes can produce some spectacular effects.

Glowing Edges is more fun because it's prettier, and because you can adjust it to have maximum impact on your picture. Glowing Edges turns the edges into brightly colored lines against a black background. The effect is reminiscent of neon signs. You can vary the intensity of the color and the thickness of the line. In Figure 9.18, I've applied Glowing Edges to the same picture. It works especially well with busy pictures with lots of edges. The more it has to work with, the more effective the filter is. Be sure to check these out in the color section. Black and white doesn't do them justice.

Figure 9.18

Some of the color remains, but the background goes black.

Trace Contours, like several of the previous filters, works better on some pictures if you apply it several times (see Figure 9.19). The Trace Contour dialog box has a slider setting for the level at which value differences are translated into contour lines. When you move the slider, you are setting the threshold at which the values (from 0 to 255) are traced. Experiment to see which values bring out the best detail in your image. Upper and Lower don't refer to the direction of the outline. Lower

Outlines specifies where the color values of pixels fall below a specified level; Upper Outlines tells you where the values of the pixels are above the specified level. This also makes a nice background page.

Figure 9.19

The image was traced several times with different settings.

I like to use the Trace Contours filter to place different tracings on different layers and then merge them for a more complete picture. To turn this into a scrapbook page background, I can put a second layer below the image with a pale color. But first I would convert the image layer to grayscale by choosing Enhance, Adjust Color, Remove Color. Then I'd reduce the opacity of the lighthouse layer to 20%. You can see this in Figure 9.20, and also in the color section.

Figure 9.20

This gives the effect of a delicate etching or pencil drawing— very nice as a background.

Posterizing

Posterizing is an easy and really awesome effect that can be used either as a scrapbook page background, as an artistic photo, or as a cover page with type. Posterizing, in effect, means reducing the numbers of colors available in the image. Instead of pixel-by-pixel full color, you see large flat areas in a photo, making it look rather like a silkscreen print. When you posterize an image in Photoshop Elements, the dialog box shown in Figure 9.21 lets you specify the number of *tonal levels* (or brightness values) for each of the three color channels (RGB) in the image and then maps pixels to the closest matching level. For example, choosing two tonal levels in an RGB image gives a total of six colors: two for red, two for green, and two for blue. Choose Filter, Adjustments, Posterize to open the Posterize dialog box in Photoshop Elements.

Figure 9.21

Start with a low number of levels.

Figure 9.22 shows before and after views of a rather blah amusement park that has been posterized. Be sure to see them in the color section, too.

If you want a specific number of colors in your image, convert the image to grayscale and specify the number of levels you want. Then convert the image back to RGB mode, and replace the various gray tones with the colors you like. Note that posterizing can also be applied to an adjustment layer, making it a no-risk method for changing a picture. (If you don't know how to add an adjustment layer, the Photoshop Elements Help screens describe the process very clearly. Always check Help when you have questions about a program.)

Figure 9.22

This was also done with Posterize set to four levels.

Posterization can be applied to both color and grayscale images, of course. Applying it directly to color gives a more random, but usually interesting, choice. As you play with it, you'll notice that lower numbers are apt to give you more satisfactory results. With too many levels of posterization, you can't really tell that much has changed.

Remember also that you're not stuck with what you get. You can change colors selectively, paint back the sky if it was lost in translation, use the Sponge tool to intensify small areas of color, and add a textured surface to the image. There's a whole arsenal of Photoshop Elements tools. Think about what they can do in combination.

Remember that you're not limited to using just one filter or only using it once. Sometimes a combination of several filters turns out to be exactly what you need. Other times, they have too much of an effect and you forget what the picture's about. But that's the good thing about working on the computer. You can always go back to your original picture, copy it, give it a new name, and start over as many times as you need to. And each time you do so, you learn a little more about how the program works and how to achieve the look you want every time you sit down to work with a new photo.

Drawing on Photos

You're certainly not limited to using the photo "as is." When you're working digitally, you can draw or paint on them. I belong to an online group of cat lovers. One of my friends, each year, designs Halloween costumes for some of the cats, and I thought that prints of those would be a fun page for my cat scrapbook. She works in Photoshop Elements, and paints the costumes on one or more layers—depending on how complicated they are—over the original photos. You can see her work in Figure 9.23, and also in the color section.

Figure 9.23

No animals were harmed in making this page (unless you count injured dignity). Photo art courtesy of Judy Blair.

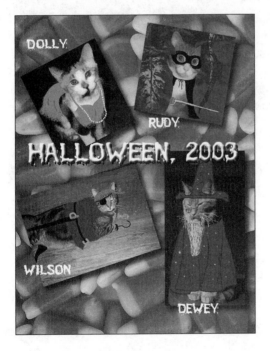

Making Composites and Collages

If you can't draw or paint as well as you want to, but still want to make some changes or additions to your pictures, consider merging a couple. I found a cute photo of a friend, seated on a camel on a trip to Egypt. You can see it in Figure 9.24.

Figure 9.24

Nice portrait, nice camel, lousy background. (Photo courtesy of Carole Harrison.)

Unfortunately, the photo was taken in a parking lot, and she appears to have a radio antenna sticking out of her head and shoulders. If I removed the antenna, it still wouldn't be a really great photo, but how about removing Carole and her camel and putting them somewhere else?

This is a job for the Zoom tool and Magnetic Lasso. I'll have to trace very carefully around both Carole and the camel, and then zoom in and refine my selections even further. Remember, to subtract from a selection, hold the Option key as you drag a Lasso around the parts you want to subtract. In Figure 9.25, I've completed selecting the woman and camel and then inverted the selection so the background was selected. Then I made the photo into a layer instead of a background layer by changing its name to Layer 0, and deleted the antenna and parking lot, leaving them in limbo.

Now I can put her anywhere I want her. Maybe in the Arizona desert? Or riding down Broadway in New York City? Or in front of the Museum of Fine Arts in Boston? All I have to do is paste her in, and then adjust the color and lighting to match the location (see Figure 9.26). The trick with composite pictures like this is simple; just use a program that lets you work in layers.

Figure 9.25

The checkerboard pattern indicates transparency.

Figure 9.26

She does get around....I wonder how the camel is for mileage.

Scrapbooking purists will probably have strenuous objections to doing this. It's changing history, and so on. You can't preserve a memory of something that never really happened. Nevertheless, I think it's a fun, and occasionally useful, technique, so I'm including it here. If you don't approve, don't do it.

Let's take a couple of pictures and combine them step-by-step. Figure 9.27 shows two, selected at random. The first thing I have to do is to decide whether to colorize the couple or turn the railroad station into black and white. The latter is, of course, easier.

1. To remove the color from the train station photo, change the working mode from RGB color to grayscale. In Photoshop Elements, Mode, Grayscale is on the Image menu.

2. The second step is to prepare the couple to be moved from in front of their house to the railway platform. This requires selecting them and cutting them out of their background. Depending on the background, you might be able to select the subject with the Magic Wand or Lasso tools. Photoshop Elements has a tool called the Selection Brush that makes this task quite easy. Working with the Selection Brush tool and a comfortably sized brush, paint around the inside edges of the couple. Then fill in the middle. It's easier if you enlarge the image to 200%, as shown in Figure 9.28. Then you can really see what you are doing. If you're working with the Lasso tool, this is especially true.

Figure 9.27

A couple of Don's relatives and the North Conway, New Hampshire railroad station. Photos courtesy of Don Maynard and Joshua Rose.

3. After they are selected, simply copy and paste them into a new layer in the other picture. You'll probably have to do some resizing because the chances are good that they'll be too tall or short for the surroundings. In Figure 9.29, I've scaled them to fit.

4. There's still one step left. If you look carefully, you'll realize that the day is sunny, but our couple isn't casting shadows. Rather than fool around with the drop shadow dialog box, I can simply paint in some soft shadows on another layer and then drag to move the new layer behind the old one. Figure 9.30 shows the finished picture.

Figure 9.28
Bigger is sometimes better.

Figure 9.29
I checked their height against the size of the train. They ought to be able to stand up inside it.

Figure 9.30

I wonder where they're headed… maybe a Niagara Falls honeymoon?

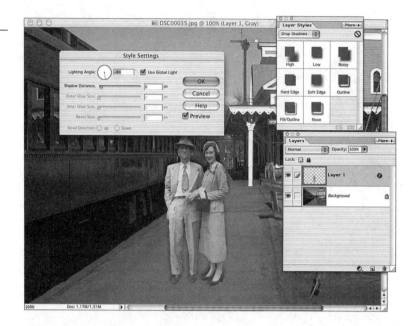

Collages (an artist's word for any picture made by combining others) don't need to be fantasy, of course. You can combine any two or more pictures in any way you want. One that's often seen, and can be very effective, is the combination of a head-on portrait and a profile of the same person. Figure 9.31 is a double portrait of my beautiful daughter-in-law.

Figure 9.31

This is simply two pictures on different layers, trimmed to fit together.

Making Panoramic Photos

People have been sticking photos together to create panoramic images for close to a hundred years, with varying degrees of success. The scissors and glue method rarely succeeded. Shooting a panorama all in one photo with a very wide-angle lens almost worked, until you realized that the ends of the Grand Canyon were very fuzzy, or the two outermost bridesmaids in the wedding line-up appeared 50 pounds heavier than reality. Distortion is the main problem. Wide-angle lenses aren't that good. The more curve you apply to the front of the lens, the more glass the image has to pass through. Glass adds distortion. The more logical way to shoot a panorama that stays in focus from one end to the other is to take a series of pictures and splice them together. Prior to computers, that was exceptionally difficult, although it certainly was done. Now, thanks to clever software, it's easier than ever to get good results with panoramic photography. First, you must shoot the pictures, and that takes a bit of skill. Then you assemble the panorama.

Considerations When You Shoot a Panorama

Obviously, the main thing to consider when you shoot pictures for a panorama is to hold the camera steady at one height. Don't take it away from your eye while you're shooting. If you get interrupted mid-sequence, start again. Better yet, if possible, use a tripod to keep the camera steady. Remember, digital photos don't waste film. Stay away from the focus and zoom buttons. Auto-focus the first picture and let that one dictate the rest.

Practice the panorama shuffle. Start shooting with your body aimed at one end of the scene. Take small steps circling to your right as you shoot your pictures from left to right.

Don't use a flash. Particularly, don't use auto-flash because it throws varying amounts of light as it sees a need. These make the exposure all but impossible to correct.

Use a normal lens for best results. Set your zoom lens about halfway between zoom and telephoto, and leave it there. Don't use a wide angle or a fisheye. They defeat the purpose of the panorama, which is to have everything in the same focus and not distorted. Nothing distorts more than a fisheye. That's how they got the name.

Make sure you have enough overlap between pictures, but not too much. Somewhere around 20% is good. As you pan across the scene, remember what was on the right side of each picture you take, and just cover it again on the left of the next shot.

Take a picture of something clearly different, even your foot, between shooting panorama sequences. That way you won't use Photomerge to try to assemble pictures that don't go together. Keep each set of pictures in a separate file as you download from the camera.

Once you have the pictures loaded into the computer and sorted out into separate folders, one per panorama, the rest is easy. You can either do the assembly yourself, or use software that does it for you. We'll look at both.

Photomerge

Photomerge is a Photoshop Elements plug-in that automates the process of assembling a panorama. After you've photographed the shots, you plug your camera or flashcard into the computer, and download the pictures. Then you open Photoshop Elements, choose File, New, Photomerge Panorama, and tell it where to find the pictures you want to use. The dialog box is shown in Figure 9.32.

Figure 9.32

It's easiest if you download your pictures to a single file. That way you don't have to go hunting around your hard drive for them.

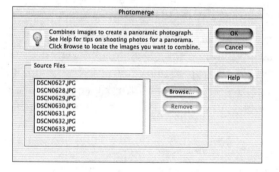

When you click OK, the magic begins. First, Photoshop Elements downloads all the photos you specified and opens a new page. Then it puts them down in order, matching the edges where images overlap. At this point, the window in Figure 9.33 opens so you can watch the progress.

The pictures appear to come in at 50% opacity, so the computer can easily line up areas of major contrast. In this series of pictures, tree trunks seemed to be the major point for matching. Pictures that can't be matched in are left at the top of the strip, so you can manually drag them in and match them later. When all the pictures have been merged, Photomerge continues the process (in Figure 9.34) by adjusting the brightness and contrast of each pair of pictures so you have a consistent exposure from one end to the other. If the sun goes behind a cloud and emerges again, as it did for me, you have to do some extra tweaking. Apparently, it can only cope with *logical* changes.

Figure 9.33
Panorama in
progress.

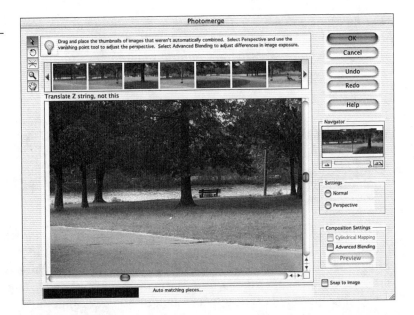

Figure 9.33
Panorama in
progress.

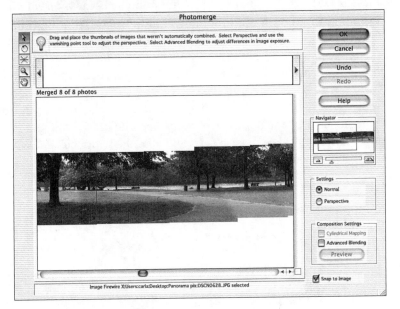

Figure 9.34
Processing the
exposures.

Your final product is an untitled file with all the pictures assembled and matched as well as possible (see Figure 9.35). Unfortunately, when you get it, the image has already been flattened, making it difficult to adjust the exposure of one frame that's a little off.

Figure 9.35

The edges do help suggest that this is more than one photo.

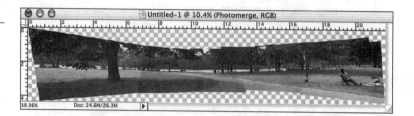

It's still up to you to crop the picture, if you want to. Some photographers argue that the slanting edges and unevenness of the raw panorama somehow add to the experience. Others, myself included, prefer to crop. A lot depends on whether, and how, you intend to print the picture. The eight images I assembled for this test of Photomerge produced a strip 4 inches high by 36 inches long. At 300dpi resolution, that's a 37MB file. I actually *can* print it at home because one of my inkjet printers takes banner paper. But if I want a real panorama, I'd probably take it to a service bureau and have them print it 8 inches high by 6 feet long, and wrap it around the top of my office. That, of course, is much too big for a scrapbook, but if you have or can locate a printer that handles 11×17-inch paper (tabloid size), you can make a foldout scrapbook page. You need to size the photo up or down to a size that's no wider than 15 inches. Print the image centered on the page, as in Figure 9.36. Then, trim one inch off the right side of the paper, and after running a piece of Mylar tape up the left side, punch holes so it fits in the scrapbook. Make your fold precisely 8 1/2 inches from the left edge, so it fits right in.

Figure 9.36

Bring the cut side over and fold it so the edge of the paper is the same size as a regular page.

If this were a real page, I'd also add some journaling about where the picture was shot (Digby, Nova Scotia) and some other smaller pictures from the same area.

If you're working in an earlier version of Photoshop Elements that doesn't include Photomerge, all you need to do is import the photos into a new document and place each one on a separate layer. Make sure you set up the page wide enough to hold all of the pictures. This also avoids the automatic flattening by Photomerge mentioned previously, so you can match colors and brightness of the individual pictures. Adjust the opacity of a layer to see "through" it to the next layer so you can easily match the images. Then slide them as needed until you've matched the overlaps as closely as possible. Crop and save as usual. This method is also easier than Photomerge if you need to combine only two shots into a single picture.

If you need to scan something larger than your scanner can hold, like a full page of a newspaper or a calendar photo, use the same technique. Scan as many pieces as you need, and then import them to separate layers and match the overlaps.

Summary—What You Need to Remember

The main point of this chapter is to show you that you can do things to your pictures other than just cleaning them up and pasting them on pages. You can filter them, paint on them, and combine them in interesting ways. You can move people from one place to another, if you want. You can make collages and panoramic photos. The only limits are your creativity and your willingness to go beyond what's in the photo. Have fun!

Adding Type

To keep things simple, I'm calling it *type*. You might call it a title, text, a caption, a journal entry, lettering, or words on the page. A lot of advantages exist to using the computer to set type. First, and most important, it's neater and easier to read than most handwriting. If you happen to be a master calligrapher and really enjoy intricate Gothic script, go for it. But for the rest of us, the computer makes typesetting a lot easier. It's certainly quicker, and you don't mess up the page when the kids or dog jog your arm while you're writing. You don't have to deal with a clogged or leaky pen. Photoshop Elements can even check your spelling!

The Language of Typography

Before you start working with type, there are a few terms you need to learn. The first is *point size*. This is a standard measurement based on the distance between the bottom of the lowest descender and the top of the highest ascender, with a little bit added on. The space is added so lines of type *set solid* (without any additional space between them) do not run into each other. Body text is typically somewhere around 12 points, and headings, titles, and so on are set in larger type. A subhead might be 18 to 24 points high and a headline anywhere from 24 to 144 points high. Because a single point is 1/72 of an inch, 72-point type is normally about an inch high. However, certain fancy fonts have elongated ascenders and descenders. On such fonts, the point size is determined by a more typical letter, such as lower case *n* or *o*.

Alignment is the way the type is positioned on the page. You have three choices: flush left, flush right, and centered. Figure 10.1 shows some examples.

Figure 10.1

This typeface is called Helvetica.

Type set flush left
is lined up against the
left margin of the page.

Centered type has the
same amount of space
on either side of
the lines of type.

Type set flush right
is lined up against the
right margin of the page.

There's also an alignment style called *justified*. It forces each line in a column to be the same width. To achieve this, the spacing between letters and words is adjusted. Most graphics programs aren't that sophisticated, but if you need justified type, you can set it in almost any word processor and paste the type onto your scrapbook page.

When you have multiple lines of type, you sometimes have to deal with line spacing, also called *leading* (rhymes with sledding). Back in the early days of metal type, the typesetter placed lead bars in between the lines of letters to separate them and make them easier to read. Both leading and type are measured by point size. If there's not enough leading between lines of type, it's hard to read, makes the page look too crowded, and the block of type looks too black. Too much leading is also a problem. If the lines are spaced too far apart, the text seems disconnected, and your eye doesn't flow as it should from one line to the next. Type designers build into the font a suggested amount of leading, usually two points more than the height of a typical lowercase letter (They call it *x-height*, referring to the height of a lowercase x). They also build in *kerning*, or kerned pairs. Kerning refers to the amount of space between two adjacent letters. Some letters look better and are easier to read if they are closer together. The combination *To*, for example, looks best in larger point sizes if the letter *O* is moved closer to the *T*, even allowing the top of the *T* to extend over it.

If you set type in a word-processing or page-layout program, you can control the amount of leading yourself, or use auto-leading. Most graphics programs use auto-leading, and the type looks quite good.

Putting the Words on the Page

The *Type tool* in Photoshop Elements works very intuitively. You simply place the type cursor on the page and start typing. There's no text box, as there is in some other graphics programs. To begin a new line of text, you must press the (Return) [Enter] key.

The Photoshop Elements Type tool is actually four tools in one: the Horizontal and Vertical Type tools and the Horizontal and Vertical Type Mask tools (see Figure 10.2). The regular Type tools set type on its own (vector) layer. Thus, you can edit the type and apply layer styles to the layer. You can change the type from horizontal to vertical and back again, change display options (discussed next), and warp the type into waves, flag shapes, or even fish. You can move, copy, and change the position or layer options of a type layer just as you can with a normal layer. However, filters and edits involving distortion or perspective can't happen until the type is *simplified*, or rendered into bitmap (raster) form.

The Type Mask tools allow you to do some very cool tricks with type and photos. When you use the Type Mask tool, you are making a mask in the shape of the letters you type. You can fill the mask with a picture, or cut the letters out of a picture. I'll show you how to do this later on in this chapter.

Figure 10.2

The Photoshop Elements Type tools.

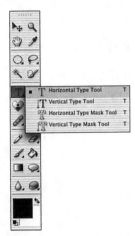

Before you start entering your type, you'll probably need to adjust the settings on the Tool Options bar (see Figure 10.3). Other graphics and scrapbook programs have similar settings in a Type dialog box or toolbox, although they might not have as many.

Figure 10.3

I had to cut the Type Options bar into two pieces so it would fit on the page.

The first four choices on the Tool Options bar are the same as in the toolbox, namely which kind of type to set—horizontal or vertical, masked or not. Next, there's a pull-down menu that displays a list of fonts installed. The next pull-down menu is of type styles. This menu changes according to the fonts you have installed, but generally you can choose from regular and italic styles, and often light, bold, or demi-bold, as well. The menu after that offers a choice of point sizes. If you don't see the size you want, enter it into the window, or click the window and use the up and down arrows to adjust the point size up or down, by one point per click.

The next button determines whether to anti-alias the type. *Anti-aliasing* smoothes out "jaggy" type. It's important to apply anti-aliasing if readers will view your work on the screen. Few things look worse, or less professional, than jagged type. Figure 10.4 shows the difference. If your type is to be printed, however, turn off anti-aliasing. The same process that makes it look better on-screen adds a blur when the page is printed.

Figure 10.4

Notice the curves in the non-anti-aliased type. They appear lumpy, as if made of bricks.

Anti-aliased type
Not anti-aliased

The next choices give you false (or faux) bold and italic, and underlined and strikethrough type. You can use the bold and italic options to enhance a plain font or to increase the boldness or slant of already bold or italic faces. Strikethrough and underline have very limited uses, as far as I can see. Underlining was a way of indicating emphasis back in the days of the typewriter, but it was always read as if it were italic. Because you now have lots of options for italics, underlining isn't typographically correct. Nor is strikethrough because of the invention of the Delete key. Use them if you think you must, but *please* don't tell me about it.

Those little stacks of lines indicate alignment: flush left, centered, or flush right. The color swatch, black by default, lets you choose a type color independent of the foreground and background colors. Just click it to open the usual Color Picker.

The two *A*'s stacked with an arrow next to the lower one and the entry window are where you control leading between lines. Photoshop Elements 3 gives you the option of auto-leading, or setting a precise amount. That sort of twisted letter with the curved line under it takes you to one of the more interesting aspects of setting type in Photoshop Elements, namely Warp Text. I'll come back to it in a moment, I promise. But first, let's finish discussing the Tool Options bar. The final icon lets you change

tip

If you learned to type on a typewriter rather than a computer, one of the rules you learned was that you always place two spaces after a period. Right? On the computer, it's wrong. Computer type, even in so-called monospaced fonts such as Courier, is designed so it leaves an appropriate amount of space between characters. You don't need to add the extra space, and when you do, it looks wrong.

One other no-no for computer users: Never use those initials, abbreviations, and smiley faces you use in chat rooms and emails such as "LOL," "hw r u?" and ":-)" for anything you want most people to understand. Your scrapbooks are going to be around for a lot longer than that online shorthand will. You don't want your grandchildren to think you were illiterate, do you?

horizontally set type to vertical type, or vice-versa. It's most useful if you tend to use type as a design element rather than as a means of communication. Simply click it to change a selected string of letters or symbols from reading left-right to up-down.

A Bubble for Your Thoughts?

Comic strips have taught us that people speak and think in bubbles or balloons. Adding a thought bubble or speech bubble to your photos is easy and fun. Photoshop Elements has talk and thought bubbles available on the Tool Options bar when the Custom Shape tool is selected. Don't forget that you can rotate or flip the bubble as needed, using the Image, Rotate subcommands. In Figure 10.5, I placed the type and the balloon on separate layers and moved them around until they looked right.

tip

Horizontal type is what we're used to seeing in the English-speaking world. Other cultures use many different alphabets and different typographic styles. Outside of short words on neon signs, we rarely see English, French, or similar languages intended to be read vertically. It's unnecessarily difficult for readers to decipher, which doesn't mean you can't do it—just that you might want to think before you do. If you're featuring an old movie marquee, a theater, or hotel sign, some vertical type on the page might be a nice addition.

Figure 10.5

Thought balloons work very well with animals and babies. (Photo by Matt Purcell.)

Choosing Fonts

There are literally thousands, if not millions, of fonts available. And that's before you start adding styles and special effects to them. Fonts come in many styles but two basic categories, with serifs or without (sans serif, in typographer's terms). *Serifs*, if you're not familiar with the word, are those little strokes at the ends of letters. Serif type is supposedly easier to read, which is why it's used so much in children's books, and especially in reading primers. Here's an example in Figure 10.6, from the Baskerville font. For comparison, Figure 10.7 shows a typical sans serif font.

Figure 10.6
Maybe it's easier to read because it's what we learned to recognize.

See Spot.
See Spot run.

Figure 10.7
This font is called Techno.

See Spot.
See Spot run.

There's also a distinction that needs to be made between display type and body type. What you're reading right now is *body type*. The chapter and section titles are in *display type*. The main difference is size. Body type is usually 12 points or less in size. Usually, but not necessarily—if you have a journal entry and the space for it, set it in 14-point type to make it easier to read.

Display type is always a bigger point size than body type. It can be precisely the same font, or not. Because it's bigger and placed more prominently on the page, it's easier to see, even if you're using a fancy or funky font. Fancy? Funky? Believe it. Figure 10.8 shows a few of the stranger examples.

Figure 10.8

Not all of these are right for all occasions.

Hello from
STRANGE THINGS
AND SILLY ONES
Hash House   Graduate
Phooey *Handsprings*
ORIENT *Sailor knots*

Your choice of font can either help convey the message or interfere with it. These *character fonts* are good for setting a mood, and really help communicate what your scrapbook pages are about, as much as the words you apply them to. There are fonts that suggest holidays, fonts that relate to sports or places you've been, and fonts that look like handwriting or a child's crayon printing. The trick is choosing the right one for the right kind of page. Here's the same scrapbook title set in a bunch of different fonts (see Figure 10.9). Which one tells most about the subject?

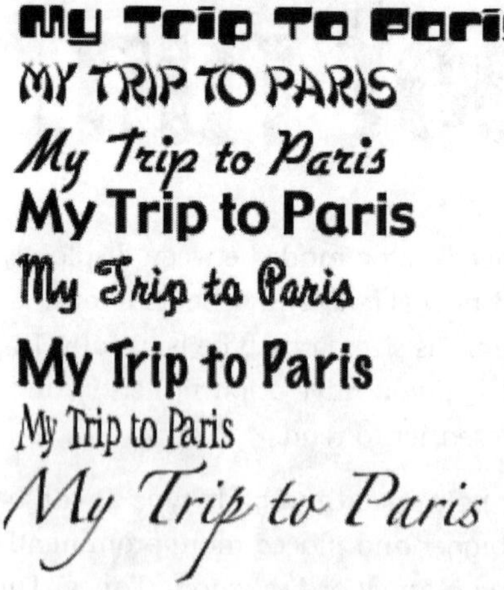

Figure 10.9

The person in the top line traveled there by spaceship; the one in the last line stayed at the Ritz.

My Trip To Paris
MY TRIP TO PARIS
My Trip to Paris
My Trip to Paris
My Trip to Paris
My Trip to Paris
My Trip to Paris
My Trip to Paris

You can find fonts all over the Internet, as well as in your local computer store, in catalogs, and so on. Some you can get free; others cost money. As mentioned in an earlier chapter, some scrapbooking programs come with dozens of free fonts. I've also found several CDs full of useful fonts at office supply stores and advertised in the back pages of computer magazines at very reasonable prices. Start by checking out http://www.1001freefonts.com. They have an amazing collection, for both Mac and Windows users.

How many fonts do you need? That's going to depend on what you intend to use them for. Certainly, you already have some useful ones, probably Helvetica and one or two other sans serif faces like Arial or Verdana, and some of the classic serif ones like Palatino and Garamond. You have something like Courier, which imitates a typewriter, and you probably have one or two script fonts, such as Chancery or Dom Casual. Beyond that, why not wait and see what you need?

Tasteful Typography

With all those fonts waiting for you, it's hard not to get carried away and lose sight of the real reason for the type. Words mean something. You're putting type onto your page or picture for a reason, and most of the time it's to help communicate an idea. Maybe it's a title. Maybe it's a caption or a journal entry. Whatever it is, you want people to be able to read and understand it. Otherwise, why clutter up the art?

Using bizarre fonts and too many special effects gets in the way of communication. If the words are hard to read, only the most devoted readers will even try. If the message is "Get Well," but the font came from a circus poster, there needs to be a reason. Perhaps the recipient is a circus fan, or a part-time clown. Otherwise, you've just given him one more thing to make his headache worse.

Keep the type in proportion to the rest of the page, size-wise, as well as stylistically. Don't let one element overpower another, unless there's a reason to do so. However, don't make the type too small to read, either. Print a copy, and see whether you can read it from five feet away, without your glasses. If so, other folks probably can, too.

If you're going to say it, why not say it in colors? Colored lettering looks really nice if you've chosen the right colors, and it's a feature you might as well make use of. To change the color of the letters, look for the color swatch on the Text Options bar. By default, the selected color is whatever happens to be the current foreground color. Clicking the swatch leads you to the Color Picker so you can choose a custom color, if none of the swatches are what you need.

Adding Drop Shadows

Be sure that the color you choose for the type is different enough from the background that the letters stand out. If you want to make the letters really stand out, add a *drop shadow* behind them. Drop shadows are so-called because they drop away behind the type or object you apply them to. Figure 10.10 shows part of a page I'm working on. (It's also in the color section.) It has several things going on, but one of the most obvious is the drop shadow behind the letters.

Figure 10.10

There are two kinds of drop shadow here. Under the type there's a hard edged shadow, and under the picture a softer, noisy one.

Drop shadows are particularly easy to add in Photoshop Elements. You simply choose the one you want from the Styles and Effects palette shown in Figure 10.11. After you have applied it, if you click on the script letter *F* that appears on the Layers palette next to the layer you have styled, you can adjust the way the effect is applied. This opens the dialog box shown in Figure 10.12, which lets you define the shadow by its direction and offset. The size, color, and amount of blur are preset according to which shadow you select. Options that appear grayed-out in this window become available as needed for other kinds of layer effects.

Figure 10.11

There are shadows, bevels, and lots of great special effects on this palette. Use the pop-up menus to view them.

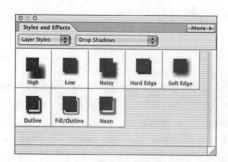

Figure 10.12

The dial-like device in the upper-left corner of the window controls the direction of the shadow.

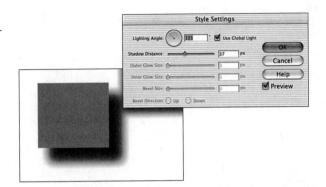

You can also create reasonably effective drop shadows from scratch, if you don't like any of the ones on the Styles and Effects palette. You need to set the type twice or copy the object you're applying the shadow to, and fill it with a dark gray, or whatever color you want the shadow to be. Select the layer that becomes the shadow in the stack and choose Filter, Blur More to add a nice soft edge to the shadow. You may need to apply the filter several times to get the amount of blur you want. Make sure the type layer ends up on top of the blur layer, as in Figure 10.13.

Figure 10.13

Notice how the shadow helps make the type stand out.

Using Masked Type

Now go back and take another look at Figure 10.10. This time, notice the cut-out lettering. This is a trick Photoshop Elements does really well. Choose a photo you want to show through your type, and select the Horizontal Type Mask tool. The Type tools are shown in Figure 10.14. Place the type cursor on the picture where you want to start typing. As soon as you do, the picture turns light red, telling you there's a mask on it. As you type, the letters are cut out of the background. After you're done typing, the mask disappears and you see the letters as "marching ant" marquees, as shown in Figure 10.15. You can then drag them wherever you want, even to a different page. To use the type marquee to copy a section of the photo, position it where you want it and then choose Layer, New and either make a Layer via Copy or a Layer via Cut. If you want to copy a section of the background with your type marquee and not make a hole in your background image, choose Layer via Copy. Layer via Cut cuts a hole in your image in the shape of the type you entered.

Figure 10.14

The Type Mask tool converts each letter to a little selection marquee.

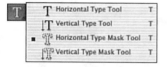

Don't forget that the Type Mask tool is essentially another Selection tool rather than a Type tool, so you won't be working on a type layer. Your letters appear as a raster graphic shape on whatever layer is selected, and are not editable as regular text is. Therefore, you need to select your font, style, and size before you use the Type Mask tool. Don't forget to check your spelling, too.

Figure 10.15

Now you can drag the type wherever you want it or copy it to a new page.

Obviously, this only works with large bold type. Otherwise, your letters are so thin nothing really shows through from the background image well enough to be recognized. What you do with them from here is up to you. You can paste them into another picture, use them as a title, and add some layer effects.

Embossing and Other Special Effects

Traditional hand embossing requires tracing around the edges of pictures or type with a tool of some kind—either a stylus or ball-end burnisher, pressing a line into the paper and thus forcing it to sort of billow upward next to the impression. Press embossing uses brass dies and a combination of heat and heavy pressure to make raised images. Powder embossing uses plastic based powders applied to wet ink and heated so they melt and form raised lines. Embossing on the computer screen gives the same look, but much more easily. In Figure 10.16, you can see the bevel and embossing styles available in Photoshop Elements.

Figure 10.16

Bevels have angled or chiseled edges, whereas embossing gives a rounded edge.

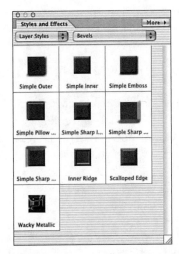

You can vary the effect of these tools by changing the blending modes, by varying the opacity, and by changing highlight and shadow colors. As always, the best way to see what they do is to experiment with different settings. Be sure to make a copy of your original digital image before you experiment.

Creating Metallic Effects

There are lots of ways to create metallic type using the layer styles, particularly with the Bevel and Emboss options, and of course, Jack Davis's excellent Wow Chrome effects, which he's allowed Adobe to use along with his Neon and Plastic styles in Photoshop Elements. For many more tricks like these, take a look at his column in the *Photoshop Elements Techniques* newsletter. For a preview, visit http://www. photoshopelementsuser.com.

Choose appropriately metallic colors, such as pale blues for silver and light yellows for gold. Remember to also set highlight or shadow colors to something appropriate, not necessarily black or white. Then just start experimenting. Try adding noise for a brushed metal finish. Figure 10.17 shows an example of liquid gold type. This example uses a combination of a drop shadow, simple emboss, and small outer glow, applied to yellow text. Remember, you can use as many layer styles as you want, not just one. If you go too far and make the type hard to read, just undo them and start again.

Figure 10.17

Be sure to see this effect in the color section.

Warping Text

Warped text is simply text that's set in a curve, along a wavy line, or forced into a shape. It can definitely add interest to a page title and be a lot of fun, as long as it's readable. If your word processor happens to be Microsoft Word, you have pretty good collections of warping styles that you probably never knew about. Figure 10.18 shows the Word Art dialog box from Word (choose Insert, Picture, Word Art). After you choose a style, you see a window into which you enter your text. It's that easy.

Figure 10.18

You can set titles here and simply copy them to the Clipboard and paste them on your page.

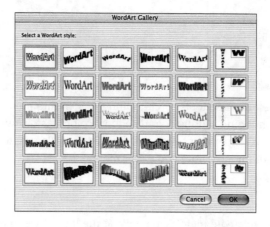

In Photoshop Elements, you can select among 15 preset warp styles, and you can also drag and distort these until you have exactly the look you want. Figure 10.19 shows Photoshop Elements Warp Text styles. You can open this dialog box by selecting the Type tool and then clicking on the icon that has a warped letter *T* with a curved line beneath it in the Tool Options bar.

The Warp Text dialog box settings, shown in Figure 10.20, are a little bit tricky at first. Use the sliders to increase the amount of Bend applied to the path. Moving to the right bends words up; to the left (negative numbers) bends them down. Distortion makes the line of type appear to flare out on one end (*Horizontal Distortion*) or from top to bottom (*Vertical Distortion*).

Figure 10.19

Some of these styles need multiple lines of text or large point size text to be effective.

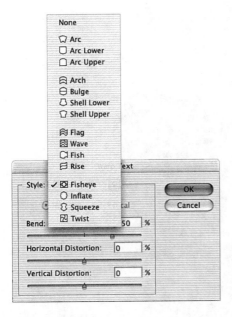

Figure 10.20

You need to experiment with the settings to really understand them.

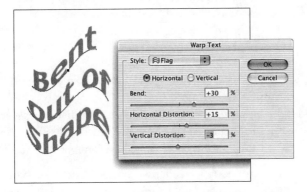

In Figure 10.21, I've used two kinds of type warp. The first is Flag, and the second, used for the photo caption, is Lower Arc. The striped effect is the result of setting the type twice, once in red, and the same text on a layer over that, in blue. Then I warped both text layers exactly the same way, and dragged an eraser over the blue layer to let the red text layer show through, making the stripes. Be sure to see this in the color section.

Figure 10.21

Warped type is very effective, when you don't overdo it.

Journaling

Journal entries are a major part of many scrapbooks. *Journaling* can be loosely defined as any text that goes beyond a simple title or photo caption. Because journal entries tend to be at least a paragraph long, and sometimes several paragraphs or continued across multiple pages, it's generally much easier to write them in a word processor, rather than setting them directly in type on the page.

When you write for a scrapbook, consider who might be reading your words. This is a chance to tell your stories, relate your family history, and make daily happenings into memories your family will cherish. Write in your own voice. Don't use what Grandma Figg called "high-falutin' words" if that's not who you are. Just try to write concisely, clearly, and well, and say something worthwhile. When you want to use a journal entry, but don't know what to say, ask yourself why you chose the items you have put on the page, and then turn that concept into an explanation. Say what they mean to you, or what you remember most about the people in the pictures, or the place where they were taken.

Be sure to check your spelling, and always proofread your words before you put them on a page. You can't trust the spelling checker to know whether you meant "to," "too," or "two" or "whether" or "weather."

Usually, after you decide which photos and other items to include on a scrapbook page, you'll have a specific amount of space on the page for your journal entry. One way to make sure that what you write will fit and be legible is to choose the font and type size that you think works best, and then set the page margins in the word processor to give you a block to fill that's the same size as the space on your scrapbook page.

There's a good deal of discussion in the scrapbooking forums on the Internet about what fonts to use for journal entries. I like to use "antique" fonts if I'm writing about family history. I use a font that gives the impression of handwriting when I'm journaling my own thoughts and ideas, and I often use a font that looks like comic book lettering if I'm entering something a child has said. Figure 10.22 shows some examples of different fonts.

tip

If you're not sure about questions of grammar or how best to say what you mean, there's a wonderful little book by William Strunk and E.B. White called *Elements of Style*. This is a book that should be in every home, and packed into every college freshman's suitcase. It's not just for writers or English majors, but for anyone who has to write anything that needs to be read and understood.

Figure 10.22

The first font is called Didot, the second is Hans Hand, and the third is called Zapfino.

My great grandfather fought in the Civil war. He often said "There warn't nothin' civil about it."

*I used to wonder what I'd be when I grew up. Now I wonder if I'll **ever** grow up...*

Mothers are special people...

Many handwriting fonts are available online. You can even have your own hand-writing turned into a font you can use for all your computer correspondence, as well as your scrapbook. Do a Google search of handwriting fonts to find sources for free and shareware versions as well as companies that create your own handwritten font. This is a great gift idea, if someone you know wants to give you a very useful and personal present. Of course, you'd have to know about it because you have to provide samples of your handwriting in capitals, lowercase, numbers, punctuation marks, and specific letter combinations.

Online Sources for Clips and Quotes

You know you want to say something, something significant. But you can't think of anything. The chances are fairly good that someone else already has said it, and there are many books of quotations you can use, either as a source for quotes or to inspire your own messages. I used to keep a battered copy of Bartlett's *Familiar Quotations* on the shelf next to my desk. Then I discovered that the same excellent book is now available online. Go to http://www.bartleby.com/100/. You can search by author, alphabetically, chronologically, or by topic. Another good source is The Quotations Page (http://www.quotationspage.com). Finally, let me suggest two of my favorites, Quoteland (http://www.quoteland.com) and Quotations for Creative Thinking (http://www.creativequotations.com). Quoteland is organized with an alphabetical list of topics, as well as some quotes for special occasions, sports quotes, literary quotes, and a listing by author. They have many contemporary quotes from favorite TV shows. Quotations for Creative Thinking has proverbs, quotes from 3,000 or more famous people, and several indexing systems, all intended to help you find the words you want to use.

When you use a quotation, please don't forget to credit it to the person who said it first. Aside from being honest, it makes your pages more interesting and informa-tive if quotes are attributed to their sources. Another idea, courtesy of my tech edi-tor, Jennifer Burke, is to give credit to family and friends for their own "famous" quotes. People say interesting things all the time and sometimes become known for always giving the same piece of advice or using a favorite phrase (such as "Button your jacket. I'm cold," or "Great galloping grapefruit," one of my dad's favorites). When you add a line that someone always says and place their name next to it on your scrapbook page near their photo, you are enhancing everyone's memory of that person, as well as enhancing your page layout.

Summary—What You Need to Remember

There's obviously a great deal I can say about type. I could relate the history of type, from the first Sumerian script incised on clay tablets to Gutenberg and moveable type, and so on. But you don't need to know the entire history of typography to use it effectively. All you need to keep in mind when you use type is that the purpose of writing is to communicate. Anything that helps the communication is good. Anything that doesn't is bad.

Using fonts that somehow relate to the theme of the page helps get your message across. Using a delicate wedding invitation script font to caption the picture of your son's football team doesn't help the communication. Make sure your type is big enough to read easily and is well spaced, so the reader can follow logically from one word or phrase to the next. Restrain yourself to a limit of two or three fonts per page or section. Type can help you tie related pages together as much as colors and styles can.

Using fancy type is fun, as long as it doesn't get in the way of the message. Warped type and other special effects add character. Drop shadows behind type make it appear to stand out from the page, just as a drop shadow behind a photo makes it look as if it's been stuck on rather than printed there.

Be sure to check your spelling and grammar before you print your pages. You don't want your family and friends to laugh at your work, and you certainly don't want to be embarrassed about showing it off.

Well-chosen words in legible fonts really help your scrapbooks tell their stories.

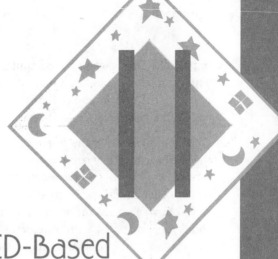

Creating Web/CD-Based Scrapbooks

You've probably heard about the paperless office of the future. The idea is that everything will happen on computer and cell phone screens. All the files will be stored on some kind of disks, whether enormous hard drives, DVDs, memory sticks, or whatever other storage medium the future brings. It's a good idea for a number of reasons. First, and most important to me, it saves trees, and I love trees. Tons of paper are copied on, scribbled on, and thrown away every day. True, some of the paper is recycled, but most of it is either burned, polluting the air, or dumped in a landfill, polluting the soil. Also, the paperless office means that important information can be shared by as many people as need to have access to it over the Internet or by distributing the material on a CD or DVD. If you're not at your desk, you can look at your cell phone or PDA, and call up the data you need, whether it's the babysitter's phone number or the company's annual report.

If you're at all like me, you enjoy the feel of the paper your scrapbook is made of, and the textures of the objects you have chosen to put in it. That's great, but suppose you want to show it to your mom and dad in another state, or give the same book to several grandchildren. With a paper scrapbook, that's difficult, if not impossible. This is when the computer becomes your working partner. You can put your scrapbook pages into a digital album other people can look at on their computer screens or using an ordinary TV and DVD player. Sharing is easy, and you can send a disk for the same price as a letter.

Of course, there's also the Internet. Your family and friends don't have to wait for the mail carrier. They can look at your scrapbooks online whenever they're in the mood. With Internet access practically everywhere—from the public library to the corner coffee shop—the Internet is a simple and reliable place to store your memories. Your web pages can be as public or private as you want to make them. You can share your scrapbook with other scrapbookers if you want, or password-protect them so only the people who know your password can get in.

Understanding the World Wide Web

You've probably done some web surfing, checked the weather report online, or found ideas for scrapbook pages from websites such as http://www.scrapbooking.com, but you might not understand the technology behind the Web. There are three things involved: the Hypertext Markup Language (HTML for short), servers, and addresses. You don't need to know how they work, but if you want to have your own web pages, you at least need to know what they are.

HTML—You Can't Pronounce It but You Can Learn to Love It

Hypertext Markup Language controls how a page looks: which images are shown and where on the page they appear, what size a headline is and what it says, what color the background is, and anything else on the page. When you access a web page, the information sent to your computer is not the collection of words and images you see on the screen. It's plain text—called the page's *source code*—that usually contains the words that appear on the displayed web page, along with a bunch of *tags*. The tags are short pieces of HTML code that tell your computer what size or color to make the words, and where to find and copy other text or images.

The *hyper* in hypertext refers to *links,* underlined words on the screen that, when clicked, take you to other pages, play sounds, and activate other web features. Making links is child's play; most web page creation software does it for you automatically, or, if you're hand-coding your HTML, you can type a few words that serve the same purpose. Web browsers, such as Internet Explorer, Macintosh Safari, Netscape Navigator, or the web-viewing software in America Online, understand HTML and use it to create an image of the page on your computer screen.

HTML is fairly simple and is based on English. Many people teach it to themselves by surfing to a page, and then using the View, Source command in their web browsers. You'll look more specifically at HTML tags in the section called "How HTML Works."

Are You Being Served?

Server? Let me explain. The second part of the equation that is the World Wide Web involves the server. When somebody looks at your web page, they're not connecting directly to your computer. In fact, your computer can be turned off and the page still appears on their web browser. Instead, they're contacting a *server*—a fast computer with lots of storage and a good Internet connection. The server stores your web page's text and images in a folder, and transfers the web page contents to anyone's web browser on demand.

Big companies, like car manufacturers, news media, and search-engine services like www.google.com, usually have their own servers. But there are plenty of companies that are simply in the server business. They maintain the computer and storage devices, and rent or, in some cases, give away space for individuals and businesses to store their web pages. These companies are called *web hosts*.

After you assemble your web pages, you upload them to the server, and then other people can connect to them in exactly the same way they connect to any other website, by entering the address in their browsers.

The Right Address

People can't find you if they don't know where to look. That's why your website needs an address. Every website has a unique numeric address assigned to it, called an *IP address*. For example, the IP address for my site is 64.33.79.84. If you type that number into your browser, you'll see some of the digital photos I've taken. But all those numbers can be hard to remember, especially if you want to visit several sites. That's why each site also has a unique *domain name*. Internet registrars, such as VeriSign, keep track of domain names for a fee and send lists of the names and their matching IP address numbers to your Internet service provider (ISP), where they're entered into a sort of giant phone book called the *domain name server*. It's updated frequently because there are always new websites coming online. So if you enter my website's name, http://www.graphicalcat.com, into your browser, the domain name server at your ISP translates that to my unique string of numbers (my IP address) and displays my web page.

How to Get on the Web

If you have access to the Internet, you can have a website of your own. There are several ways to do it, depending on your budget and your tolerance for pop-up ads and flashing banners.

Free Websites

Companies like GeoCities at Yahoo! host your web pages with simple page-building tools. Most make their money by putting ads on your pages or sending pop-under windows that appear when you close the original page, but these are generally unobtrusive and you can choose an appropriate category for the ads (such as "family," "cars," or "music"). Your website will have a domain name such as www.geocities.com/graphicalcat (a site I just set up to demonstrate some typical pages). There are plenty of others, including FreeServers and ProHosting (http://free.prohosting.com). The list of hosts keeps changing, but if you enter "free web hosting" in your favorite Internet search engine, you'll get hundreds of names. Check their terms. Some free hosts offer more storage space on their servers, so you can have more pictures on your web page; others limit the size of file transfers, which can prevent you from adding sound or video to your website because the files would be too big.

America Online has a free website called AOL Hometown (hometown.aol.com). It comes with a page designer called 1-2-3 Publish, which is one of the easiest I've ever seen. It's also completely inflexible. However, they also allow you to upload pages you have created offline in some other program.

Your ISP might also have free web space available. The disadvantage of using an ISP's server for your website is if you change providers, your web address changes as well.

Websites for (Almost) Free

If you don't want to see ads, many free hosts can upgrade your account to a non-advertising version for as little as 5 dollars a month. Mac users might also want to look into http://www.mac.com, a $100/year web-hosting service that also includes mail, an address book, online storage for important files, and other features. Actually, all these hosting sites are cross-platform—you can access them from Windows or Macintosh. However, some of the advanced mac.com features don't work with the Windows OS. Delphi Forums (http://www.delphiforums.com) has a low-cost web-hosting service, along with related bulletin boards and chat rooms.

Be Master of Your Own Domain

If you sign up for a free web host service such as GeoCities, they'll assign you an address that takes visitors to your folder within their domain (such as www. geocities.com/graphicalcat). Similarly, if you have your website hosted by your phone company or cable company, your address might be something like www.cabletv.com/users/johndoe or users.cable.com/harpomarx. It's not quite as classy as having your own domain, but it's less expensive. For most scrapbookers, this isn't a problem. But if you also want to provide a service or run a small business or organization on the Web, it's a good idea to get your own domain name. It can also be a major ego boost. By the way, domain names are also used for email. If you want to contact me, I'm author@graphicalcat.com. Another advantage to having your own domain is that you can have as many mailboxes as you want. Perhaps there is one you only give out to family and friends, and one you use only as an address for signing up for freebies. (It'll fill up with spam.)

Web addresses don't have to be "dot-com," which is a good thing because almost all the good `.com` names have been taken. The dot-something is called a *top-level domain*, and there are others available. Businesses can be a `.biz`, organizations can be `.org`, or individuals can be `.name`, `.net`, or something else. There are even specialized top-level domains for museums and their managers, licensed professionals, and cooperatives.

To get a domain of your own, do a web search for "domain name registrar." There are dozens of registrars such as VeriSign and they're competitive—fees vary. Also, some might not have access to a particular top-level domain. The registrar will help you search for an available name, and make sure it gets properly registered. After you have a domain name, you'll still need a host. (It's possible to host a site on your own computer, but not recommended unless you're a serious computer geek.) Many domain name registrars offer low-cost hosting as well.

Assembling Web Pages

Unfortunately, there's no way to take your existing scrapbook pages and just post them as they are. You could, conceivably, take each page and scan it, and then save the scanned page as a JPEG. Or, if you created them entirely on the computer, you can simply save a low-quality JPEG version. In Figure 11.1, I've used the Adobe Photoshop Elements Save for Web feature to reduce a 9MB TIF page to a low-quality JPEG that's only 152KB. As you can see, the quality doesn't suffer too much.

However, that's still a fairly large file if you're on a dial-up modem. If you have a 28.8Kbps dial-up connection, loading the page takes 55 seconds. Some of your friends might not be willing to wait that long.

Figure 11.1

I also reduced the page size to 5×7" to save more file space.

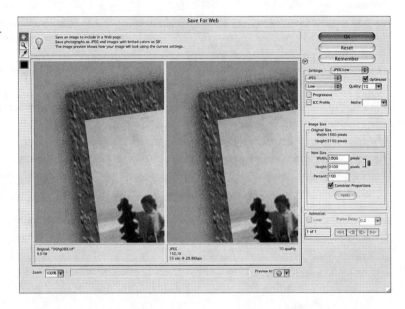

The greater file size/more download time equation limits the usefulness of this technique for posting your scrapbook on the Web. That's why most people lay out their web pages, in scrapbook form or otherwise, as HTML documents. You really don't need to be a computer whiz to make your own pages.

Sites that offer personal web pages often have *wizards*, a kind of step-by-step, fill-in-the-blanks utility. With a wizard, you can choose from a variety of themes and backgrounds, select photos from your computer, automatically upload them to the website, and then add titles and captions. Figure 11.2 shows an example from the page wizard at GeoCities.

The wizards make some rather boring and bland pages, but there are workarounds, of course. If you save your pictures with a block of color behind them, that's what appears on the web page. If you set fancy type for a title and save it as a GIF, you can place it as if it were a photo and not have to deal with the limited fonts available in most wizards. Typically, these utilities restrict themselves to the two fonts everybody *has* to have on their computers—Times and Helvetica/Arial.

Figure II.2

Choose a style and then click Next to place your photos on the page.

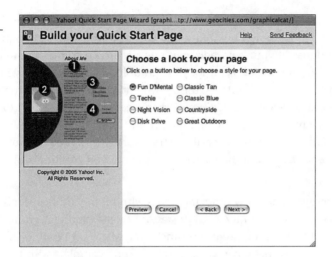

For the Do-It-Yourselfer

There's plenty of web page design software available that doesn't require you to write your own HTML. One of the nicer ones for Windows is Cool Page. Download a free trial from http://www.coolpage.com. You add your own photos and text, as if you were building a scrapbook page, and the program converts everything to uploadable HTML. This concept, by the way, is called WYSIWYG (wizzy-wig) and stands for "what you see is what you get." As you add elements to the page, you see exactly what will appear on the finished web page.

Figure II.3

Cool Page includes backgrounds, icons, and even animations you can use on your pages.

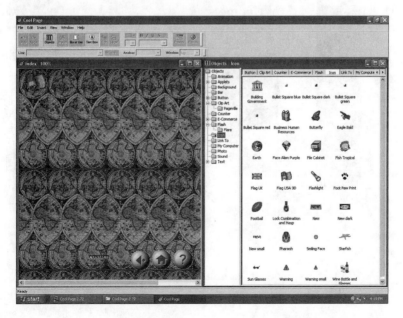

One of the advantages of using web design software, rather than the free wizards, is that you have more design flexibility. You can also work *offline*, designing and perfecting web pages at your own pace, without needing a connection to the Internet. After you're happy with everything, you can upload your pages to your server. There are lots more page builders, all the way up to high-powered tools such as Microsoft FrontPage and Macromedia Dreamweaver MX, which sell for $200 and $400 respectively. As you can tell by the prices, these last two are intended for professionals, and are probably overkill for the average scrapbooker. But if you have access to one of them, and the patience to learn it, you can turn out some amazing pages.

You can turn out some fairly amazing pages without any of these tools, if you have a recent edition of almost any word processor or text-editing program. Many word processors and text-editing programs—including Microsoft Word, Microsoft Works, WordPerfect, and iWork—save pages in web format, complete with text styling and pictures. You simply design your pages in one of these programs, and when you save, the program writes HTML source code. Then, you can upload it to your server along with the images and other graphics you want to use. I was quite surprised when I started revising a page with Microsoft Word and found that I could apply graphics filters and add drop shadows and other effects right within the word processor. (This applies to the current version, not necessarily to earlier ones.) Check out Figure 11.4. You can even fix red eye, as well as crop and fix color on your photos.

Figure 11.4

Who knew a word processor could do all this? I didn't.

Web Page Design Basics

There are a few things to think about when you create a web page, as opposed to a normal scrapbook page. The first is to keep the graphics files small. You can save web graphics in JPEG, GIF, or PNG format. Which one you choose depends on what kind of a graphic it is. Photos are best saved as JPEG or PNG, and they can be compressed to very small files. Line drawings, backgrounds, single or limited color blocks, or anything with fewer than 216 colors save smallest as GIFs.

When you choose type to add to a web page, you have two options. You can set the type in a graphics program and save it as a GIF if you want a particular font. If "close enough" is good enough, just set your type in the web page program, using one of the headline or text settings, and specify a common font your viewers are likely to have installed, such as Times or Arial. Why? Well, suppose you want to use a character font like Chalkboard, or Rodeo, or your own handwriting font. The chances are good that the people who visit the page won't have that font available on their computers. So, their web browser chooses a generic font instead, which probably won't even be close to what you wanted. If you set the type as a GIF, you can apply any special effects you like, and crop the block small, make the area surrounding the type invisible so the page's background or color shows through, or add a different background color behind it. Check the program's help files or manual for information on creating these effects.

Can This Page Be Saved?

When you save a web page on the server, you have to give it a name ending in `.htm` or `.html`. People access your page by entering the domain name and your folder, followed by the name of the page. In the case of the site I just set up, it might theoretically be something like geocities.com/_graphicalcat/MainScrapBookPage.html. (It's not.) But you can save your friends some typing by naming the main page `index.html`. That magic name is automatically used for the page name when someone enters your website without specifying a page. That's why you can see my GeoCities page by just entering geocities.com/graphicalcat. It automatically takes you to the page I made called `index.html`.

> **tip**
>
> If you want to put your email address on your web page so people can write to you, set it as a GIF, instead of as regular type on the page. They'll have to copy it rather than just clicking on the address to send an email, but the search programs that crawl through the Web looking for email addresses for spammers can't find you this way.

How HTML Works

You don't have to know this. As you've seen, there are plenty of WYSIWYG page-building software and websites that translate your layouts into HTML, the universal language of web pages. But if you have a basic understanding of how this authoring language works, you can better tweak your pages and make them look different from others.

Although HTML is a computer language, it's one of the simplest to understand. The commands (known as *tags*) are either abbreviations of English words, such as <b> to turn a font bold, or the words themselves. Many tags control font formatting, others let you put multiple columns on a page, but the most important ones tell the browser which images to put on a page, or where to go when someone clicks on a link. Links take you to other pages on your own website, or someone else's website, if you want. You might want to link to your favorite scrapbooking store or to your friends' pages. I have a link to Amazon.com so people who come to my website can buy my books. (And I make a few extra pennies per book from Amazon for providing the link.)

There are three important points to remember about HTML:

- Tags have to be enclosed in *angle brackets* < > (also known as lesser-than and greater-than symbols), which are found above the comma and period on a keyboard.

- Tags that affect formatting have to be closed, which you do by using another tag with a slash mark. For example, if you type <i> in front of a word to make it appear italic in the browser, every word that follows it will also be italic until you type the closing tag, </i>.

- The source code for your HTML pages—the text files that contain all the tags and content—in your website aren't formatted themselves. Everything's in the same dull typeface, and there are no colors or pictures. The magic happens after your browser downloads the page and interprets the tags.

Table 11.1 shows the HTML source code that displays the wedding scrapbook web page in Figure 11.5, with an explanation of what the tags are doing.

Table 11.1 HTML Source Code for the Web Page Shown in Figure 11.5

Tag	Purpose
`<HTML>`	Tells browser this is an HTML document, so it should draw the page based on these tags.
`<HEAD>`	This is the beginning of the page's header. The `<HEAD>` tag can contain info for search engines, as well as style and script information.
`<TITLE>Josh & Melissa's Wedding</TITLE>`	The text contained within the `<TITLE>` tags is displayed in the browser's title bar.
`<META http-equiv="Content-Type" content="text/html; charset=_iso-8859-1">`	Tells browser which version of code to interpret.
`</HEAD>`	End of page header information…
`<BODY background="papertexture.jpg">`	…and beginning of the body of the page. The `background` command tells the browser to find an image called `papertexture.jpg` in the same folder as the HTML document, copy it as many times as necessary to cover the page, and put all the type and other images over it. The `<BODY>` tag always follows the `<HEAD>` tag in HTML documents.
`<TABLE border=2 bordercolor=#808080 bordercolorlight=#C0C0C0 bordercolordark=#404040 width="90%" cellspacing="2" cellpadding="6">`	This places those nice embossed rectangles around the words on the left, and the picture on the right, by actually drawing a two-column table. The attribute `border=2` indicates that the border is two pixels wide. The text `bordercolorlight` gives the highlight color around the border, whereas `bordercolordark` gives the shadow color. The colors are represented by numbers as shown.
`<TR>`	Start one row of cells in the table.
`<TD>`	The `<TD>` tag defines the contents of a cell in a table.
`<H1 ALIGN=Center>`	H1 means "heading size 1," the largest the browser can display.
`<FONT COLOR="#FF0000"> <BIG><I>Mr. and Mrs.  Joshua & Melissa  Rose </I></BIG></FONT></H1>`	`FONT COLOR` specifies the color, and `FF0000` means bright red. The `<BIG><BIG/>` tag obviously defines text that should be displayed in a larger font than usual. Text contained within `<I></I>` tags appears italicized. The ` ` tags force a break between lines of type. Note how all those formatting commands are closed with slash marks.
`<H3 ALIGN=Center> <FONT COLOR="#FF0000"> September 1, 2001</FONT></H3> <FONT></FONT>`	Changes the font size and color, as shown in the source code at left. H3 is two sizes smaller than H1.
`<IMG SRC="palm2.gif" WIDTH=123 HEIGHT=114 ALIGN=BOTTOM>  <I><BIG><FONT COLOR="#FF0000">`	Find the palm tree image and make it the element after the previous text.

Continues…

Table 11.1   Continued

Tag	Purpose
`<A HREF="message.htm">` `A Message in a Bottle </A>`	`<A HREF>` is a link to another page. When someone clicks on the words "A Message in a Bottle," they're taken to a different web page (`message.htm`) that features a poem the groom wrote.
`   `	Adds some space…

`<A HREF="pictures.htm">`
`To more pictures</a></FONT>`
`</BIG></I>`
	…and then adds a link to the page that has more pictures.

`</TD>`	End of the first column in this row of the table.
`<TD>`	Start the next column.

`<IMG SRC="kiss.jpg" WIDTH=327`
`HEIGHT=350 ALIGN=CENTER ALT=`
`"The Kiss">`
	Finds the kiss image and put it here. The `ALT` attribute displays the words "The Kiss" while the picture is loading, or if the browser can't find the image.

`</TD>`	End of this column.
`</TR>`	End of this row.
`</TABLE>`	End of this table.
`</BODY>`	Okay, browser, you've displayed everything on the page.
`</HTML>`	End of HTML code.

Figure II.5

Josh and Melissa's wedding page.

And that, in a nutshell, is very basic HTML source code. There are lots of good books about it, including one in the *Sams Teach Yourself in 24 Hours* series, and if you want to learn even faster, there's *Sams Teach Yourself HTML in 10 Minutes*.

Enhancing Your Site with Sound and Video

A website or CD can be an electronic version of a traditional scrapbook, with pictures and text arranged as they might appear on paper pages. But it can be more: Electronic scrapbooks can also include sound and video. Why just have a still picture of baby's first step, when you can hear and see him walking? Home movies and amateur sound recordings have been around for well over half a century, as a way to share family events and as a more personal communication than a letter. I still remember seeing my mother's movies of the 1939 New York World's Fair, and hearing a very early tape recording of my grandfather telling stories about his days as mate on a sailing ship. The film and tape are long gone, of course. Computers, CDs, and DVDs allow people to preserve these memories. Services exist for transferring old home movies, photos, negatives, and VHS video tapes to digital data. The biggest benefits are that digital data doesn't break down over time like film or video tape, and the digital format allows people to share these memories online easily.

File Formats and Sizes

Top-quality movies and sound can be extremely large. Full-screen movies eat 30MB per minute or more, depending on video quality; CD-quality sound needs about 10MB per minute. Sizes like this are impractical for a web page—even at a paid host. They use up too much space on the server, and take too long to download.

Fortunately, there are ways to shrink the files. You can do it brute-force, getting small improvements in file size by drastically lowering the image or sound quality. Or you can use modern compression techniques that take advantage of the way we see and hear to significantly shrink the file without too much compromise in quality. The best known of these is MP3, the almost-universal format for compressed sound and music on the Web. Music files in MP3 format can be almost as good as a CD, yet use less than 1MB per minute; voice-only files can be a quarter that size and still sound acceptable.

Popular web formats for video are Microsoft's Windows Media Player (.wma) and Apple's QuickTime (.qt). Both are cross-platform, so you can create and play either file format from a Windows PC or a Mac. Both can transfer streaming video, so viewers can start watching your movies without waiting for the whole thing to download. File sizes for video depend on a lot of variables, including image size, frame rate, and compression method, but a medium-small image without too much flicker can use as little as 3MB per minute.

These formats for sound or video are not part of the HTML specification. That means that a computer has to have Windows Media Player or QuickTime software installed to play them. They play directly in the browser only if the right plug-in has been installed. The plug-ins, in versions for just about any kind of computer, are available free from http://www.microsoft.com and http://www.apple.com.

Copyright Issues

It's illegal to put copyrighted music or video on your web page without the owner's permission, and that pretty much rules out anything you can get at a music or movie store or over the air. Using even very short clips can be copyright infringement, no matter how appropriate they are to your pages. For more information, check http://loc.gov—the Library of Congress's website. They administer copyright law.

Unfortunately, the large music companies have convinced some web hosts that all MP3 files are illegal copies of copyrighted music. They're not, of course. You can make perfectly legal MP3s of your daughter playing songs she wrote, or Grandpa talking about his war experiences. But these web hosts refuse to let users post them, basically because they're scared.

The workaround is to turn your sound recordings into Windows Media Player or QuickTime files instead. These file formats can be used to shrink audio-only files as well as ones with video, and—as of now—don't make web hosts nervous.

Creating Sound and Video Files

Sorry to say, this book isn't about how to make movies or sound files. There are lots of good ones that tell you how and what to do. I liked *QuickTime for the Web: For Windows and Macintosh, Third Edition* (QuickTime Developer Series), but there are many others too. Software such as Apple's iMovie for the Mac is a good way to edit your movies, and it's included in Apple's OS X packages. Windows users, check out Magix Movie Edit Pro 2004 (at http://www.magix.com). It's less than $100 and has some nice features for video editing. Microsoft offers Movie Maker software as a free download to Windows XP users. It's simple to use with drag-and-drop features and allows you to save to video tape for playback in a camera or VCR. Movie Maker is compatible with third-party software that allows you to make your movies into DVDs, too.

Putting Your Audio and Video Creations on a Web Page

Better page-building software lets you select a compressed movie or sound on your desktop, upload it to your host, and generate the proper link. All the consumer-oriented software programs do this for pictures, but not necessarily for movies or sound.

If the wizard or software you're using doesn't let you select movies or sound, you have to follow a few extra steps:

1. Find the movie or sound file on your computer and upload it to your host. Most hosts have site-management tools that help you do this.

2. Decide where on your web page you want that file to appear. Note what text is near it.

3. In the wizard or page-building software you're using, activate the Manual Edit feature. This shows you the page's source code and lets you type additional tags into it. Find the beginning or end of the text you noted in step 2.

4. Make sure the cursor is right next to the text, and not inside angle brackets. Enter the following: `<EMBED SRC="myFilm.mov" WIDTH="240" HEIGHT="195" CONTROLS="SMALLCONSOLE" AUTOSTART="FALSE">`.

The angle brackets (also known as greater-than and lesser-than) are important; they tell the web browser that this is an HTML tag. You can get those characters by holding Shift and pressing the comma or period key.

Of course, you should replace `myFilm.mov` with the name of whatever file you've just uploaded. Capitalization is important—it must match the actual filename exactly. So is the three-letter filename extension after the period. Windows users might have to manually view their file extensions. Choose View, Folder Options. Open the View tab and uncheck Hide File Extensions for Known File Types in your computer to see that extension. (In Windows XP, look in Folder Tools, Folder Options after you open a folder.)

`WIDTH` and `HEIGHT` indicate the size of the movie or sound player in pixels. You have to experiment to find the best numbers for your movie. If you change `Autostart="False"` to `Autostart="True"`, the movie or sound starts playing automatically when the page is loaded.

note

In case you ever wondered, ROM is an acronym for *read-only memory*. After it's recorded, the CD-ROMs or DVD-ROMs can't be erased or reused. Thus, whatever you put on them is going to stay there. That's also why they're good for backing up your important files and photos. (You do make frequent backups, don't you? Many things can go wrong with computer hard drives, and a backup CD-ROM is cheap insurance.)

Finally, upload your new source code. Go to your website and see how it looks. It'll probably take some experimentation to make everything work perfectly.

Creating CD-ROMs and DVD-ROMs

If you have a CD-ROM or DVD-ROM burner, either built-in or plugged into your computer, you can make multiple copies of your scrapbooks, and send them to family and friends. The most reliable way to create them is to use what's now an old friend—HTML. That way, anyone with a web browser can view them. Making a CD or DVD is often referred to as *burning* because the mechanism in the drive uses a laser beam to inscribe the data on the blank disk. When you take it out of the drive, it's often still warm from the process.

If you want your work to be seen and enjoyed, be considerate. Organize your digital files before you burn the CD-ROM. Give the disk a title, too. Don't make your viewers face a bewildering collection of files, as in Figure 11.6.

Your CD-ROM will be a lot more inviting if you organize it. Figure 11.7 shows how a properly organized CD-ROM looks.

Figure 11.6

Faced with this mess, most folks would click at random or just give up.

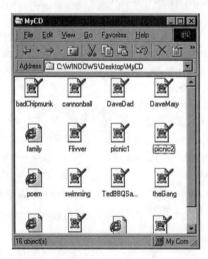

Figure II.7

Isn't this much easier to figure out?

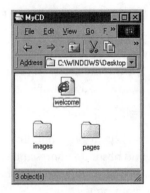

The following are some easy steps to help organize the disk:

1. Before building the pages, create a folder on your desktop with a descriptive name, such as Vacation Scrapbook or Lisa's First Year. Then create two folders inside it, one called Images and the other Pages. (If you or your viewers are using much earlier versions of the Windows operating system instead of XP, be sure to use legal filenames, omitting spaces and most punctuation. Macs don't have that restriction.) Be sure to include those "dot-three" filename extensions, too, so your files are compatible with computers of all ages and operating systems, PC or Mac.

2. Drag all the photos you plan to use into the images folder. These can be copies if you want to keep the originals somewhere else, or you can move them there while building the scrapbook and then put them back after you've burned the CD-ROM.

3. Start building the CD's home page, using your favorite web design tool. Give it a name such as welcome.htm and save it in the first folder you created in step 1 (perhaps Vacation Scrapbook).

4. When you select images to place on this page, be sure you choose them from the images folder you created in step 1—not from anywhere else in your computer. Your CD-ROM scrapbook page should link to images on the CD-ROM, rather than your computer. Your friends and family won't have your computer when they look at the finished CD-ROM scrapbook, and you don't want them to see broken links.

5. You can create additional pages that are linked to the Welcome page. Save them in the pages folder, so they don't clutter the CD-ROM.

6. When you think the electronic scrapbook is complete, check it by opening welcome.htm in your browser. Make sure all the links work and the images display as they should. Check your spelling in any titles, captions, or journal

entries, and if a link isn't working, check its spelling as well. Ensure that all the quotes and brackets are in their proper places. Save your `.htm` page.

7. Launch your CD-ROM burning software, and start a new CD with the same descriptive name you chose in step 1. Drag the `welcome.htm` file and the images and pages folders to it. You're now ready to burn as many copies of your digital scrapbook as you want.

There are just two things to be aware of. First, if your page-building software asks you to choose between relative addressing and absolute addressing, use relative. Otherwise, the links might not work. If it doesn't ask, don't worry about it. The software automatically does the right thing for your page.

Second, if your CD-ROM burning software lets you choose between Windows and Macintosh formats, select Windows—even if you know some of your friends have Macs. All modern Macs can open Windows CDs, but some Windows machines can't open Mac discs.

As a final touch, you might want to make a custom label and/or jewel case insert for your CD. You can find precut blanks at your local computer or office supply store and matching templates on the Web. I use Avery 8696, which has a CD label, CD box insert, and spine labels all on one sheet for easy printing. There's even a downloadable template for it at http://www.avery.com. Even though you can print nice round CD labels, don't try to label the disc without a special alignment tool; if it goes down wrinkled or off-center, the CD might not play. The label alignment tool is available wherever the labels are sold. You can also write on the top of a CD/DVD with a Sharpie permanent marker. Not as pretty, but it works.

Summary—What You Need to Remember

The stuff in this chapter is very technical, compared to the contents of the previous chapters. If there were things you didn't understand, ask a computer-savvy friend or family member for help. I am not a bit ashamed to admit that my husband takes care of my web pages. He also helped out a lot with this chapter. (Thanks, Jay!)

What I really want you to remember is that wonderful things are possible, on the web and on the computer, as well as on paper. You can take your scrapping to new levels with the techniques you've learned here. Go for it!

Above all else, have fun!!!

Appendixes

Other Uses for Your Pictures

You have all these beautiful scrapbooks now, and because you used the computer and a digital camera or scanner, you also have all the pictures digitized and ready to use for something else. What are the possibilities? Let's start with some simple projects.

Iron-On Photos

You can buy iron-on paper for inkjet printers. It's simple to use. Your regular inkjet ink is fine for fabric printing. All you do to print on a white or light-colored cotton or cotton blend fabric is reverse the original photo, either in your graphics program or as part of the page setup when you get ready to print. Then you print onto the special paper. Figure A.1 shows this step.

Iron your fabric and put a piece of cardboard under it so the ink won't bleed through and damage anything. Place the transfer paper on the fabric, design-side down, and iron according to the iron-on transfer package directions. Time and heat might vary with the material or brand of transfer paper, so I can't give you a definite direction. When it's done, let it cool and then peel off the transfer paper. Enjoy. Figure A.2 shows my finished T-shirt. You can also buy transfer paper to print pictures on a dark background, such as a black or dark blue T-shirt. These work a bit differently, so be sure to follow the manufacturer's instructions carefully.

Figure A.1

The transfer is ready to iron on. Note the backward lettering.

Figure A.2

He's definitely got "catitude."

Pictures can go on anything from a T-shirt, tote bag, or hat, to placemats, napkins, and curtains…. Use your imagination. How about pictures of your prize-winning roses at the four corners of a linen tablecloth? Smaller photos on matching napkins? How about making a family photo quilt? Iron your photos onto squares of sturdy cotton cloth and alternate them with squares of brightly colored fabrics. Then quilt as usual for a family heirloom you'll be proud to display.

In Figure A.3, I've drawn a cartoonish flamingo and made it into an iron-on transfer that I put on a canvas tote bag. As a final touch, I hot glued feathers and sequins on the bird. It'll be a gift for a dear friend who has a thing about flamingoes. Embellishments like these can add extra zip to your iron-ons.

Figure A.3
Without the feathers, it's just another bird.

Printing on Fabric

If you have some smooth all-cotton fabric and a bit of patience, you can print directly on the fabric using your inkjet printer. First, you have to prepare it. Cut the fabric to 8 1/2×11 inches, and either cut a piece of freezer paper to the same size, or use a full-sheet adhesive label. (You use these to stiffen the fabric so it can pass through the printer.) Freezer paper works well because it has a waxy coating that melts as you heat it, holding the fabric in place. Pretreat the fabric with an ink fixative. The best is Jenkins Bubble Jet Set 2000, which you can order from the website (http://www.cjenkinscompany.com) or find at some of the larger craft stores. Follow the directions for pretreating and drying, and then iron the fabric to remove any wrinkles.

If you're using freezer paper, place the fabric face down on a firm surface, such as a sturdy table, kitchen countertop, or board, lightly padded with a couple of layers of old sheeting or something similar. An ironing board is too soft. Put the paper, shiny side down, on top of the fabric. Starting in the center, iron toward the edges with a hot iron, until the paper is bonded to the cloth. Use a dry iron and the cotton setting. Then turn the sheet over and iron out any wrinkles. Trim any uneven edges to prevent the fabric from snagging in your printer's guide rollers. Brush the fabric with a lint brush and you're ready to print on it.

If you are using adhesive labels, make sure to use the kind for printers and not for copiers. They use heavier paper that holds the fabric better. Be careful to avoid bubbles as you apply the peeled label to the fabric back. Use a cool iron or a roller if necessary to get rid of any wrinkles or bubbles.

If all this sounds like too much work, Jenkins also stocks prepared fabric sheets at a very reasonable price. A 10-pack of letter-size cotton sheets is less than $17. And here's a news flash. I just came back from my friendly local computer store (part of a national chain) where I bought a pack of printable cotton fabric sheets. They're about 3 dollars a sheet, so they're not cheap, but an enormous time-saver. They have an iron-on coating on the back, so all you do is print and press. Unfortunately, none of these comes in anything other than plain white cotton. If you want to print on something more interesting, you have to use the labels or freezer-paper backing.

In Figure A.4, I've printed a photo from my Nova Scotia trip onto a piece of cotton, and I'm getting ready to iron it onto a pillow cover. I can hold it in place with straight pins or a bit of tape, which I then remove after I iron the center part. After the picture is applied, I glue some moss green velvet ribbon around the edges of the photo to serve as a frame, and to hide the edges. The iron-on fusing tape called Stitch Witchery is very good for this, and less messy than the hot glue gun. Corners of the ribbon frame can either be mitered (cut at an angle) or hidden with a decorative button or embroidered rosette.

Figure A.4

Soon I will have a useful and pretty souvenir.

Printing on Frosting

Imagine a birthday cake with a photo of the guest of honor on it! Or cookies for baby's christening with her picture? There are lots of places that can turn your photos into edible images on sugar sheets. Last time I checked, even the local supermarket bakery could do so. If you've tasted supermarket cakes, though, you might prefer to bake your own. This, too, is feasible. Many online companies accept your emailed photos and send back an edible sheet printed with your photo in edible inks. You frost the top of the cake with flat white icing and place the sheet on it. Maybe add a few rosettes around the edges, and wait for the compliments. The frosting sheets are even kosher! Here's a cake I designed for a friend (see Figure A.5).

If you really want to get into this and have one of several specific models of Canon printer, you can buy the special, edible inkjet ink cartridges and edible image sheets and nozzle cleaner, and start your own cake business. For more information, visit http://www.photofrost.com. They can also make the icing sheets for you.

Figure A.5

Yummy! (Photo courtesy of Ali Williams.)

Bibelot Boxes and Other Tchotchkes

Tchotchke is one of my favorite words. It's Yiddish for "little bits of decorative things." Some people buy their tchotchkes from places like the Franklin Mint or the Lillian Vernon catalog. I like to make my own. In Figure A.6, you can see a little Bibelot box I put together. It has a photo of my pretty part-Siamese boy cat, Ari, on top. I bought a simple papier-mâché box at one of the craft stores, and covered it with bits of colored tissue and some torn Mulberry paper, all applied with thinned out Elmer's glue. (I use a scant tablespoon of water with a generous tablespoon of glue.) You brush the glue on the box first, and then slap on some paper and brush another layer of glue over the top. Don't worry about gluing the top onto the box. You can open it when it's dry by cutting along the seam with a razor blade or X-ACTO knife.

I tried printing the photo on Mulberry paper, but the printer didn't accept it. So I used a print on ordinary paper, which was still translucent after adding lots of glue.

note *Bibelot* comes from an old French word meaning trinket or treasure. Bibelot boxes are not only decorative themselves, but can serve as a repository for other trinkets or things you need to keep track of.

As a final touch, I applied some rub-on butterflies. Ari likes to chase them. Now I use the box to keep track of the rabies tags, and of any medicines the vet prescribes for any of my three cats.

Figure A.6
You can decorate any kind of a box. Metal ones, like Altoids tins, can be spray painted, and then you can add decoupage photos and whatever else you like.

Stationery, Calendars, and Cards

Many word processors and crafts programs, such as American Greetings Scrapbooks and More, include preformatted calendars. You can also find calendar templates online. Avery (http://www.avery.com) has a set in their Home Corner section, and there are many styles at the Calendar Template web page (http://www. printablecalendar.ca/). Why not make your own personalized business cards, note pads, and stationery? You can have business cards, paper, envelopes, and note pads made up from your artwork at any instant print shop, usually for very little money, unless you choose a particularly expensive paper stock. Figure A.7 shows a few simple examples.

If you just need a few business cards at a time, and not a thousand, you can buy blank business cards at most office supply stores. These come in standard letter size sheets with micro perforations so you can run them through your inkjet printer and then separate them easily and without shaggy edges. These are available in many colors and with preprinted designs as well as blank, so you can customize to suit your home business or your personality.

Figure A.7

The calendar template came from Avery. The other pieces were designed in Photoshop Elements.

The End, or the Beginning?

In these pages, I've shown you just a few of the literally millions of possibilities. Now it's up to you to put your computer and your visual skills to work. How many crafts can you combine in one piece? How many new ways can you think of to show off your favorite photos? The only limit is your own creativity.

If you have questions—or great ideas you want to show off—you can always reach me at author@graphicalcat.com. Please send your files zipped or stuffed, make them as small as possible, and mention *Scrapbook* in the subject line.

Glossary of Computer Graphics and Scrapbooking Terms

acid migration   The transfer of acid from one source to another on your page through physical contact or acidic vapors. Placing acidic items, such as newspaper clippings, on a page can pass the acid from the source to your photo if you don't take steps to buffer and prevent this.

acid-free paper   Paper that resists deterioration from age, and won't destroy items, such as photos, attached to it. Also called alkaline paper, archival paper, neutral pH paper, or scrapbook paper. Paper and other materials that have a pH balance between 7.0 and 7.5 are considered acid-free. Acid is neutralized during manufacturing. Acid-free papers and other scrapbooking supplies are labeled as such. Newsprint and construction paper are not acid- or lignin-free! (See also *buffering* and *lignin*.)

acids   Acids weaken the cellulose in paper, which leads to its breakdown, causing discoloration and disintegration. Acid turns litmus paper red. To test the acid content of paper materials, purchase a pH test pen from a scrapbook, office, or archival supplier. A small mark in a corner reveals acid content. (See also *pH* and *pH testing pen*.)

Acrobat   Acrobat is part of a set of applications developed by Adobe to create and view PDF files. Acrobat is used to create the PDF files, and the freeware Acrobat Reader is used to read the PDF files.

adhesive   The glue used to secure items in the scrapbook, including tape or glue. For scrapbooking, you should always use acid-free and lignin-free adhesives. Adhesives used in scrapbooking include double-sided tape, photo corners, photo splits, acid-free spray adhesive, and glue sticks. Rubber cement is an adhesive, but is not archival and not recommended for scrapbooking.

airbrush   Pen-shaped tool that sprays a fine mist of ink or paint to retouch photos and create continuous-tone illustrations. In most graphics programs, the paintbrush tool also can serve as an airbrush.

album   An album is a book typically used to protect and store photographs and other memorabilia items; also sometimes called a scrapbook album. (See also *brag book, scrapbook,* and *strap-hinge album.*)

aliasing   Aliasing occurs when a computer monitor, printer, or graphics file does not have a high enough resolution to represent a graphic image or text. An aliased image has jagged edges as if it was made from bricks, and is often said to have the "jaggies." (See also *anti-aliasing.*)

alignment   The positioning of a block of text. Text can be placed to the left, right, or center of a page, and can be justified, so both margins are even. Otherwise, type set flush left is also ragged right, and type set flush right is ragged left.

alkaline   The opposite of an acid; substances having a pH greater than 7.0 (between 7.5 and 14). (See also *pH.*)

analogous colors   Any three colors that are side-by-side on a 12-part color wheel (one that includes tertiary colors), such as yellow-green, yellow, and yellow-orange. (See also *color wheel, complementary colors,* and *tertiary colors.*)

anti-aliasing   The appearance of smoothing or blending the transition of pixels in an image. Anti-aliasing a raster graphic or text adds shading along the curves and diagonals, which the human eye interprets as a smooth edge rather than a serrated one.

archival   Products rated to last without changing chemically or fading for many years. There are currently no organizations defining or policing this rating, so check the manufacturer's reputation before you invest.

bevel   Adding a beveled effect to a graphic image gives the image a raised appearance. You do this by applying highlight colors and shadow colors to the inside and outside edges.

bibelot box   A small, decorated box for keepsakes too valuable or too thick to put in a scrapbook. Can be decorated with decoupage, stamps, stickers, lace, velvet, or whatever else is available.

binder   A notebook cover, commonly found in office supply stores, with rings or clamps for holding and protecting sheets of paper. To use a binder as a scrapbook, make sure it is not made with PVC or vinyl plastics. Also binder's board, a thick paperboard used to add stiffness to book bindings. Most binder's board has a high lignin content, although acid-free and lignin-free board is available. (See also *acid-free paper, lignin,* and *three-ring binder.*)

bitmap (.bmp)   A graphic image stored as a specific arrangement of screen dots; also known as raster graphics. The opposite of a vector graphic. Web graphics are often saved as bitmap images. Common types of bitmap graphics are GIF, JPEG, Photoshop (PSD), PCX, TIFF, Macintosh Paint, Microsoft Paint, PNG, FAX formats, and TGA.

bleed or bleeding edge   When a page or a cover design extends to and off the edge of the paper, it is called a bleed.

bleed-proof/resistant   Adhesives and colorants that do not soak (or bleed) through to the reverse side of the material to which they are applied (such as a sheet of paper). This term also refers to coated or specially finished paper stock that prevents substances from soaking through to the opposite side.

blow-up   An enlargement made from an original image, normally used with graphic images or photographs.

BMP (Windows Bitmap)   The standard filename for Windows Bitmap graphics files, represented by the extension .bmp. (See also *file extension.*)

bond paper   Category of paper commonly used for writing, printing, and photo-copying. Also called business paper, typing paper, copy paper, and writing paper.

book paper   General term describing a category of paper suitable for books, magazines, catalogs, advertising, and general printing needs. Book paper is divided into uncoated (also called offset paper) and coated paper (also called art paper, enamel paper, gloss paper, or slick paper).

bookmarks   When using an Internet browser, electronic bookmarks are used to bring you to a website or other site you want to return to. The Netscape Navigator browser saves bookmarks in a file you can recall at any time. Microsoft Internet Explorer uses the term favorites instead of bookmarks for the same concept.

brag book   A small scrapbook or photo album that is easily transported. It usually contains photographs of children, pets, or grandchildren.

browser   Short for web browser. Software used to locate and access web pages by interpreting hypertext and hyperlinks. The two most common browsers are Netscape Navigator and Microsoft Internet Explorer. Web pages often appear differently when viewed using different browsers, depending on the brand and version number of the intended viewing browser. (See also *HTML.*)

buffering   Process of adding alkaline substances to paper materials after production, removing the acids to protect the product against acid migration in the future. The most common buffers used are magnesium bicarbonate and calcium carbonate. (See also *acid-free paper, archival,* and *lignin.*)

calligraphy   Hand-written lettering created by using a quill pen, fountain pen, or other split metal nib that carries ink to the paper. Calligraphy is popularly used to decorate formal invitations to weddings, scrapbook pages, and photo albums.

caption   The line or lines of text that provide information identifying a picture or illustration.

card stock   Sturdy, solid colored, printed, or textured heavy papers commonly used in catalog covers, brochure covers, and business cards, as well as in scrapbooking and rubber stamping.

chalking   Using special artist's chalks to enhance edges and cutouts on scrapbook pages.

circle cutter   A tool designed solely for the purpose of cutting a perfect circle in different sizes.

clip art   Simple graphics, both in color and in grayscale, that you can find online and in computer programs to print out and use. Clip art began as generic illustrations sold to newspapers and advertising designers, who would literally clip the picture they needed to drop into their layout. Computers, the Internet, and CD-ROMs have made finding the clip art you need for a specific theme very easy.

CMYK   Abbreviation for cyan, magenta, yellow, and key (black), the four offset printing process colors.

color picker   A window that opens when you click on a foreground or background swatch, allowing you to choose a color by clicking anywhere in the full spectrum.

color wheel   The basic tool of color theory, a color wheel is a circle showing the relationship between colors in a logically arranged sequence of hues. Red, yellow, and blue are primary colors. They are separated from one another on a color wheel by the secondary colors. Tertiary colors are formed by mixing the primary and secondary colors, and so on. (See also *analogous colors, complementary colors, primary colors, secondary colors,* and *tertiary colors.*)

collage An artistic composition of materials, objects, or photographs layered together on a surface, often with a unifying theme or color. Also the method of combining borrowed images with original elements to create a new artistic creation. A montage of photographs is a type of collage. (See also *montage.*)

complementary colors Any two colors that are directly opposite each other on any color wheel, such as red and green or orange and blue. Complementary colors create strong contrast when used together in images. (See also *analogous colors* and *color wheel.*)

composition In graphic design, the arrangement of type, graphics, and other elements on the page.

compression A method of storing data in a format that saves disk storage space or takes less time to transmit over a network such as the Internet. JPEGs are compressed bitmap graphics files. (See also *lossless compression* and *lossy compression.*)

contrast The range of tones in an image from the brightest white to the darkest black. High-contrast photos have more pure blacks and whites. Low-contrast photos have many shades of gray but few strong highlights or shadows. Also called *contrast ratio.*

copyright Copyright laws protect the originator of material to prevent commercial use without express permission or acknowledgement of the originator.

corner punch Similar to the corner rounder but these come in many decorative styles when you want something fancier than a rounded edge. Victorian, snowflakes, flowers, and lace are examples of some different styles.

corner rounder A punch specially designed to round the 45° angles of photograph or paper corners.

crop Trimming the photo to highlight a certain area, to remove unwanted background, or to change the photograph's shape. (See also *cropping.*)

cropping The elimination of parts of a photograph that are not required. Cropping can improve composition, and allows the remaining parts of the image to be enlarged to fill the space. Also a scrapbooking workshop or party where people work on their own or a group project.

cutout A photo from which the background has been removed to produce a silhouette.

dauber   A kind of small stamp pad that can be dabbed onto a stamp to apply ink.

dauber duo   A dauber applicator with a different color or shade on each end.

de-acidification   The act of removing acid from newspaper clippings, certificates, and other scrapbook items using such products as Archival Mist, one brand of spray that neutralizes acid content.

decorative ruler   A normal ruler with a special edge used in designing scrapbook pages.

decorative scissors   Any kind of specialty scissor that cuts a decorative pattern when the blades are applied to paper. Some examples are zigzag, deckle, Victorian, and waves.

desktop publishing   Technique of using a personal computer to design images and pages, assemble type and graphics, and then use a laser or inkjet printer to output the assembled pages onto paper.

die cut   Shapes or letters cut from card stock by special machines. You can purchase precut paper designs or the cutting machine and a selection of dies to make your own.

digital image   Visual data stored electronically, as on a computer hard drive, rather than an image that is produced chemically or physically, as is a photograph or a drawing. Digital images can be made using digital cameras, video recording devices, scanners, and other input devices that capture and store images without film. Digital images can be manipulated using computer software and transferred over the Internet. (See also *scanner.*)

dither   To create the illusion of new shades or tints of color by alternating the pattern of black and white dots within the image. For example, photos printed in newspapers are dithered. In computer graphics, dithering can occur if the color palette is too limited to show all of the shades and tints of color within an image. GIF files, limited to a 256-color palette, often show dithering. (See also *GIF.*)

dot   A single point; the smallest identifiable part of an image. A dot is not synonymous with a pixel. (See *dots per inch, pixel,* and *resolution.*)

dots per inch   Measure of the resolution of an image. Abbreviated dpi. (See also *dot* and *resolution.*)

drop shadow   A black or gray patch "dropped" in place behind an object, photo, or type to give it depth by creating an apparent shadow behind the item.

duotone   The application of two colors to provide a richer sepia or other colored tone than a single-color image, usually grayscale, can provide. A good duotone image can simulate a wider range of the color spectrum than two colors used separately.

embellishment   Any extra decorative items used to enhance scrapbook pages. Examples include stickers, die-cut paper designs, punches, buttons, raffia, ribbon, and so on.

embossing   Creating the effect of a relief image (actual or imagined). Embossing a graphic image adds dimension to it by making the image appear as if it were carved as a projection from a flat background. Also, creating actual raised edges or relief textures on paper by applying heat or pressure to the paper. (See also *bevel*.)

embossing powder/ink   Embossing powder is sprinkled on stamped images, and then heated using a craft heat gun to melt and create raised lines.

encapsulation   Sealing memorabilia between two sheets of stable transparent polyester film (not to be confused with lamination) for the purpose of protection from handling, moisture, and acid migration. No adhesive is applied to the items being encapsulated. (See also *acid migration, de-acidification,* and *polyester*.)

ephemera   Objects that have special meaning to you, but will not last without preservation. Ticket stubs, matchbook covers, postcards, and other souvenirs and memorabilia are considered ephemera.

export   To save a file in a different format. For example, many Adobe Photoshop files (PSD) are exported to GIF or JPEG format for use on the Web. (See also *import*.)

eyelet   A round metal stud with a hole, applied by punching a hole in the page, inserting the two parts of the eyelet and flattening the back half of the eyelet. Used to durably attach objects or layers of paper or card stock to a scrapbook page, or sometimes as a decoration. Available in various sizes at sewing, craft, and hardware stores. Also called *grommets*.

feathering   Feathering the edge of a graphic image gradually dissipates the edge, making the edge look blurry.

file extension   Three or four letters separated from a filename by a ".", called a period or dot. Most computers use a dot-three standard, meaning that the file extension has three letters, such as `.jpg`, `.gif`, `.htm`, and `.bmp`. The dot-four extension is less common and not compatible with all computers or web browsers. Examples include `.jpeg` and `.html`.

filter   In Adobe Photoshop and Photoshop Elements, filters are mini-applications that work within the main program to add extra functions, such as sharpening, blurring, or modifying photos to look like drawings or paintings.

filter gallery   A window that displays the effect of many of Adobe's filters on a typical photo, allowing you to see the effect before you apply the filter to your own work.

Fiskars   A very reliable scissors brand. They make both regular and decorative scissors and shears in many sizes. (See also *decorative scissors*.)

flush left   Text aligned along the left margin.

flush right   Text aligned along the right margin.

focal point   An element of page design where lines converge. The eye is naturally drawn to the focal point of an image or a page design.

font   A complete set of characters in a particular size, design, and style. This includes the letter set, the number set, and all of the special character and diacritical marks you get by pressing the Shift, Option, or Command/Control keys. For example, Times New Roman Bold Italic is one font, and Times New Roman Bold is another font in the Times New Roman typeface family. (See also *typeface*.)

freeware   Copyrighted software distributed for free by the author. (See also *shareware*.)

FTP   Abbreviation for File Transfer Protocol, the standard format on the Internet for exchanging files. An FTP website works the same way as HTTP for transferring web pages from a server to a user's web browser. FTP is commonly used to download from or upload to a server using an Internet connection. One example is to upload your scrapbook web page to a server, so you can share it with your family over the Internet. (See also *HTML*.)

GIF   Originally developed by CompuServe for use on its proprietary World Wide Web online service, GIF has become a popular file format for displaying graphics on websites. Pronounced "jiff" or "giff" (hard g), GIF is the abbreviation for graphics interchange format. Using the file extension .gif, a GIF is a bitmap graphics document that uses lossless compression to store image data. Because it uses a limited 256-color palette, GIF is better suited to simple logos and images rather than photographs.

glow   The opposite of a shadow in that it creates a highlight around an image. A high radiance creates a soft, subtle glow and a low radiance creates a hard, bright glow, such as a neon glow.

gradient   A gradient is a gradual transition of colors. Many metallic images are gradients. Web images that use gradient fills as a special effect need to be saved in a JPEG rather than a GIF format, to preserve the subtle transition without dithering. (See also *dither, GIF,* and *JPEG.*)

graphic backgrounds   The bottom-most layer on a web page, usually with either a design or color that highlights the copy above it. A small graphic can be tiled to create a background texture for a web page.

graphic design   Arrangement of type and visual elements along with specifications for paper, ink colors, and printing processes that, when combined, convey a visual message.

graphics   Visual elements that supplement type to make printed messages more clear or interesting.

grayscale   An application of levels of black ink (for print) or shades of the color black (for the screen) that simulate a range of tones between black and white. Grayscale images have no hue (color). In print design, a grayscale graphic image appears to be black, white, and shades of gray, but only uses the black ink in your printer. Converting to grayscale assigns each dot within an image a specific shade of gray, using between 16 and 256 shades. Basically, the more levels, the better, but with correspondingly greater memory requirements.

grid   A systematic division of a page into areas to enable designers to ensure consistency. The grid acts as a measuring guide and shows text, illustrations, and page sizes.

heat gun   Also called a thermal or embossing gun. A heat gun is a hobby tool that heats without producing air, unlike a hair dryer, which would blow your project away.

heirloom   Used in regard to many aspects of scrapbooking. It can mean an old-fashioned-looking page, or an actual antique photograph or object.

highlights   Lightest portions of a photograph or piece of artwork, as compared to midtones and shadows.

hinge album   A plastic strap binding allows these albums to expand. These tend to lay more flat than the post bound albums. (See also *post bound album* and *strap-hinge album.*)

HTML   Abbreviation for Hypertext Markup Language; a cross-platform page-layout system for creating web pages, including copy, images, sounds, frames, animation, and more.

hue   The actual color of an object. Hue is measured as a location on a color wheel, expressed in degrees. Hue is also understood as the names of specific colors, such as blue, red, yellow, and so on.

import   To use data created by another program, such as a JPEG or GIF file. Many programs are capable of importing (reformatting) graphics in a variety of file formats. The opposite of export. (See also *export*.)

inkjet printing   Method of printing by spraying droplets of ink on to a sheet of paper or other print media. Inkjet printers are generally less expensive than laser printers. The print produced by an inkjet printer can be smudged or damaged by water unless special inks are purchased.

Japanese papers   Especially thin and strong art papers made in Japan from long fibers, such as mulberry. They are largely handmade, the fibers pulped by hand rather than acid; the lengths of the fibers give the paper exceptional wear capability. The edges tear with an attractive feathered effect. (See also *mulberry paper*.)

journal entry   Writings included in a scrapbook or journal describing a mood, feeling, scene, or event.

journaling   Process of writing journal entries.

JPEG (Joint Photographic Experts Group)   The JPEG file format uses a method of lossy compression that reduces image file size by selectively reducing the amount of detail contained in the image and by transforming the image data into a format that is better suited for compression. Images with fewer details compress extremely well, whereas pictures with a high degree of random detail do not compress as well, or suffer some degree of image degradation. The relative amount of detail removed can be specified in most applications. At the default value of 75, relatively little picture degradation takes place, but a significant amount of compression is obtained. At lower values, you experience still better compression, but with a marked loss of image quality. JPEG images support up to 16 million colors and are typically RGB color or grayscale (256 shades of gray). The default file extension for JPEG files is .jpg. (See also *grayscale*, *lossy compression*, and *RGB*.)

justify   The alignment of text along both the left and right margins. This is achieved by adjusting the spacing between the words and characters as necessary so each line of text finishes at the same point.

K   In computer terms, K or KB stands for kilobyte, 1,000 bytes of data, as in 256K of RAM (random access memory). In print design, the K stands for key, represented by the ink color black in the CMYK (cyan, magenta, yellow, and black) color process. (See also *CMYK*.)

kerning   The horizontal spacing between the letters in a word. Some pairs of letters, such as *AV*, *To*, and *Ta*, look better and are easier to read when the space between them is closed up.

laminate   A thin transparent plastic coating applied to paper or board to provide protection and give it a glossy finish.

lamination   Sealing an object between translucent plastic pieces for the same reasons as encapsulation, although lamination is not as safe for some photos and other scrapbook items because of heat exposure and pressure.

landscape   Any page orientation in which the width used is greater than the height. Also used to indicate the horizontal orientation of tables or illustrations that are printed sideways.

latex pages   Usually found in magnetic albums. They discolor anything placed on them in a very short period of time. Do not use for scrapbooking.

layout   A sketch of a page for printing showing the position of text and illustrations, exploring color options, and giving general instructions before final design decisions are made. Layouts also refer to groups of scrapbook pages that go together. Also the process of designing a page by placing elements in a harmonious and logical pattern. (See also *graphic design*.)

leading   (Pronounced to rhyme with "sledding.") The vertical spacing between lines of text. In early typesetting, metal strips made of lead were placed between lines of metal type, thus the name.

Letraset   A proprietary name for rub-down or dry-transfer lettering used in page titles and the like.

library picture   A picture taken from an existing photo or clip art library and not especially commissioned.

light box   A small light table used for viewing negatives or embossing.

lignin   Substance found in trees that holds cellulose fibers together. Acid-free papers have most lignin removed; ground wood paper such as newsprint contains lignin.

lossless compression   In graphics programming, lossless compression refers to a data compression technique whereby the file quality is preserved and no data is lost. Lossless compression can reduce file size to about half of its original size. Lossy compression, by contrast, eliminates some data but can further decrease file size.

lossy compression   A term coined by graphics programmers to refer to a technique of shrinking file sizes by giving away some precision of detail. JPEG is an example of a file that is compressed this way. By reducing the so-called quality of a picture when you save it, you can make the file size smaller. Many photos can take some loss of fine detail before it becomes noticeable.

magnetic album   A widely available and inexpensive type of photo album not to be used for scrapbooking. It uses a special adhesive to hold photographs in place and creates static for the plastic page cover to cling to. These deteriorate over time and damage photos.

mask   A mask is used either to hide the part of the picture you don't want to change or to reveal only the part of the picture you do want to change. Masks are applied in Photoshop Elements using the Selection Brush tool to paint over the area to be masked.

mat or matting   Placing a piece of acid-free paper behind the photo to accentuate it or act as a buffer between the photo and the page. Also, a cardboard frame around a piece of art.

memorabilia   Anything that reminds you of an historical or family event or time in your life. Artwork, certificates, matchbooks, postcards, tickets, badges and medals, and brochures are all memorabilia.

memory book   Another name for a scrapbook.

montage   A single image formed by assembling several images. A panorama is one kind of montage. Another type of montage is a scrapbook page formed entirely of photographs collaged or layered together. (See also *collage*.)

mount   To attach a photo or other memorabilia to a piece of paper or card stock, such as the background page in a scrapbook. Also the wood or plastic handle of a rubber stamp.

mounting squares   A small square of double-sided tape-like adhesive generally dispensed from boxes.

mulberry paper   A type of handmade paper with long fibers that create a feathered edge when torn. Often acid-free due to a handmade process rather than an acid pulp production. Available in many textures, weights, and colors. (See also *Japanese papers*.)

neon glow   Type of glow on a graphic image that gives the appearance of neon lighting.

neutral   Having a pH of between 7.0 and 7.5; neither acidic nor alkaline.

neutral gray   Gray with no hue or cast, that is, neither warm nor cool.

nonpermanent mounting   Using photo frames, photo corners, or pocket pages to hold photographs and other items on or near a scrapbook page without permanently adhering them. (See also *photo corners* and *pocket page*.)

opal laminate   This is the film that is stuck to the top of opal stickers. It has a pearl look to it.

origami   The Japanese craft of paper folding. Sometimes used to add embellishments to pages.

outline   In graphic design, tracing the outer edge of text or a graphic image. If the outline is feathered, the effect is generally referred to as a glow.

overalls   A shortcut used in scrapbook page layout, overalls are printed on card stock with a title and borders or pictures to cut out. It's an easy way to decorate a page because it comes with everything but your own photos. (See also *page toppers*.)

page protector   A PVC-free (photo-safe) plastic sleeve or cover used to protect and display your scrapbook pages. They can be sleeves that fasten directly into your album or covers that slide over your page; the latter are especially useful in spiral bound albums. Page protectors can be top- or side-loading and are generally available in 8.5" × 11" or 12" × 12" page sizes. Top-loading page protectors are best for pages with glitter, beads, or anything that might come loose.

page toppers   Like overalls, a product that can be used as-is or cut up to create a title and die-cut paper accents on a scrapbook page. (See also *overalls*.)

panorama   A wide format photograph, made either with a special panoramic camera or pieced together from several "normal" shots. In Photoshop Elements, select File, New, Photomerge Panorama to merge pictures automatically.

paper piecing   Die cuts and decorative punches used in multiple layers together to create an image for your scrapbook page.

PDF   Stands for Portable Document Format. Created by Adobe Systems in its software program Adobe Acrobat as a universal file format. Files can be downloaded via the Web and viewed page by page, provided the user's computer has the necessary plug-in, Acrobat Reader, which can be downloaded free from Adobe's own website. (See also *Acrobat*.)

perforated punches   Precut shapes that can be used as embellishments on a scrapbook page simply by punching out the precut perforations. (See also *embellishment, overalls,* and *page toppers*.)

pH   The measure used for acidity and alkaline. The scale runs from 0 to 14, with numbers greater than 7.0 being alkaline (and therefore scrapbook-safe).

pH testing pen   A pen used to test the acidity of paper or other scrapbooking materials. It contains an indicator dye that discolors the material it is applied to if the pH is highly acidic.

photo corners   Small paper corners with adhesive backs. Used to attach the four corners of photographs, postcards, or other items with four corners to pages of scrapbook and photo albums without applying adhesives directly to the item. (See also *nonpermanent mounting*.)

photo splits   Squares of double-sided tape. Also called photo squares. Can be either flat or based on foam tape to add dimension to a pasted object.

photo tape   Double-sided tape on a roll with a paper backing. Good for sticking larger items like mats and frames.

pixel   Also called *picture element,* refers to a single point in a graphic image. It has some attributes associated with it, for example, a certain color, texture, and so on, that are assumed to be constant over the whole area covered by it. All pixels are assumed to have the same shape and size. A pixel is the smallest element of a picture whose attributes can be controlled independently of the other pixels. Pixels refer to screen resolution, not print. The print equivalent of a pixel is a dot.

plug-in   A software extension that works with a graphics program, such as Photoshop Elements, to apply particular transformations to a photo or piece of art. Also, plug-ins can be designed to work with a web browser for viewing, hearing, or saving especially formatted files such as audio or video. Most plug-ins are available via the creator's web page for downloading.

PNG   Stands for Portable Network Graphics format and is generally pronounced "ping." PNG is used for lossless compression and displaying images on the Web. The advantage of PNG is that it supports images with millions of colors and produces background transparency without jagged edges. The disadvantages are that PNG images do not show up on older browsers, do not support animation, and still can be comparatively larger in file size than GIFs. (See also *GIF* and *lossless compression*.)

pocket page   A scrapbook page with a built-in pocket. Useful for holding memorabilia you might want to take out and look at, such as programs or other booklets or two-sided postcards.

point size   A measurement of height used in typesetting. One point is typically equal to approximately 1/72 of an inch, although this can vary if the font has elongated ascenders and descenders. In general, a capital letter in 72-point type is about an inch high. (See also *font*.)

Polaroid   A type of camera that prints a photo instantly. These photos cannot be cropped because they are made in layers, and have acidic chemicals inside that develop the instant photo. Cutting into them allows the chemicals to leak out and destroy both the photo and anything with which it comes in contact. If you need to crop a Polaroid, scan it and crop on the computer. Because Polaroids are small, you might want to enlarge them as part of the scanning process.

polyester   The common name for polyethylene terephthalate (PET), a clear plastic resin safe for scrapbooking, not to be confused with polyvinyl chloride. (See also *polyvinyl chloride*.)

polyethylene   A chemically stable, transparent plastic safe for storing photographs and other memorabilia, not to be confused with polyvinyl chloride. (See also *polyester*.)

polyvinyl chloride   Also known as PVC, this plastic is not stable and damages photographs and albums. PVC plastic page protectors, binders, photo enclosures, and other products, often found in office supply and discount stores, should never be used with photographs or in scrapbooks. (See also *polyester*.)

portrait   An upright image or page where the height is greater than the width. Opposite of a landscape.

post bound album   This album type uses metal posts to bind the pages in the album. This gives you the most flexibility in size, because you can continually screw in extra posts to add more pages. (See also *album, strap-hinge album,* and *three-ring binders*.)

PPI   Stands for pixels per inch. Pixels per inch is a measurement of the screen resolution at which a monitor displays image data. The number of pixels contained within one square inch of monitor space.

primary colors   In traditional color theory, the primary colors are red, yellow, and blue. They are considered primary because they cannot be made by mixing any other colors, and all other colors are derived from these three. (See also *color wheel*.)

punch   A small gadget similar to a hole punch that creates die-cut shapes and comes in a variety of sizes and styles.

punch art   Similar to paper piecing but is art solely made up of punches.

punches   The product made by using a punch; the middles of the die-cut holes. These embellishments can be used in paper piecing or pasted on to decorate scrapbook pages. (See also *embellishment*.)

quilling   A paper art featuring curls of long, slim pieces of paper, sometimes used as a scrapbook page decoration. Often curled and arranged to produce patterns and floral designs.

raffia   A natural, grass-textured fiber that can be used to embellish scrapbook pages, providing a country or farm flair.

rag paper or board   Any paper or board produced with a high content of long, cotton fibers. 100% cotton rag paper or board is considered safe for most scrapbooking because of its low acid content.

RAM   The acronym for random access memory, the most common type of memory found in computers and printers. Computers and printers with more RAM perform tasks more quickly.

raster   What your image is when using most paint programs; also called a bitmap image. They are composed of individual picture elements, or *pixels* that, when viewed from a distance, appear to form a complete image. You can tell if you are looking at a raster image by the extension on the filename. The extensions `.bmp`, `.pcx`, `.gif`, `.tga`, `.jpg`, `.png`, and `.tif` are common raster image filename extensions. (See also *bitmap* and *resolution*.)

rasterize   To convert an image from a vector graphic to a bitmapped graphic. (See also *BMP* and *vector graphic*.)

red eye   An effect that happens when the flash of a camera hits the back of the eye and reflects. Human eyes literally look red in the photograph. Some animal eyes look green or yellow. Can easily be corrected on the computer.

repositionable   A type of adhesive that holds photos and objects temporarily, but doesn't stick permanently. You can remove the object without damage and put it somewhere else. Sometimes called reversible adhesive. (See also *nonpermanent mounting*.)

resolution   Refers to the sharpness and clarity of an image. Measured in dots per inch (dpi). The greater the numbers of dots, the more smooth and clean the image appears. 300 dpi is generally enough resolution for small photos. (See also *raster* and *bitmap*.)

retouching   A means of altering artwork or photographs to correct faults or enhance the image. Retouching is much easier on the computer than on an actual paper photo.

RGB   Abbreviation for red, green, and blue, the additive color primaries. In web design and design for computer monitors, colors are defined in terms of a combination of these three colors.

rubber cement   An adhesive made from liquefied rubber and solvents. It is not safe for scrapbooking because it eventually stains your photos and any paper surface to which it is applied.

sans-serif   A style of typeface that means "without feet." Common sans-serif typefaces include Arial, Helvetica, Avant Garde, and Verdana. (See also *serif*.)

saturation   The color intensity of an image. An image high in saturation appears to be very bright. An image low in saturation appears to be duller and more neutral. An image without any saturation is also referred to as a grayscale image.

scaling   A means of calculating the amount of enlargement or reduction necessary to accommodate a photograph within the area of a design.

scanner   A device that attaches to a computer and scans or *digitizes* a page using light sensitivity to translate a picture or typed text into a pattern of dots that can be manipulated in software and stored by the computer. (See also *BMP* and *resolution*.)

score   To compress paper along a straight line so it folds more easily and accurately. Also called crease.

scrapbook   An album used to display photographs and ephemera.

scrapbooking   The craft of organizing your photos and other memorabilia into albums. Also the hobby of using photos, images, decorative papers, embellishments, and journaling to create archival memory albums.

secondary colors   The secondary colors on the color wheel—green, orange, and purple—are formed by mixing the primary colors in pairs. (See also *primary colors* and *color wheel*.)

self-healing mat   A mat used as a surface for cutting papers with a knife or razor blade. The cut edges reseal themselves, so the mat is good for many work sessions.

serif   A type style that has little feet. Also refers to the foot itself. Common serif typefaces include Times Roman, Garamond, and Palatino. (See also *sans-serif*.)

setter   A tool used in attaching rhinestones, eyelets, or studs. It applies pressure to force the metal to bend and grip the paper or cloth.

shade   Hue made darker by the addition of black; the opposite of a tint. (See also *tint*.)

shadows   Darkest areas of a photograph or illustration, as compared to midtones and highlights.

shareware   Copyrighted software distributed by its creator using an honor system of payment. Most shareware is free of charge, but the author usually requests a small fee if you like the program or use it regularly. By paying the fee, you become a registered user, eligible to receive service help and updates to the shareware program. You can copy shareware and pass it to friends, but they are expected to pay the same small fee to the author if they use the product. (See also *freeware*.)

silhouettes   Just the shadow of an object or person. An old-fashioned practice of tracing the shape of one's shadow as a keepsake or form of art.

spiral bound   An album or notebook that is machine-bound by winding a metal wire or plastic rings through holes in the pages in a circular pattern.

sticker   A self-adhesive cutout picture or tag. Often used to decorate scrapbook pages. (See also *embellishment*.)

sticker art   Combining any number of stickers to create a larger project.

straight scissors   Regular straight-bladed scissors, without any decorative edges, used in cutting continuous lines. (See also *decorative scissors* and *Fiskars*.)

strap-hinge album   A type of memory book, photo album, or scrapbook that is secured with plastic straps. The straps run through guides attached directly to the pages themselves and into guides on each cover. (See also *album, scrapbook,* and *post bound album*.)

template   Any predesigned page layout. Commonly used in computer scrapbooking programs, a template contains a page background, some art, and places for you to insert your pictures and titles. In traditional paper scrapbooking, a template is made of sturdy plastic and has shapes, such as circles, squares, and ovals, cut into it that you can trace onto your paper.

tertiary colors   On a 12-part color wheel, the tertiary colors are formed by mixing the primary and secondary colors in pairs, forming yellow-orange, red-orange, red-purple, blue-purple, blue-green, and yellow-green. (See also *color wheel, primary colors,* and *secondary colors*.)

theme album   An album in which all the photographs and memorabilia belong to a specific subject, such as a birthday, holiday, wedding, or vacation.

three-ring binder   A basic loose-leaf binder that you can use as a cover for your scrapbook. Three-ring binders are found with office or school supplies. (See also *binder*.)

thumbnail   A small representation of a larger graphic image. Image browsers show thumbnail views of your photos. (See also *HTML*.)

TIFF (Tagged Image File Format)   Computer file format used to store bitmap images. Typically uses LZW, a lossless compression scheme, to decrease file size. TIFF files can be any resolution and support black and white, grayscale, and all color depths. The default file extension for TIFF files is .tif. (See also *file extension* and *lossless compression*.)

timeline   A spread containing one subject over a certain amount of time, such as your child's birthday parties, year by year.

tint   A hue made lighter by the addition of white. (See also *shade*.)

typeface   A typeface is a family of fonts. For example, the typeface Arial includes the fonts Arial, Arial Bold, Arial Italic, and Arial Bold Italic. (See also *font*.)

value   The shade (darkness) or tint (lightness) of a color. Also called brightness, lightness, shade, and tone.

vector graphic   A graphic image drawn in geometric formulas visually represented by shapes and lines, called paths. Images created in Adobe Illustrator and Macromedia Freehand are vector graphics.

vellum   A lightweight, translucent paper that is generally thicker than tracing paper. It can be plain, printed, white, or colored.

VersaMark   A brand of ink pad or pen that, when used on a solid color of paper, produces a subtle effect similar to a watermark. Other stamping effects can be created on many types of paper using the VersaMark watermark stamp pad.

vignette   Decorative design or illustration fading to the background color around its edges.

WYSIWYG   Pronounced "wiz-zee-wig." Abbreviation for what you see is what you get. A popular feature in desktop publishing, a WYSIWYG program shows you onscreen exactly what you see when the document is printed.

X-ACTO knife   A brand of precise, sharp hobby blades used to cut intricate designs. The #11 size blade is the most versatile for use in most crafts. Available in art, hobby, and office supply stores.

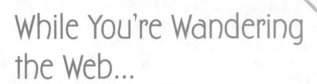

While You're Wandering the Web...

Be sure to check out some of the many Web resources for scrapbookers. You can use the following list, and you can also find a whole bunch of good sites by searching on Google (or whatever your favorite search engine is) for "scrapbook," "journal," and "scrapbooking." Of course, if you are looking for specific tools or items such as stickers, scrapbooking papers, and so on, try them as Google search terms, too.

I've also included a list of websites for various scrapbooking and craft projects. I'm not specifically recommending any of these. As always, buyer beware. Be especially wary of companies that only have email and website addresses, but no postal mailing address or phone number. This is common-sense advice that is found in many consumer guides. Also, websites come and go, so a year from now you might not find the ones mentioned. This list is correct as of January 2005.

Here are some good scrapbooking sites to get you started:

- Avery Labels (http://www.avery.com/homecorner/)
- Epson (http://www.epson.com/cgi-bin/_Store/PrintLab/PrintScrap.jsp)

- Learn2Scrapbook (http://www.learn2scrapbook.com)
- Scrap Circle (http://www.scrapcircle.com)
- Scrapjazz (http://www.scrapjazz.com)
- Scrapbook Sites (http://www.scrapbooksites.com)
- Scrapbooking.com Magazine (http://www.scrapbooking.com)
- Stamping Links (http://www.rubberstampinglinks.com)
- Two Peas in a Bucket (http://www.twopeasinabucket.com)

Company Name	Products	Web Address	Phone
3L	Mounting corners, pockets, and adhesives	http://www.3L.dk	+45 63 76 86 00 (Denmark)
7Gypsies	Albums, paper, and tags	http://www.7gypsies.com	800-588-6707
A Stamp in the Hand	Stamps	http://www.astampinthehand.com	310-884-9700
Adobe	Software	http://www.adobe.com	800-833-6687
American Art Clay Co.	FIMO clay and embossing supplies	http://www.amaco.com	800-374-1600
American Tag Company	Eyelets, grommets, tags, tassels, and cords	http://www.americantag.net	800-223-3956
Anima Designs	Stamps, journals, and ephemera	http://www.animadesigns.com	
Art Gone Wild	Stamps	http://www.agwstamps.com	800-945-3980
ARTchix Studio	Stamps, art bits, and more	http://www.artchixstudio.com	250-370-9985
Artisan's Choice	Make your own stamps and transfers	http://www.artisanschoice.com	877-7-ARTISAN
Artistic Wire	Colored wire and tools	http://www.artisticwire.com	630-530-7567
Avery Dennison	Paper goods, templates, and free clip art	http://www.avery.com	800-GO-AVERY
The Beadery	Plastic beads and rhinestones	http://www.thebeadery.com	401-539-2432
Bo-Bunny Press	Papers and stickers	http://www.bobunny.com	801-771-4010
The C-Thru Ruler Company	Scrapbook pages, add-ons, and drafting tools	http://www.cthruruler.com	800-243-8419
Canson	Fine art papers	http://www.canson-us.com	
Carl Mfg.	Paper cutters and trimmers	http://www.carl-products.com	847-956-0730
Carolee's Creations	Papers, tags, and punch outs	http://www.caroleescreations.com/?pg=carolees	435-563-1100
Chatterbox	Papers, frames, rivets, and nails	http://www.chatterboxinc.com	888-416-6260
Cheap Joe's Art Stuff	Art supplies	http://www.cheapjoescatalog.com	800-227-2788
Clearsnap	Inkpads, stamps, and stones	http://www.clearsnap.com	888-448-4862
Close to My Heart	Stamps	http://www.closetomyheart.com	888-655-6552

Company Name	Products	Web Address	Phone
Club Scrap	Color-coordinated kits	http://www.clubscrap.com	888-634-9100
Colorbök	Coordinated kits	http://www.colorbok.com	
Colors by Design	Cards and add-ons	http://www.cbdcards.com	800-832-8436
Craf-T Products	Chalks	http://www.craf-tproducts.com	
Crafts Etc!	Artists supplies	http://www.craftsetc.com	800-888-0321
Creative Imaginations	Papers and add-ons	http://www.cigift.com	800-942-6487
Daisy D's Paper Co.	Papers and themed pages	http://www.daisydspaper.com	888-601-8955
Daler-Rowney	Art supplies	http://www.daler-rowney.com	+44(0)1344 461000 (UK)
Darice, Inc.	Art supplies	http://www.darice.com	800-321-1494
Delta Technical Coating	Stamping supplies and glass paints	http://www.deltacrafts.com	800-423-4135
Deluxe Designs	Laser cuts and tags	http://www.deluxecuts.com	480-497-9005
Dick Blick Art Materials	Art and craft supplies	http://www.dickblick.com	800-828-4548
Dymo	Label makers and label tape	http://www.dymo.com	800-426-7827
Emagination Crafts	Punches, papers, corners, and scissors	http://www.emaginationcrafts.com	630-833-9521
Epson	Ink jet printers, scanners, inks, and paper	http://www.epson.com	800-463-7766
European Papers	Papers, kits, and charms	http://www.europeanpapers.com	614-316-3948
Fibers by the Yard	Fiber, raffia, and hemp	http://www.fibersbytheyard.com	405-364-8066
Fiebing Company	Leather dyes	http://www.fiebing.com	414-271-5011
Fiskars	Punches, trimmers, scissors, and embossing tools	http://www.fiskars.com	800-500-4849
FoofaLa	Tags, envelopes, and charms	http://www.foofala.com	
Frost Creek Charms	Brass and pewter charms	http://www.frostcreekcharms.com/	763-684-0074
Frances Meyer	Scrapbooking supplies and stickers	http://www.francesmeyer.com	
Funky Fibers	Yarns and fibers	http://www.funkyfibers.com	480-659-5616
Glue Dots International	Adhesives	http://www.gluedots.com	
Golden Artist Colors	Acrylic paints and archival varnish	http://www.goldenpaints.com	800-959-6543
Gone Scrappin'	General scrapbook supplies	http://www.gonescrappin.com	435-647-0404
Harbor Freight	Hand tools and craft knife sets	http://www.harborfreight.com	800-444-3353
Hero Arts	Stamps and supplies	http://www.heroarts.com	800-822-HERO (4376)
Hillcreek Designs	Hand-dyed buttons	http://www.hillcreekdesigns.com	619-562-5799

Continues...

Company Name	Products	Web Address	Phone
Hot Off the Press	Templates	http://www.craftpizazz.com	800-227-9595
Inkadinkado	Rubber stamps	http://www.inkadinkado.com	781-938-6100
Inspire Graphics	Fonts and journaling art	http://www.inspiregraphics.com	801-235-9393
International Typeface Corporation (ITC)	Type	http://www.itcfonts.com	866-823-5828
Jacquard Products	Textile paints and dyes	http://www.jacquardproducts.com	800-442-0455
Jest Charming	Charms and embellishments	http://www.jestcharming.com	702-564-5101
JewelCraft	Beads, charms, and shaker kits	http://www.jewelcraft.biz	201-223-0804
Junque	Rubber stamps and supplies	http://www.junque.net	
K&Company	Papers, frames, and themed kits	http://www.kandcompany.com	888-244-2083
K&S Engineering	Metal tooling foils	http://www.ksmetals.com	773-586-8503
Karen Foster Design	Papers and stickers	http://www.karenfosterdesign.com	801-451-9779
Keeping Memories Alive	All kinds of scrapbooking supplies	http://www.scrapbooks.com	800-419-4949
Kolo	Photo albums	http://www.kolo-usa.com	888-636-5656
Kopp Design	Papers, cut-outs, and tags	http://www.koppdesign.com	801-489-6011
Kreinik	Iron-on metallic thread, yarns, and so on	http://www.kreinik.com	410-281-0040
Lazertran	Transfer papers	http://www.lazertran.com	800-245-7547
The Leather Factory	Leather goods, tools, and dyes	http://www.leatherfactory.com	
Limited Edition Rubberstamps	Stamps, ink pads, ephemera, beads, tags, and die cuts	http://www.LimitedEditionRS.com	877-9-STAMPS
Linotype Library	Type	http://www.linotype.com	+49 (0) 1805 79 3339 (Germany)
Lucky Squirrel	Shrink plastics	http://www.luckysquirrel.com	800-462-4912
Ma Vinci's Reliquary	Rubber stamps	http://www.crafts.dm.net/mall/reliquary	
Magic Mesh	Decorative mesh	http://www.magicmesh.com	651-345-6374
Magic Scraps	Embellishments and supplies	http://www.magicscraps.com	972-238-1838
Making Memories	Scrapbook supplies	http://www.makingmemories.com	801-294-0430
Marvy Uchida	Markers and art supplies	http://www.uchida.com	800-541-5877
McGill Inc.	Punches and craft tools	http://www.mcgillinc.com	800-982-9884
Michaels Arts and Crafts	Everything!	http://www.michaels.com	800-MICHAELS
Micro-Mark	Small tool specialists	http://www.micromark.com	800-225-1066
Midori	Handmade papers and ribbons	http://www.midoriribbon.com	800-659-3049
Monotype Imaging	Type	http://www.agfamonotype.com	978-284-7201
Mustard Moon	Papers, piercings, and tags	http://www.mustardmoon.com	408-229-8542

Company Name	Products	Web Address	Phone
Nankong Enterprises, Inc.	Punch art and stamps	http://www.nankong.com	302-731-2995
Nature's Pressed	Pressed flowers and leaves	http://www.naturespressed.com	800-850-2499
Offray	Ribbons	http://www.offray.com	800-327-0350
Once upon a Scribble	Stickers and supplies	http://www.onceuponascribble.com	702-896-2181
P22	Type	http://www.p22.com	800-P22-5080
Paper Adventures	Papers and rub-on letters	http://www.paperadventures.com	800-727-0699
The Paper Loft	Stationery	http://www.thepaperloft.com	909-694-4420
The Paper Patch	Binder covers, papers, and stickers	http://www.paperpatch.com	800-397-2737
Patchwork Paper Design Inc.	Papers, die cuts, and patchwork pieces	http://www.patchworkpaper.com	239-481-4823
Pebbles in My Pocket	Papers and tools	http://www.pebblesinmypocket.com	800-438-8153
Plaid	Craft supplies, All Night Media rubber stamps	http://www.plaidonline.com	800-842-4197
Polyform Products	Polymer clay	http://www.sculpey.com	847-427-0020
Princess Crafts	Paper and tutorials	http://www.princesscrafts.com/index1.htm	719-683-5780
Provo Craft	Scrapbooking supplies	http://www.provocraft.com	800-937-7686
Prym-Dritz Corporation	Sewing supplies and notions	http://www.dritz.com	
PSX	Papers, stamps, inks, and tools	http://www.psxdesign.com	866-779-9877
Ranger Industries, Inc.	Stamping inks and glitter glues	http://www.rangerink.com	732-389-3535
Red Castle	Templates and stamps	http://www.redcastle.com	
Rubba Dub Dub	Rubber stamps and supplies	http://www.artsanctum.com/RubbaDubDubHome.html	209-763-2766
Scrapworks	Embellishments	http://www.scrapworks.com	
ScrapYard 329	Embellishments	http://www.scrapyard329.com	775-829-1118
SEI	Albums, stickers, and embellishments	http://www.shopsei.com	800-333-3279
Shutterfly	Digital photo printing	http://www.shutterfly.com	
Sizzix	Die cutting machines, dies, embossing tools, and molds	http://www.sizzix.com	877-355-4766
Snapfish	Digital photo printing	http://www.snapfish.com	301-595-5308
The Stamp Doctor	Stamps and accessories	http://www.stampdoctor.com	208-342-4632
Stamp It!	Rubber stamps and accessories	http://www.stampit.com	757-425-0721
Stampendous	Rubber stamps, stickers, and papers	http://www.stampendous.com	800-869-0474

Continues...

Company Name	Products	Web Address	Phone
Stampin' Up!	Rubber stamps and accessories	http://www.stampinup.com	800-STAMPUP
Tandy Leather	Leather tools, stamps, and dyes	http://www.tandyleather.com	800-433-3201
Target	Craft and office supplies	http://www.target.com	800-440-0680
Therm O Web	Tapes and adhesives	http://www.thermoweb.com	847-520-5200
Tsukineko, Inc.	Inkpads and temporary tattooing supplies	http://www.tsukineko.com	800-769-6633
Two Busy Moms	Tags and embellishments	http://www.twobusymoms.com	480-497-9005
Two Peas in a Bucket, Inc.	Papers, stamps, stickers, and glues	http://www.twopeasinabucket.com	608-827-0852
The Uptown Design Company	Stamps, inks, and embossing powders	http://www.uptowndesign.com	253-925-1234
USArtQuest, Inc.	General craft supplies	http://www.usartquest.com	517-522-6225
Westrim Crafts	Embellishments, albums, and paper	http://www.westrimcrafts.com	800-727-2727
Winsor & Newton	Paints	http://www.winsornewton.com	
Wordsworth	Rubber stamps, stickers, and quotations	http://www.wordsworthstamps.com	719-282-3495
Young Bros. Stamp Works	Brass stencils and metal type	http://www.youngbrosstampworks.com	800-553-8248

Index

Want to learn more?
Check out these other books
by Carla Rose!

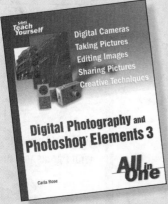

You know how to use Photoshop Elements for scrapbooking. Now see what else it can do! In *Sams Teach Yourself Adobe Photoshop Elements 2 in 24 Hours*, Carla digs deeper into this popular photo-editing software, teaching you how to fix red eye, create original digital images, and build customized patterns and brushes to reuse.

Taking the next step? Learn to use the more advanced Adobe Photoshop CS with the *Sams Teach Yourself* series. Work through 24 proven one-hour lessons and learn everything you need to know. With Carla's friendly, conversational style and step-by-step instructions, you will be up and running in no time.

Sams Teach Yourself
Digital Photography
and Adobe Photoshop
Elements 3 All in One
ISBN: 0-672-32688-4, $34.99

Sams Teach Yourself
Adobe Photoshop 7
in 24 Hours
ISBN: 0-672-32388-5, $24.99

Sams Teach Yourself
Adobe Photoshop CS
in 24 Hours
ISBN: 0-672-32755-4, $24.99

Find out about the software and technology in

Scrapbooking with Adobe Photoshop Elements 3

with other great titles from **Que** and **Sams**,

available at fine retailers everywhere or online.

Easy Digital Cameras
ISBN: 0-7897-3077-4
$19.99 US

**Absolute Beginner's Guide
to Digital Photography**
ISBN: 0-7897-3120-7
$18.95 US

**Digital Photography with
Photoshop Album in a Snap**
ISBN: 0-672-32568-3
$24.99 US

**Absolute Beginner's Guide
to Adobe Photoshop
Elements 2**
ISBN: 0-7897-2831-1
$18.95 US

**Easy Adobe
Photoshop Elements 3**
ISBN: 0-7897-3330-7
$19.99 US

**Adobe Photoshop
Elements 3 in a Snap**
ISBN: 0-672-32668-X
$29.99 US

www.quepublishing.com

www.samspublishing.com